ELECTRONIC DREAMS

*How 1980s Britain Learned
to Love the Computer*

Tom Lean

BLOOMSBURY
sigma

Bloomsbury Sigma
An imprint of Bloomsbury Publishing Plc

50 Bedford Square   1385 Broadway
London   New York
WC1B 3DP   NY 10018
UK   USA

www.bloomsbury.com

BLOOMSBURY and the Diana logo are trademarks of Bloomsbury Publishing Plc

First published 2016

Quotes on p. 181, 192 from *Sinclair User* © ECC Publications/EMAP 1984, 1987. Quotes on p. 71, 238
from *Personal Computer World* © Felix Dennis/VNU 1979, 1986. Quote on p. 124 from *Your Computer*
© IPC 1982. Quotes on p. 142, 201, 204, 208 from *Crash* © Newsfield 1984. Quote on p. 184 from
Big K © IPC 1984. Quote on p. 208 from *Beebug* © Beebug 1984. Quote on p. 230 from
Personal Computer News ©VNU 1984. Quote on p. 243 from *The Guardian* © The Guardian 1985.

Photo credits (t = top, b = bottom, l = left, r = right, c = centre) Colour section: P. 1: School of
Computer Science/The University of Manchester (t); Tom Lean (b). P. 2: Rick Dickinson (t). P. 3:
Mel Croucher/Automata Software (b). P. 4: Bill Bertram/Creative Commons Attribution-Share
Alike 2.5 (t); Factor-h/Creative Commons Attribution-Share Alike 3.0 (background modified)
(tcl); Liftarn/Bill Bertram/Creative Commons Attribution-Share Alike 2.0 (bcl); Evan Amos (bl);
Bilby/Creative Commons Attribution-Share Alike 3.0 (br). P. 5: Science and Society Picture
Library/Getty Images (t, b). P. 6: Jon Ritman (t); Mel Croucher (b). P. 7: Malcolm Evans (tl); Frontier
Developments (cr); Jon Ritman (b). P. 8: Tom Lean and Jacob Lindberg (t); Ian Mckinnel (b).

British Library Cataloguing-in-Publication Data
A catalogue record for this book is available from the British Library.

Library of Congress Cataloguing-in-Publication data has been applied for.

ISBN (hardback) 978-1-4729-1833-8
ISBN (ebook) 978-1-4729-1835-2

2 4 6 8 10 9 7 5 3 1

Typeset in Bembo Std by Deanta Global Publishing Services, Chennai, India
Printed and bound in Great Britain by CPI Group (UK) Ltd, Croydon CR0 4YY

Bloomsbury Sigma, Book Ten

MIX
Paper from
responsible sources
FSC
www.fsc.org   FSC® C020471

To find out more about our authors and books visit www.bloomsbury.com. Here you will find
extracts, author interviews, details of forthcoming events and the option to sign up for our newsletters.

MAR 2 8 2016

Contents

Introduction

In the 1980s, computers invaded British homes for the first time, a wave of cheap and futuristic *microcomputers* that allowed millions of people to discover for themselves what a computer was and how it worked. For most of their earlier history, computers were too large, too expensive and too complicated for the general public to understand; they were machines for big science, big government, big business and perhaps even Big Brother. Yet with the development of the microprocessor in the 1970s, the tiny 'computer on a chip', dramatically reduced the cost and size of computing, and brought prophecies of an information technology revolution that would change the world. Against this backdrop, Britain embraced home computers as introductions to information technology, passports to the future that would prepare people for the changes to come.

As home computing boomed manufacturers developed a staggeringly diverse array of computers to meet the demand. They came in different shapes and sizes, but shared many common features too. Most were intended originally as affordable and user-friendly introductions to computing; comparatively simple devices of limited power and sophistication, but with enormous potential for people to tinker with and learn to program. Home computers were there to be explored, experimented with and understood, but beyond this there was only a vague idea of what they were actually for. They were open to a wide range of different interpretations, and 1980s Britain imprinted itself on this eminently malleable technology in many different ways: to the state and educationalists it became a tool of computer literacy, a way to remake the British economy and workforce; to bedroom programmers computers were a means of expressing themselves in creative ways, as they wrote games to push machines beyond designers' expectations; to Thatcherites they were a symbol of the nation's enterprise and inventiveness; to millions of people around the country computers became entertainment platforms, information terminals, household aides, office tool, or whatever other uses users could conceive. The home computer boom was not just about computers, but a huge period of experimentation to find out what they could do, and the coming together of all these different groups and agendas created a curiously British cultural event.

After every boom follows a bust. By the mid-1980s disillusionment with cheap home computers was setting in: familiar computer companies went bust; home computers were reduced to the status of toys as gaming blossomed and users turned to more sophisticated 'real' computers; the IBM PC standard killed much of the diversity of the boom years. The home computer should have died then and there, but it did not. Embedded in personal and popular memory, and kept alive by collectors and retrocomputing fans, the machines of the 1980s are living an active semi-retirement three decades later. But more than that, the legacies of the home computer boom are all around us in a world where computers have become boringly commonplace. Yet as news today fills with stories of digital revolution and digital literacy, the promises of information technology to deliver disruptive change remain as strong as ever; twenty-first century Britain is rediscovering and recreating the promises of 1980s home computing anew. This is the story of the home computer boom, and how Britain stopped worrying about microchips and learned to love the computer.

CHAPTER ONE

Electronic Brains

In June 1948, in a drab laboratory in the Gothic surroundings of the Victoria University of Manchester, a small team of electronics engineers observed the success of an experiment they had been working on for months. The object of their interest was an untidy mass of electronics that filled the tall, bookcase-like racks lining the walls of the room. At the centre of this bird's nest of cables, radio valves and other components glowed a small, round display screen that allowed a glimpse into the machine's electronic memory, a novel device sitting off to one side hidden in a metal box. This hotchpotch assembly of electronic bits and bobs was officially known as the Small-Scale Experimental Machine (SSEM), but has become better known as the 'Manchester Baby'. It was the world's first electronic stored program computer, a computer that used an electronic memory to store data and the program that instructed it what to do, the basic architecture still used by most computers today.

Baby's creators, Tom Kilburn, Geoffrey Tootill and Freddy Williams, were all electronics engineers seasoned by years of work developing wartime radar systems under great secrecy and urgency. It took them months of methodical work to complete the computer, building, testing and installing each of the computer's units before moving on to the next. 'The very last thing we could contemplate doing was to design the whole thing, and have it all built, and wire it all up, and then find out why it didn't work,' recalls Geoff Tootill. 'We went on with this process of adding the units and making the whole lot do something together at every stage, until we got to the stage when we'd made a computer.'[1] They began testing the machine, and eventually on the morning of 21 June 1948 Kilburn's first program ran successfully. For 52 minutes, binary digits danced across the display screen as the computer repeatedly divided numbers as it searched for the highest proper factor of 262,144. By lunchtime it had produced a result, 131,072, displayed as a series of dots glowing on the display screen.

It is nice to imagine Baby's creators pausing to think of how their creation could change the world, the green glow of its small display screen marking the dawn of a new age. In fact it was a low-key moment. No photographs were taken at the time and no press conferences were called. Years later Williams would say that 'nothing was ever the same again',[2] after the machine completed its first run, but it needs hindsight to appreciate this as a great event. As Tootill recalls it, Baby's first run was an understated moment: 'We congratulated each other and we went to lunch together, which we quite often did anyway.' To those there, this was an experiment that had worked, rather than a world-changing event. At the time, Tootill had thought that computers might be useful for complex calculations in weather forecasting or the development of atomic energy, and that 'there would be scope for another one, or perhaps two big computers in the UK, and three or four in Europe, and probably half a dozen in the US, and that was the eventual scope of our invention'.

In this modest way the world's first modern computer came to life, born in a Victorian laboratory amid the post-war shortages and soot of Manchester. For a short time, Baby placed Britain at the very forefront of computing, before well-financed laboratories in the US and elsewhere raced far ahead. Forty years later a very different Britain once again lead the world in computing, as millions of people purchased their first personal computer, and the country boasted the world's highest level of computer ownership. Between a single experimental machine in post-war Britain and the millions of 1980s personal computers was a story of swift technological development and huge changes in the ways that people thought about computers. This book is a history of how computers entered the homes of 1980s Britain, but to appreciate the nature of this development it helps to have a little historical context of what computers were like in the decades before they became technologies of everyday life.

Computers before stored program computers

Baby was the world's first electronic stored program computer, able to store its instructions and data electronically. It was the first machine to share the basic architecture of the computer on desks today, but it was far from the first big computing machine, to be built. 'Computer' originally referred not to a machine but to a person who did computations. Organisations that needed mathematical problems solved often employed large numbers of human-computers, and many of them had sought ways to improve the speed and accuracy of calculations. One of the earliest to try was the irascible Victorian polymath Charles Babbage, who became frustrated with errors in human-computed mathematical tables, apocryphally declaring, 'I wish to God these calculations had been executed by steam.' Babbage's solution was to begin development of a giant mechanical calculator, the Difference Engine, but unfortunately Babbage fell out with his funders and the engineer contracted to build his machine, so he never completed it.* In any case, He had become preoccupied with schemes for a more sophisticated successor, the Analytical Engine. This would have been much like a modern computer in concept, albeit realised in brass cogs and Industrial Revolution terminology; instead of information passing through memories and processors, Babbage wrote of 'stores' and 'mills'. Babbage died in 1871 with his engines incomplete, and sadly his ideas had little direct influence on the development of computing afterwards.

Two decades later, the American Herman Hollerith was more fortunate in his development of punched card tabulators. Tabulators were not computers as we would understand them

---

*Although Babbage did not complete his engines, his schemes were validated in 1991 when the Science Museum in London built a working Difference Engine to his plans.

today, but machines for swiftly processing stacks of punched cards. The holes punched in different locations on the cards represented different types of data, which could be read by the tabulator and the results recorded as the cards whisked through the machines at a rate of over a hundred a minute. The tabulators were first used on a large scale in the 1890 US census, processing the data in a single year, whereas with traditional methods the 1880 census took seven years. Hollerith's Tabulating Machine Company eventually merged with other office-equipment firms to form International Business Machines, IBM, in 1924. Following Hollerith's example, other companies were soon building comparable equipment, which proliferated through the statistics and accountancy departments of governments and businesses. As well as the general-purpose tabulators, other machines were built for specialist scientific work, such as the mechanical differential analysers built for several universities and research centres in the 1930s to solve differential equations.

By the end of the Second World War, mechanised information processing had reached new levels of sophistication. Some of these machines were electromechanical, with the logic that did the 'thinking' built of a mix of electronic and mechanical components. Best known today, though ultra-top secret at the time, were the Bombe code-breaking machines of Bletchley Park. Designed principally by mathematicians Alan Turing and Gordon Welchman, and building on earlier work in Poland, the Bombe were invaluable in the deciphering of secret messages encoded by German Enigma machines. Over in the US, the physicist Howard Aiken and IBM developed the Harvard Mark I, a 50-foot long electromechanical calculator used for a variety of purposes, including calculations for the development of the atom bomb.* In Germany, an engineer named Konrad Zuse had

*Howard Aiken was perhaps the only computing pioneer directly influenced by Charles Babbage, after discovering part of the Difference Engine while scheming a calculating machine of his own in the 1930s.

been building electromechanical and mechanical computing machines since the 1930s. Zuse's Z3 was used in aeronautical research, but with little support from the Nazi government, and with two of his machines destroyed in air raids, his work had little impact on the war. The principle problem with electromechanical computers such as these was speed. The Bombe, for example, had mechanical rotors, which physically rotated as they tested different possible Engima settings. Zuse's machines were mostly built with relays, small switches that flicked on and off as data clicked through the logic. Because their parts had to physically move, electromechanical computers were far slower than purely electronic machines could be.

Electronics in the 1940s did not mean microchips or integrated circuits, but bulky radio valves, each about the size and appearance of a light bulb, and used as the basic building blocks of everything from wireless and radar sets to the logic circuitry for computing machines. The first machine to be entirely electronic was Colossus, another of Bletchley Park's code-breaking machines, designed by Post Office engineer Tommy Flowers to crack the Lorenz code. Capable of faster operations than any machine before, there were ten Colossus machines at work at Bletchley Park by the end of the war. In 1945 most were broken up on the orders of Winston Churchill to preserve their secrets, which did not come to public notice until the 1970s.[*]

Most technically impressive of all the wartime efforts was the Electronic Numerical Integrator And Computer, or ENIAC. Developed in an American project led by J. Presper Eckert and John Mauchly, ENIAC was a monstrous 30-ton computer built from over 17,000 electronic valves. Initially developed for solving ballistic calculations, it could actually be used for all sorts of different problems, making it the first

---

[*]Although their logic circuits were entirely electronic, the Colossus machines relied on punched paper tape to feed data into them. At least two of the machines survived the war and were used in secret at GCHQ until about 1960.

general-purpose electronic computer. However, the instructions that controlled it were hard-wired into the machine itself. Reprogramming ENIAC for a new task essentially meant physically reconfiguring wiring and settings, rebuilding bits of its logic to make a slightly different sort of machine for every new job. But what if the instructions could be stored electronically rather than in the wiring of the machine?

Historians, computer scientists and even lawyers have spent a great deal of time since squabbling over who got the idea first, but by about 1945, scientists, mathematicians and engineers in Britain and the US had arrived at the concept of the *stored program* computer. Unlike ENIAC, it would have some sort of electronic memory in which a program of instructions could be rapidly stored, accessed and altered. Making the machine do something different would be simply a matter of swapping one set of electronic instructions for another, what we would regard today as loading a different program. Putting the concept into practice was not a simple matter. Like any computer of the time, it would be complex to build, and rely on hundreds of inherently unreliable components working perfectly with each other. It would also need a new type of device, a store or memory to hold the data and instructions, whose contents could be accessed and easily changed by the computer.

In the late 1940s there were several teams working towards such a machine, principally in Britain and the US. It perhaps appears more like a race in hindsight than it did to those taking part at the time. The different groups were working on the same basic concept, but with different technologies, different designs and different aspirations for what they were trying to build. Alongside Manchester, there were large computer projects underway at the National Physical Laboratory (NPL) in Teddington, where Alan Turing planned the ambitious and logically elegant Automatic Computing Engine (ACE); and the University of Cambridge, where former wartime radar developer Maurice Wilkes was building the Electronic Delay Storage Automatic Calculator (EDSAC), intended as a practical tool to help scientists with their calculations.

That the Manchester machine was first was largely due to the relative simplicity of its design and the wartime-honed skills of its developers. Kilburn, Tootill and Williams had spent the war at the Telecommunications Research Establishment (TRE), the centre of British radar development. 'We were accustomed to working under extreme time pressure,' remembers Tootill, 'to developing electronic equipment with a deadline, or if not with an actual deadline "we'd like it yesterday please".' As the war came to a close, Williams and Kilburn developed a new use for the Cathode Ray Tubes (CRT), which were used to display what a radar could see. Rather than just using the screen of the CRT to *display* the location of German bombers, they used it to *store* information as electrically charged dots, each a simple binary 1 or 0 of digital data, a 'bit', which could be changed at lightning speed.* By 1947, they had a device that could electronically store 1,024 bits of data, about the same number of bits as there are letters in this paragraph. What they did not have was any way to test whether it would actually work in a computer, because in 1947 there was none. To test the store they would have to build a computer of their own.

With the war over, Williams became a professor at Manchester, taking Kilburn with him to continue work on the CRT store, and was joined a few months later by Tootill. Gradually during 1947 and 1948, their computer took shape. In the rationed world of post-war Britain, where basic necessities of life were still in short supply, many of the components

---

*In the binary system commonly used to measure the size of computer memory, a bit is a single binary digit, capable of being a 1 or a 0; eight such bits make up a byte (b), for example 10101010; a thousand and twenty four such bytes is a kilobyte (k or kb); a thousand and twenty four such kilobytes is a megabyte (mb). The electronic memory of my desktop computer could accommodate that of over 30 million Manchester Babies.

for the computer were war surplus, raided from TRE's well-stocked stores of radar parts. Rather than try to build the best computer they could conceive, Baby's designers made it a relatively simple machine. It had just seven instructions, and was only built with the circuitry to subtract numbers.* For all the complex electronics used to build it, Baby was a surprisingly basic machine, largely an experiment to test if the CRT memory worked. The creation of the first computer was merely a side effect of testing the first electronic computer memory.

Electronic brains that can play chess

Baby was revealed to the wider world in autumn 1948, when a short note from Kilburn and Williams appeared in the prestigious science journal *Nature*, modestly noting that their small computing machine had been running for a few weeks, and giving its particulars.[3] Understated or not, Baby was born into a world where the computer was a strange new scientific novelty for many people. Already the unveiling of ENIAC had come to the attention of a wider public, when in 1946 the *Daily Mirror* reported on it under the headline 'Science Makes A Brain That Can Play Chess'.[4] Meanwhile in the letters pages of *The Times*, scientists debated just what was meant by the idea of a machine being able to 'exercise judgement'. Among those writing in was Charles Darwin, grandson of the famous naturalist, and director of the National Physical Laboratory. Darwin reassured that computers would not replace thought, as scientists were only trying to imitate the 'unconscious automatic' functions of the brain, not 'higher realms of intellect'.[5]

In 1949 a photograph of the Manchester machine, by now expanded into a more powerful form, appeared in *The Times*, dubbed a 'mechanical brain'.[6] In the terms of the day there

---

*Addition was done by subtracting negative numbers. For example, adding 1 and 1 together could be achieved by subtracting − 1 from 1.

was probably no other way of describing what a computer was, other than an electronic or mechanical brain. They were sometimes described as 'high-speed calculators', but this did not really do justice to the flexibility of computers to do things other than add numbers. That they reacted differently depending on the data presented to them, 'those hitherto human prerogatives of choice and judgement', as the *Daily Mirror* put it, attracted much comment and an impression that the machines might somehow have a will of their own. As journalists compared radio valves to brain cells, and began commonly referring to computers as 'he' rather than 'it', the term 'electronic brain' stuck, to the disgust of experts concerned that such terms misled people over the nature of computers.

In spite of experts' protestations, the personification of the electronic brain over the 1940s and '50s was striking. The first computers were generally one-off experimental machines, dubbed with individual names that almost gave them personalities, such as ACE, EDSAC, Meg, LEO and HEC. Journalists described them not as soulless machines, but almost as living things. On viewing ESDAC, *Daily Mirror* journalist Roland Bedford reported that it behaved 'just like a human being... It does not scratch its head, but it hesitates a little. You can almost see it "thinking."'[7]

Among the earliest users of the Manchester computer was Alan Turing, who moved to Manchester after becoming frustrated with the lack of progress in building ACE. In 1950 Turing addressed the question of 'can machines think?' in a seminal article for the journal *Mind*. Turing considered the question in its broadest sense, considering such issues as animal intelligence, and if immortal souls or emotions were necessary for thought. As it was hard to satisfactorily define 'machine' or 'think', Turing suggested that the question be replaced by a game, better known today as the Turing Test. Turing reasoned that if someone asked questions of another person and of a computer, and could not tell from their answers which of them was human, then the computer's intelligence would be demonstrably indistinguishable from a human being's. More than 60 years later computer scientists' creations still compete to pass the Turing Test, and the concept has been a foundation of artificial intelligence studies.

The nature of the computer was blurred further as journalists began reporting on the novel uses to which computers were put by designers, who were finding out for themselves what the machines could do. At Manchester, the upgraded university computer was soon being used for more varied purposes than just complex mathematics. It was soon playing chess and writing love letters in awkward prose, such as, 'YOU ARE MY WISTFUL SYMPATHY: MY TENDER LIKING'. The BBC even recorded the machine hooting out the national anthem and the big-band jazz number *In the Mood*. With most people used to household wireless sets that contained perhaps two or three valves, massive machines built from many hundreds of them seemed incredible works of engineering. Amid the novelty of tons of expensive electronics performing tricks for its human masters, there was also a palpable sense of awe at the machines' abilities. News stories suggested that the new machines could solve problems impossible for human minds, and disquiet at humankind's new-found inferiority was often implicit. One journalist complained that Pilot ACE, the NPL's computer, let out a 'buzz of triumph' every time it beat him at noughts and crosses, and he could only beat it by cheating.[8] News from the US in 1952 hinted that computers may have had even greater powers, when a UNIVAC computer appeared on CBS television on election night. With human pollsters predicting that Adlai Stevenson would be the next president of the USA, UNIVAC's verdict was a landslide victory for Dwight Eisenhower. A doubtful CBS initially fudged its reporting to announce that UNIVAC had only predicted a close result. Later in the evening, when Eisenhower won his landslide victory, CBS had to admit that the machine had been right all along.

Since industrialisation brought the replacement of manual workers by machinery, there had been a sense of concern over the ability of machines to work faster and more relentlessly than humans. However, there was something about the ability of the computer to out-think people that went beyond worries over jobs and fear of change. The thinking machine struck more fundamentally at notions of what makes human beings different, the privileged ability to perceive, analyse, decide and be conscious in a way that separates people from other animals and from machines. As Alan Turing noted, man liked to believe he was superior to the rest of creation: 'it is best if he can be shown to be necessarily superior, for then there is no danger of him losing his commanding position'.[9] The electronic brain challenged this position, but in only a philosophical sense at first. The computer was far too rare, remote and engaged in far too esoteric pursuits to be that much of a concern to most people. In 1950, the year that Turing pondered whether machines could think, there were only three of these new electronic brains in the whole of Britain; one at Manchester, the National Physical Laboratory and the University of Cambridge. Each lived in a laboratory and filled its days churning through the thousands of calculations involved in such tasks as designing atomic weapons, crystallographic research, computing the strength of new jet aircraft and esoteric mathematical pursuits such as searching for ever larger prime numbers. For now, at least, the electronic brain was restricted to research in science, mathematics and engineering, and the occasional whim of a boffin who wanted to see what else it could do. However, scientists were not the only ones in need of a faster way of doing calculations.

The tea-shop brain
In the early 1950s, the idea of using something as magical as an electronic computer for something as dull as business administration seemed rather absurd. *The Economist* mused in 1954 that putting a 'thinking robot' to such mundane tasks as counting the contents of wage packets was an

idea commonly greeted with 'general scepticism'.[10] In fact, far-sighted businesses had long been users of mechanical calculators and punched card tabulators to automate parts of their business administration. Nevertheless, the adoption of the computer as an office tool came as something of a surprise to many people, not least because the first business computer was built by a company best known for baking cakes and brewing tea.

J. Lyons and Co was one of the largest catering firms in 1950s Britain, controlling a nationwide organisation of factories, restaurants and tea shops. Already an enthusiastic user of punched card data machines, Lyons became interested in using a computer in its operations as early as 1948. With no computers available to buy, it set about building its own, the Lyons Electronic Office (LEO), based on Cambridge University's EDSAC computer. LEO was running by 1951 and was soon put to a variety of uses by Lyons to run regular business operations, such as payroll and stock control. Early scientific computers were explicitly complicated in appearance, normally laboratory racks of components, naked for the world to see, and festooned with untidy cables. LEO was hidden in closed metal cabinets, formed into walls surrounding a control desk. It had a neat and orderly appearance that exemplified the business efficiency the machine was meant to bring, and heralded a new era of office automation. Despite Lyons's workmanlike applications for its new pet, journalists delighted in the startling juxtaposition of the robot brain and the tea shop. Press reports on LEO, 'the tea-shop brain', questioned whether 'his' duties would involve counting the numbers of beans on toast, or calculating the mileage of Swiss roll required during the school holidays or how the weather would affect how many cups of tea would be sold. Incredulous though the journalists might have been, these were just the sorts of matters that LEO was soon concerning himself with. One early task, the tea-shop job, automated the ordering and delivery of pies and cakes to Lyons's 200 cafes.

Another task was to help tea blending. On the back of LEO's success, Lyons formed its own company to make the machines for other companies, just one of several British firms to dabble in making computers in the 1950s and '60s. Indeed, Britain was soon home to a lively and innovative computer industry as such companies as Ferranti, Elliott Brothers, English Electric and British Tabulating Machinery began selling machines around the world. Sadly, this early British lead in computing was short lived. Powerful competition emerged from well-funded US companies, significantly IBM, which came to dominate the market for electronic computers worldwide.

LEO is a classic example of how computing first made itself felt outside the air-conditioned lairs the machines lived in, as they began to serve bureaucracy in the 1950s. Joining philosophical concerns over whether machines could think, and disquiet over their ability to add numbers faster than people could, came worries about what their capabilities would mean for employment. At first LEO had been presented as a marvellous means for saving office staff from the drudgery of repetitive clerical tasks, and Lyons was at pains to point out that no staff would be made redundant by the machine. However, there was no escaping the fact that LEO did the work of over 300 clerks at the annual running cost of just 50 clerks, a considerable saving of manpower and money.[11] Just as industrialisation had replaced manual workers with factory machinery, clerical workers faced a future where computing machinery might be able to do the jobs of secretaries, filing clerks, payroll accountants and other administrators far faster then they. As the *Daily Mirror* remarked in 1955, electronic brains and robots could not only play draughts, but do everything from writing love letters and baking pies, to mathematics and manufacturing, and they were intimidatingly good at it: 'Whatever your job is, the chances are that one of these machines can do it faster or better than you can.'[12] As the 1950s turned into the 1960s, the computer was starting to be seen as a potential threat to livelihoods.

Mad machines

In 1966, WOTAN, a new computer recently installed in London's brand new Post Office Tower, suffered a series of spectacular errors that caused chaos across the capital. Built at a time when the British computer industry was threatened by IBM and other US competitors, WOTAN had been proudly presented to the press only days before as a great advance for the nation. The machine's appearance, the typical panels of blinking lights, spinning reels of tape and teletype printers, betrayed little of the advances built into it. WOTAN was not just tied to punched cards, but had a crude form of voice input. Years ahead of its time, it could network with other computers around the world, a revolutionary feature that pre-dated the US ARPANET, the predecessor of the Internet, by three years. For the day, WOTAN was a remarkable machine, a shining achievement of the 'White Hot Technological Revolution' recently declared by Prime Minister Harold Wilson. However, as the machine was being prepared for networking to other supercomputers at strategic locations around the world, all did not go quite according to plan...

Much to the surprise of WOTAN's designer, Professor Brett, who had confidently declared to the press that the machine was merely a brain that thought logically without political or personal opinions, it became sentient. Computing that mankind had reached the limit of its potential and, logically, the world would be better run by computers, WOTAN unleashed an army of robotic war machines to bring swinging 1960s London under coldly logical computer control. WOTAN, of course, was fictional, the villain of the 1966 *Doctor Who* story 'The War Machines'. Written at a time when very few people had direct experience of electronic brains, it demonstrates how computers came to be portrayed in ways that made them seem threatening, but confused their nature for dramatic effect. Surprisingly, WOTAN was not just a wild flight of fantasy, but an idea of the programme's scientific adviser, the scientist Dr Kit Pedler, who had been hired to base *Doctor Who* more in 'real' science.* Despite assertions from computer scientists that their creations were perfect slaves, intellectually stupid and capable of doing only what they were told, the potential for the machines to turn on humankind was irresistible to writers. In the real world, stories about computers sending out absurd utility bills for '£NIL' were already circulating by the 1960s, but in science fiction the logical but mindless nature of computers became far more threatening.

To science fiction writers the computer became a Frankenstein's monster for the electronic age; an inhuman machine, just a logic error away from turning on the inferior beings who created it. The computer 'taking over' became a common science fiction trope, in stories that often borrowed from real computing developments as much as they invented them. The homicidal HAL 9000 of Arthur C. Clarke's 1968 story *2001: A Space Odyssey* is probably the most famous of these mad machines. In a classic tale of man versus machine, HAL murders the crew of the spacecraft it controls, before a lone survivor shuts him down. The cause of this trouble, once again, was a logical error, a concept writers enthusiastically embraced as a way of explaining why a computer had gone mad, or as a way of shutting it down once it had gone rogue. Again, HAL was influenced by real-world computing developments, this time in artificial intelligence, which was making great strides in the 1960s. Massachusetts Institute of Technology (MIT) computer scientist and artificial intelligence pioneer Marvin Minsky was even a consultant on Stanley Kubrick's film version.

Elsewhere, computing development was accelerated by an influx of military funding due to the Cold War. Machines were put to work controlling missiles, simulating battles or managing the information flows in air-defence systems that

---

*WOTAN was Pedlar's first step towards the creation of an even more famous species of electronic monster, the half-man, half-machine Cybermen, another ruthlessly logical embodiment of machines taking over people.

protected nations from surprise attack. Inevitably, writers explored the risks of defence computers taking over and threatening humanity. In *Colossus: The Forbin Project*, for example, the supercomputer in charge of the American defences fulfils its mission of keeping the peace by blackmailing humankind with the nuclear weapons under its control. The AM defence supercomputer of Harlan Ellison's chilling story *I Have No Mouth But I Must Scream* goes further, destroying most of humanity, then subjecting the last survivors to an existence of never-ending torture. Not all of the computer's media appearances were quite so foreboding. They could be a source of comedy too, such as in the 1957 Hollywood romance *Desk Set*, based around Spencer Tracy's installation of a computer named EMERAC in the research department of a business managed by Katherine Hepburn. After a spirited battle of wills between Tracy and Hepburn over the machine's introduction, Tracy eventually uses EMERAC to propose to Hepburn, who decides against its logical advice not to marry Tracy and accepts his proposal anyway. Love, after all, is illogical. Yet even in comedy there was disquiet, from staff fearful of being made obsolete by an all-knowing machine, which accidentally sacked every employee in the company when it inevitably went wrong.

The takeover by the all-powerful machine was far from the only threat computing held for humanity. As computer scientists entertained people with their machines' abilities to solve any mathematical problem, fiction writers and journalists often made the computer out to be a magically all-knowing information machine, a brain with all the answers. By the 1960s, large organisations such as the government, banks, and police, were using computerised data banks to hold information on a large scale, and worries emerged in the press over the risks of a 'data-bank society'. Given how much computers have become associated with the idea of 'Big Brother' surveillance and collection of information, it is interesting to note that George Orwell never mentioned computers in his dystopian novel *Nineteen Eighty-Four*. He had no reason to – the novel took shape on his page just as Baby was being assembled in a Manchester laboratory. While the two were unlinked at the beginning, Big Brother and computers became entwined as time went by, both in their way information machines relentlessly collecting, manipulating and using data.

Just as *Nineteen Eighty-Four*'s Winston Smith spent his time rewriting inconvenient historical 'facts' to support Big Brother's new political agendas, by the 1960s and '70s the press was speculating that real-world governments or big businesses, might use computer data for nefarious ends. As British industry was racked by strikes, some wondered if civil servants could manipulate computer systems to stop benefit payments to the families of strikers. Others became concerned over the use of police computers to hold unverified gossip and rumour, or details of political beliefs. It was suggested that governments, as the largest users of computers, could use their huge stores of collected personal information to build mathematical models of how a society would behave, and then manipulate and control the society from on high. 'So subtle will be this process', warned computer expert Ray Jackson in 1967, 'that no one will be aware of how his behaviour is being influenced. Real power will lie in the hands of those at the top'.[13] The concerns of recent years over the potential misuse of personal data by Internet companies, supermarkets and governments are but a new incarceration of older worries over the implications of the data-bank society.

Miniature cities of silicon

Science fiction writers and journalists may have portrayed the computer in sinister ways, but to most people computers were so uncommon that they were perhaps more mysterious and misunderstood than overtly threatening. In everyday life few people got to see much of real computers, even those using them. To be a computer user often meant punching programs and data onto punched cards or paper tape, submitting them to the machine's 'high-priest' operators for its consideration, then returning later to collect the results, all without actually seeing the computer itself. The computer was heard, but not seen, present in people's lives more through its effects, such as printouts of calculations and wage slips, rather than 'in person'. Computer advertising from the 1950s to '70s often did not even show computers, and instead promoted computerisation to businesses with promises of speed, efficiency and order. When advertising did show the computer it was invariably a forbidding electronic monolith, a similar situation to science fiction, which favoured portraying computers as big machines. Science fiction may have occasionally featured small computers, but the star of the show was most often the giant electronic brain, a HAL or WOTAN character in its own right, inhabiting cabinets of whirling tape and blinking lights. However, in the real world, the computer technology that filled the cabinets had actually been shrinking at an incredible pace.

Early computers were huge because they had to be. The earliest machines of the 1940s had been built using hundreds or thousands of light bulb-sized radio valves in their logical circuits. In the 1950s, valves were superseded by transistors made of semiconductors, such as Germanium, fingertip-sized devices that needed a fraction of the power of valves to operate. By the 1960s many transistors were being squeezed together onto single integrated circuits, or computer chips. Noticing the trend of fitting more and more transistors onto a single chip, Gordon Moore, co-founder of American chip maker Intel, predicted in 1965 that the number of transistors on a chip would double every 18 month for at least the next decade. 'Moore's Law' has more or less held for half a century, becoming almost an industry-standard target driving the steady increase in computing power since the 1960s. The sum effect of this relentless improvement on the size and performance of computers themselves was dramatic. In the late 1970s, the computer scientist Christopher Evans, looking for a way to get over to a wider audience just what this meant, calculated that if motor cars had developed at the same rate as computer chips a Rolls-Royce should cost £1.35 with an engine capable of three million miles to the gallon yet still capable of propelling a cruise liner.[14]

Just as logic circuits became more concentrated, other components shrank too. New types of magnetic memory superseded the cathode ray tube, acoustic delay line and other primitive types of memory used by early machines. In the 1960s 'minicomputers' began appearing. Mini was a relative term – they filled a few cabinets with components rather than the rooms of equipment required by larger machines, which became know as 'mainframes'. The computer was still a large, complex and expensive machine and far from domestic. In 1969, American luxury retailer Neiman Marcus made probably the first attempt to market a computer to a home audience by offering the Honeywell 'Kitchen Computer' in its extravagant Christmas gifts catalogue. Advertised with a picture of the computer console being used in the kitchen by a pinafored housewife under the slogan, 'if she could only cook as well as Honeywell can compute', the Kitchen Computer perfectly demonstrated how impractical a home computer was in the late 1960s. Quite apart from its large size, it cost $10,600 and came with a two-week programming course to learn how to use it, making it rather a large investment of time and money just to replace a cookbook.

At about the same time that Neiman Marcus was advertising the Kitchen Computer as a laughably impracticable novelty gift, American computer chip maker Intel began developing a new technology that would make a home computer a practical reality. In 1969, Intel was approached to design the circuitry for a new electronic calculator. Rather than designing a specific set of logic chips for a calculator, they designed a set of chips which could be programmed to act as a calculator, but could be programmed for other purposes instead – a general-purpose processor. Before the 1970s the central processing unit (CPU), the thinking bit of a computer, was commonly made up of several separate integrated circuits linked together. Intel packed 2,300 transistors onto a single microchip, just a couple of centimetres across, and arranged them to form a complete CPU – a *microprocessor*. Looked at through a microscope, Intel's 4004 microprocessor resembled the plan of a city, a grid of streets laid out for data to flow around the various locations and landmarks. This tiny city of silicon was the world's first 'computer on a chip', the first commercially available microprocessor, which within a few years would change the nature of computing dramatically.

The microprocessor revolution

Revolutionary though it may have been, the Intel 4004 did not change the world overnight. Its capabilities were rather limited, and it was soon overtaken by more capable chips such as the Intel 8080 and Motorola 6800. Rather like larger computers before, it would take time for people to find uses for microprocessors, but their universal utility was far greater than any computer device before. It simply did not matter that the power of an individual microprocessor was tiny compared to that of a full-sized mainframe or minicomputer. Microprocessors were so cheap and so small that they could be used in any device where the machine had to do some form of 'thinking', and could bring dramatic reductions in cost and size.

Take, for instance, the electronic calculator, which by the end of the 1960s was typically a desktop machine about the size of a typewriter, priced at a few hundred pounds, and shared by several people in an office or laboratory. By 1973, after a few years of dramatic development and competition between manufacturers, calculators were pocket sized and, with prices as low as £25, cheap enough to be owned by individuals. Microprocessors changed the way that electronics were developed too, allowing nimble small companies to develop products far more easily than had been possible before, helping them to compete with larger firms. 'It wasn't that you had to have a lab full of wire-wrap technicians and huge investment in making a prototype of a hundred silicon chips,' explains Chris Shelton, an electronics engineer whose small company designed many microprocessor-powered products. 'It was that my little team could be as good as anyone else's in the world. We could compete with anybody. All it was, was £20 for the processor, and the rest was down to brains.' The ease of putting microprocessors to use, their low cost and useful capability, quickly led to their use in all sorts of devices: central heating, washing machines, machine tools, medical machines, television remote controls, shop tills, traffic lights, gambling machines, electronic typewriters. Even the humble bag of crisps was touched by microprocessors. 'Crisp flavouring at the time got a lot of flak, because it was either under-flavoured or over-flavoured,' Chris Shelton explains. One of Shelton Instruments' most successful microprocessor-powered products was for making more evenly flavoured crisps. 'The crisp flavour controller was great fun; it had never been done before,' recalls Shelton. 'It ended up that the supermarkets would specify that our flavour controller was used.' Computer-flavoured crisps was just one of the many unseen ways that microprocessors were beginning to creep into new applications in the 1970s. The list of their potential uses seemed endless, but worries began to grow over what this new technology would mean for society.

In 1978, developments in microelectronics suddenly came to much wider public attention in Britain thanks to a BBC *Horizon* documentary, 'Now the Chips Are Down', a powerful prophecy of how the world would be changed by microprocessors and information technology. The programme was a potent mix of incredible wonders and sinister threats, exploring the history, applications and social impact of the tiny '£5 computer'. It opened with a promise that viewers were going to see amazing things and delivered a startling showcase of new wonders, such as word processors, machines that could read books to the blind, tractors ploughing fields without drivers, and warehouses and factories run by robots.

It was a striking display of new technology, but there was something darkly Darwinian about the whole thing, a survival of the fittest and the most technologically adept. Viewers were left to wonder what was going to happen in a future where two or three word processors could do the job of ten secretaries, and where factory robots would cause mass unemployment.

The chip, it was warned, could be the reason why children would grow up without jobs, and cause dramatic changes across society. There was a relentless inevitability about what was to come, the only real question being, what was Britain to do to manage the change? Would it be a society where millions were unemployed, or one where new high-technology industries, like computer programming, created opportunities for fortunes to be made? How was British industry to beat Japan, the USA and Germany in the race to automate? What would the government do to manage Britain's transition to this new world?

Looking back from a world where microprocessor-driven technologies are a common feature of everyday life it seems hard to see what all the fuss was about, but then we need to understand both the sweeping scale of the change expected, and how it applied to 1970s Britain. With the decline of its empire, industry and economy, Britain was a country widely held to be in decline. Industry was ridden by strikes and 'the British Disease' of poor productivity, the electricity industry had problems keeping the lights on and unemployment was rising as the value of the pound was falling. In the 1978/79 'Winter of Discontent', widespread strikes saw walkouts in public services, uncollected rubbish piles in the streets and even the dead go unburied. What would mass computerisation and automation mean for a country that could barely manage the problems of the day, let alone the future?

After 'Now the Chips Are Down', microprocessors came to far greater prominence than they had before. A special screening of the programme was even arranged for members of the government, which by 1978 was already being warned of Britain's lack of preparation for dealing with the microprocessor revolution and the problems it could bring. Society, it was warned, could be split between a technologically literate elite that understood the new technology and reaped the benefits, and a mass of unemployed, second-class citizens who were left behind. British industry, already inefficient, could be unable to adapt to using the new technologies, or be held back by obstructive unions and strikes. The whole country seemed on the verge of obsolescence, ready to fall behind more adept nations that were able to exploit new technology to the full.

For all these risks there were opportunities too, if Britain was ready to grasp them. The sociologist David Skinner has described the swirl of promises and prophecies around microprocessors and information technology as a form of millennialism, a societal transformation to a new golden age.[15] Microprocessors were a threat, but if their introduction was properly managed, if businesses were ready to exploit their potential and if people were educated in their use, then the benefits could relieve Britain of many of its problems. New high-tech industries based around information technologies were widely described as potentially the new Industrial Revolution that Britain needed to renew its faltering economy. 1978 saw the government allocate £15 million to start the Microprocessor Application Project, intended to alert key decision makers and industry to the potential of microelectronics. It marked the start of what soon became a concerted effort by the state to encourage Britain to stop worrying and learn to love the microprocessor and all that the cheap information technology it allowed might do.

Mighty micros

As the government began to plan for Britian's technological future, newspapers and popular books speculated widely on what the microprocessor would mean for everyday life: fewer jobs, far more free time for everyone, the end of boring work, incredible new gadgets. These were the same sorts of stories the media had always printed about computers, but with a new urgency and a wider scope, given the rapid pace of development and the realistic possibility that computers would soon be everywhere. Among the most thought-out visions of the future was *The Mighty Micro*, a 1979 best-selling book on the computerised future of humanity, written by Christopher Evans. He was a psychologist and computer scientist, an expert on cults and a friend of science fiction authors, and worked at the National Physical Laboratory, where Turing had worked decades earlier. In *The Mighty Micro*, Evans set out a vision of how mass use of information technology would change human society over the coming decades. Thirty years later the book remains a compelling read, both for the wide-ranging scale of change it imagined, and for the comparison between the future as it was seen in 1979 and the future that we live in now.

In the abstract and in surprisingly many details, Evans was correct. Jobs, government bureaucracy, leisure time, crime; cheap computing power has changed the world in ways much like those he predicted through such technologies as 'communicative typewriters' and 'TV games'. Yet in some senses Evans's vision was too technocratic, too dedicated to all that technology could do, rather than anticipating what people would want it to do. Refrigerators that warn that food is going off, and door bells showing who is at the door exist, but are barely used; technically possible, they remain socially and commercially unappealing. He also underestimated how people fit new technologies around old ones rather than just replace them. Evans expected the obsolescence of the printed word by the year 2000, yet printed books and newspapers are still popular, even if e-books and tablet computers, the 'hand-held information terminals' that he foresaw, have joined them. Teachers, doctors, lawyers and other professionals who rely on their knowledge have not yet been replaced by computerised information systems in the ways that Evans suggested, but have adapted to use these new technologies in their work.

Evans was projecting past trends forwards, not predicting the future as such. He sought clues for the logical next steps in changes that technology had already wrought. Suggestions like a 30-hour working week, with retirement at 55, seemed perfectly reasonable given how much technology had already affected working conditions since the Industrial Revolution. Other predictions seem idealistic. Among other things, he hoped that computer-simulated war games would act against the aggressive whims of politicians and generals to bring an end to war. In other cases, Evans was overambitious in how quickly he expected developments. His suggestion that technology would soon enable 'the spread of information from human being to human being across the base of the social pyramid' is a remarkable prediction of social networking. Evans also suggested that this free flow of information would challenge authoritarian regimes, perhaps leading to the disintegration of the Soviet Union. The Soviet Union fell long before the creation of Twitter and Facebook, but the Arab Spring uprisings of 2010, in which social media has been a driving force, have vindicated Evans's basic notion.

In another 30 years, perhaps more of Evans's prophesies of how information technologies would change the world will come to pass, but more important than exactly what he got right or wrong is the magnitude of the change. *The Mighty Micro* demonstrates the sweeping scale on which change was expected in the 1970s, driven by cheap information technologies. Moreover, *The Mighty Micro* was not a definite vision of things to come, but an array of possibilities for what might be. For all the scope of his imagination, Evans offered no certainty save for the inevitability of change, as one technical step lead relentlessly to the next. For those who were adaptable and willing to learn, the new world offered great opportunities. Those who chose to remain ignorant, he warned, would find the world of the future an alien place. Yet as society at large was waking up to the potential of microprocessors, a few enthusiasts were already putting them to work in interesting ways.

CHAPTER TWO

Hobbyists Create Microcomputers

The Altair 8800 did not look much like a real computer, even in 1975. True, it had the flashing lights that one would expect a computer to have, but it was far too small to really be one. A simple metal box with rows of lights and switches on its front, it was compact enough to fit on a tabletop, when even a so-called minicomputer was the size of a few filing cabinets. MITS (Micro Instrumentation and Telemetry Systems), the company that produced it, initially referred to Altair as a 'minicomputer kit', but really it was a *microcomputer.* The secret to how Altair could possibly be a 'full blown computer' in such a small package, which cost just $397, was the tiny Intel 8080 microprocessor at the centre of it. Thanks to the microprocessor, MITS could build a machine small enough and cheap enough for individuals to own, even if they typically had to assemble the Altair from a kit themselves. Much to MITS great surprise, it sold by the thousand and triggered something seismic. Altair, historians generally agree, was the machine that sparked the personal computer revolution. It stands as the moment at which an underground interest in personal computing reached critical mass and began a chain reaction to bring information technology to the masses.

As with any breakthrough moment in technology, Altair had a number of precursors. By the early 1970s, several companies were grasping towards some sort of personal computing device. However, few of them were thinking of supplying home computers to the general public. Semiconductor-chip companies, for example, had started producing development systems intended to help engineers develop devices based around their microprocessors. Several business machine companies offered small computers, but they were expensive and not aimed at personal sales. In 1964, Olivetti launched the Programma 101, a $3,200 programmable calculator, which despite looking like an oversized cash register was architecturally a computer, albeit of limited power. The 1973 French Micral N was probably the first complete microprocessor-based *microcomputer* to be commercially available, but it sold as a sort of cut-price minicomputer not as a personal machine. In 1975, mainframe giant IBM produced a portable computer, the IBM 5100. At a weight of 50 pounds, and priced at nearly $9,000, the International *Business* Machine corporation was certainly not thinking of the home market. Even if it could make personal computing devices, the corporate computing world was not set up to think about supplying products to individuals. Indeed, many computing professionals regarded microprocessors as of laughably low power, possibly useful for running peripheral devices, but certainly not as the brains of serious computers.

While personal computing was being neglected by established computer manufacturers, calculator firms, small electronics companies and individuals were showing far more interest. In 1970, unemployed scientist John Blankenbaker began designing a simple educational computer, named the Kenbak-1, in his Los Angeles garage. The name took inspiration from the Kodak camera, which had made photography affordable to a wider audience, and Blankenbaker hoped his $750 machine would do the same with computing. Aimed at introducing elementary programming, using switches and lights as an interface, it only sold about 40 units, mainly to educational establishments, but was probably the first commercially available personal computer.[1] Far more popular, with engineers and the mathematically curious at least, were programmable scientific calculators. Among the most significant was the 1974 Hewlett Packard HP-65, a $795 calculator that allowed users to key in mathematical programs and store them on tiny magnetic strips. HP's advertising proclaimed it the 'smallest programmable computer ever', although its capabilities were largely limited to mathematical and scientific functions.

The driving force in opening up computing to a general audience came from electronics enthusiasts, or hobbyists – the sort of people who enjoyed technical hobbies such as building their own radios, electric organs or other electronic gadgets. To the hobbyists, the personal computer was a fantastic project, and even before Altair a few dedicated enthusiasts were cobbling together TTL logic chips* and other electronic components to create their own home-brewed computers. The latent demand became clear in 1974 when *Radio Electronics* magazine sold thousands of sets of plans for the Mark-8 Minicomputer. The Mark-8 was a fiendishly complicated do-it-yourself scheme for building a desktop computer around an early Intel 8008 microprocessor. Of the thousands of plans sold, probably only a fraction were converted into working Mark-8s by enthusiasts, who had to source most of the parts themselves. Nevertheless, it showed the extent of desire for a personal computer among technically interested people. In January 1975 Altair appeared on the cover of *Popular Electronics*. Not only was it more powerful machine than the Mark-8; it also sold as a relatively convenient kit, and thousands of electronics hobbyists eagerly ordered one.

'The home computer is here!'

Altair's producer, MITS, was a small company based in offices in a shopping centre in Albuquerque, New Mexico, US. Best known for producing calculators and telemetry systems for model rockets, it was about as far as possible to imagine from the corporate world of IBM. After MITS was bruised by the collapse of the calculator market, owner Ed Roberts, a former US Airforce research engineer, decided that a computer might save his company's flagging fortunes. Announced in *Popular Electronics*, the machine was cleverly pitched by MITS and the magazine, which introduced it in an editorial headed

---

*TTL (Transistor-Transistor Logic), a family of integrated circuits, or chips, offering various logic gates and other circuits that could be built together to create more complex electronic devices.

'THE HOME COMPUTER IS HERE!' Apocryphally named by Roberts's daughter after the planet the starship *Enterprise* was visiting in that week's episode of *Star Trek*, the prototype Altair got lost in the post en route to *Popular Electronics*. Undaunted by the loss of the only machine, *Popular Electronics* and MITS mocked up a case with some lights on it for the front cover and announced Altair as a 'real, full-blown computer'.

According to *Popular Electronics*, it could be used for everything from a scientific calculator or machine controller, to an aircraft autopilot or a brain for a robot. In a further appeal to the tinkering mindset of the electronics enthusiast, its capabilities could be expanded even further with additional circuit boards. Thanks to Roberts negotiating a bulk discount on 8080 chips from Intel, $75 down from the usual $360, Altair was surprisingly affordable. The basic machine cost $397, not much more than the list price of the 8080 itself, a ludicrous figure when even a basic minicomputer cost thousands of dollars. Altair was an appealing mix of technical capability, affordability and marketing. Roberts had hoped to sell a few hundred Altairs but, in a story to be repeated many times over the subsequent personal computer boom, MITS was overwhelmed with orders. However, the movement Altair sparked was a long way from truly bringing computers to the masses.

Altair was a hobbyist computer aimed largely at enthusiasts and scientific customers. Although available ready-made for $498, most people assembled their own. Indeed, that was part of the attraction. Potential users sent off a cheque in the post and waited, frequently for months, so heavy was the demand and so small was MITS. Eventually a kit would arrive in the post, packed with hundreds of electronic components to solder together, assembly instructions and circuit diagrams. MITS' advertisements warned that building an Altair would not be a piece of cake, but that it would be a rewarding experience because at the end of it builders would have a real computer, albeit a rather basic one. The machine's interface was the rows of lights and toggle switches on the front panel. Using it was not unlike programming Baby back in 1948. Programs were entered by laboriously clicking the switches on the front to input binary digits into the machines' tiny 256-byte memory.[*] A flick of another switch made the program run, and the result would appear in binary displayed on the lights; on for a one, off for a zero. Despite the rather grand claims of the adverts, the basic machine did little more than flash a few lights under computer control. However, Altair was not really a finished product, but a starting point for people to remake their machines into new forms that suited their interests by building on upgrades of various types, such as extra memory, video displays and keyboards. Indeed, a whole cottage industry soon emerged of hobbyists and electronics firms producing upgrades for the machine, and for hobbyists fitting upgrades was all part of the fun. Yet although Altairs could be made into useful tools, for most of those involved the appeal was as a technical hobby. Only a comparatively small group of people had the interest and the skills to enjoy it, but to those who did it was utterly amazing.

Before governments and big corporations had woken up to the great potential of the microprocessor, it had already fallen into the hands of electronics enthusiasts. To the hobbyists the chip was not a frightening and disruptive technology, but an object of fascination and excitement with a potential for changing the world. At a time when computers were widely associated with Big Business and Big Government, bringing computers to the people had a distinctly countercultural

[*]Computers have different types of memory. Simply put, Random Access Memory (RAM), often just referred to as 'memory', stores the program and data currently being used on the computer, and can be swiftly accessed and altered; Read Only Memory (ROM) chips cannot be altered, and are used to permanently store programs and data, such as the system software built into most computers; other types of memory, such as magnetic discs, paper tapes, punched cards and magnetic tapes, are slower to access and typically used for data storage when the computer is switched off.

appeal. Indeed, something of the freedom of the hippy years of the 1960s rubbed off on the early personal computer movement in the United States. At user groups, like the famous Homebrew Computer Club near the Silicon Valley area of California, enthusiasts met together to discuss their new hobby, shared ideas, swapped programs and helped each other out. Writing in the 1980s after interviewing many of its protagonists, technology journalist Steven Levy summed up the ideas behind the early computer movement as the Hacker Ethic; an ethos of making computers accessible and information openly available for the positive benefit of all.

Ironically, this egalitarian movement also spawned several corporate giants. In 1975, young programmers Bill Gates and Paul Allen approached MITS with a paper tape containing an Altair version of the BASIC programming language. BASIC freed Altair users from the tyranny of bruised fingers from toggle-switching in programs in ones and zeros, and allowed the machine to be instructed by keyboard using user-friendly commands like PRINT and GOTO. Altair BASIC was sold at prices starting from $60, but the very idea of selling software was something of a culture shock. In the mainframe computer world, software was generally swapped freely between users, or part of the service that a company got by buying a computer. Hobbyists were used to sharing their efforts between each other too, freely copying and adapting their efforts. Very soon paper tapes of Altair BASIC were being widely shared and copied within the community. It was theft, complained Gates in his 1976 'Open Letter to the Hobbyists', published in enthusiast newsletters. By copying BASIC without paying for it, Gates argued that people were robbing developers of the incentive to develop new software. In the eyes of Gates and others like him, software was a commodity to be bought and sold, not something free to be shared. But if it could be bought and sold, there was the potential for a whole new industry to do just that. Micro-Soft, as Gates's new company was called, went on to develop BASIC for several other personal computers before moving on to making operating systems, applications and vast sums of money in the 1980s.

There was entrepreneurship on the hardware side too. Among the members of the Homebrew Computer Club was electronics engineer Steve Wozniak. Like many others there, Wozniak built his own personal computer, a typical hobbyist machine that was simply a circuit board to plug a video display and keyboard into. After showing it to his more entrepreneurial friend Steve Jobs, the two decided to go into business together. Jobs sold his VW camper van, Wozniak his HP65 calculator. With the funds they started a business in Jobs's home, making and selling a kit based on Wozniak's machine for $666.66 as the Apple computer. Through anecdotes such as these, the early history of personal computing is normally told as a quintessentially American success story – a tale of homespun ingenuity at the hands of quirky pioneers working in garages, of fortunes made from turning digital dreams into hit products and of great corporations founded on the visions of geek-entrepreneurs. Far less appreciated is how hobbyist computing was a more international story than is generally told.

Meanwhile, back in Britain

Just as *Radio Electronics* and *Popular Electronics* had enticed droves of Americans to build their own computers, articles on silicon chips and DIY computer projects were appearing in the pages of British magazines. Between adverts for amplifier kits and diagrams for circuitry, British enthusiasts began reading about microprocessors and computers in magazines like *Practical Wireless* and *Electronics Today International*, and started building their own. The Amateur Computer Club (ACC) was founded as early as 1972 to cater for a growing body of enthusiasts around the country. With around 600 members by 1976, it was admittedly a small start compared to the estimated 50,000 hobbyists in the USA by this point,[2] but it was an active one. Through the ACC's newsletter, typewritten with crudely hand-drawn diagrams, members read about computer science topics, followed plans to build hardware projects and compared notes about their new hobby. The club's members were not just concerned with microprocessors, but with building computers from scratch using discrete integrated circuits. A few even purchased old mainframe computers at scrap value and set themselves up as computing bureaus, free from the tyranny of organisational control. Among the ACC's most ambitious projects was the Weeny-Bitter, a basic £50 DIY computer project useful, so the newsletter said, for everything from simple games and education, to controlling household devices and running train sets. In Britain, just as in the United States, the appetite for personal computing was there among those with the technical know-how to make it work.

'It started out with Mike Lord, who designed a computer for the amateur computer club called the Weeny-Bitter, made up of discrete components, switches, gates, buffers, logic,' recalled computer journalist Guy Kewney in a 2008 interview. 'With relatively little expertise you could put together a Weeny-Bitter that could process data in and out. And people were prepared to go to that sort of trouble to get their hands on a piece of working data-processing equipment.' Kewney was one of the earliest journalists to pay significant attention to personal computing in its own right, not just as the sum of its electronic parts. 'The chip business was a component story,' he explained. 'I thought this was a short-sighted and stupid approach.' Kewney began writing about microcomputers in electronics and science magazines, bringing a wry humour to what could have been a very technically dry subject, and becoming one of the most influential early figures to propagate personal computing in Britain.

It was only a matter of time before personal computing outgrew the electronics press it had started in. In 1978, *Personal Computer World* (*PCW*) began appearing on the shelves of newsagents, joining American imports such as *Byte*.[3] Like so much of the microcomputing scene, *PCW* started as a grassroots effort. Its first issue was assembled in a London cafe by Angelo Zgorelec, a newsagent and occasional journalist who had become excited by computers and the potential for a magazine about them. After making a trip to New York to attend a *Byte* magazine computer show, where he witnessed people queuing for hours to get in, Zgorelec was convinced that a British computer magazine would be a success. His instinct was spot on. The first issue's print run promptly sold out and *PCW*, soon to feature the long-running 'NewsPrint' column by Guy Kewney, became an established institution of the microcomputing world. It soon had competition from another new starter, *Practical Computing*, which began in a similarly low-key way, but had a slightly different editorial line. 'We were rather austere, middle class and intellectual. *PCW* was much more downmarket. It would happily write about any old shoebox with lights,' observes *Practical Computing*'s editor Peter Laurie mischievously. The enthusiastic *PCW* and higher-brow *Practical Computing* were both quickly joined by a great variety of other computer magazines, many with unique characters of their own, but with a largely male readership. Guy Kewney recalled a call to *PCW* from BMW, inquiring about placing advertising: 'We said, "we're not a car magazine," and they said, "no, but we've looked at your demographic and you have by far the highest ratio of male to female of any publication in the UK." And we looked at our figures and it was something like 99.6per cent male.' To Kewney and others the discrepancy was unusual given how many women worked in professional programming, but microcomputing was undoubtedly a largely male pursuit at first.

Computer magazines were vital to the spread of personal computing. Without their informing and nurturing of computer users it is hard to see how such a technical and open-ended hobby could have developed in the way it did. There may have also been computer clubs and shows, but the reach of magazines was far greater. 'We were information glue that held an amorphous mass of people, each at his own desk, each working on his own problem together,' explains Peter Laurie. 'If we had not existed no one would have known what was going on.' To readers who wanted to learn more about their new hobby, magazines were a godsend. They printed things that readers could do with their computer, answered technical questions and advised on the pros and cons of new products. Magazines even published software in the form of pages of computer code to type into a machine and run – provided, that is, they avoided typos, or the magazine had not misprinted anything or the program was not buggy to begin with. In which case the next issue might carry some corrections or an outraged letter to the editor asking what was wrong with it. There was often a certain unpolished enthusiasm to computer journalism at first. It was the handiwork of small teams reporting on a fast-moving sector, and making up the idea of what a computer magazine was as they went along, often with many contributions from readers. 'We couldn't afford to employ reporters who went out to look for stories, so we relied on stuff that was sent in, and on persuading people who were in the business and could write to do pieces for us,' remembers Peter Laurie.

As much as anything else magazines were avidly read just for the sake of interest by an enthusiastic readership. 'A magazine like this has a new, obsessive readership that will forgive a lot of journalistic ineptitudes,' observes Peter Laurie. As well as feeding the interests of a community of users, to the cottage industry springing up to produce things to go with personal computers, the advert pages of magazines were the only reasonable marketplace there was to lay out their wares. Journalists also played a role spreading news through the various personalities and small companies that made up the industry. 'We all knew each other,' explained Guy Kewney. 'I knew Adam Osborne,* the guru of the industry then. He and I used to chat two or three times a week, and then he'd say "have you seen what so and so is

---

*Although British, Adam Osborne was an influential figure of the early American hobbyist computer scene, producing many technical books on microcomputing and electronics in the 1970s, and later starting a computer company to produce the Osborne 1, one of the first portable computers.

doing?" And so I'd ring up so and so, saying "I've heard you're doing x – have you tried doing y?"' Revolutions, political or technological, rely more than anything else on the circulation of ideas and information to get them started. The electronics and computer press was undoubtedly the nerves of the popular computer revolution, but they were not the only way that information got around.

'There were lots of articles about what was happening with microprocessors and microcomputers in California and the US in general, and how this was the up and coming thing,' recalls Bruce Everiss, the managing director of a computerised bookkeeping company in the late 1970s. 'I read about these strange things called computer stores that were starting up. And I thought, "this is interesting, they're in America now and they'll come to the UK – I should start one."' In 1978, Everiss founded Microdigital in Liverpool, one of the very earliest computer shops in Europe, and soon found an untapped market of enthusiasts. 'People turned up from Scotland and Cambridge to buy stuff. And people on the phone said, "I'll just send you any money, put it in the post to me!"' remembers Everiss. 'We shipped huge amounts of stuff.' Microdigital did far more than just sell computers. It soon branched out into publishing software, doing repairs, selling components, making gadgets to connect to computers and printing the *Liverpool Software Gazette*. The customer base was typical of the hobbyist computer world. 'These people were electronics enthusiasts. They were able to build the kit computers,' Everiss explains. 'Then we had *Personal Computer World* start as the first home computer magazine, and then that created a much broader range of customers.' At a time when there were few other direct sources of information, Microdigital became a focal point for enthusiasts, offering personal advice and expertise. 'We were very sociable, because everybody was learning off everybody else,' explains Everiss. 'We'd make people a cup of coffee, then just chat for hours about how exciting it was, what's happening and what's going to happen next. It was a very convivial place.'

Computer clubs and user groups

Conviviality with other computer hobbyists was also on offer at computer clubs and user groups. In late 1978, *PCW* listed the contact details of 33 such groups across the UK. Some were national, united by newsletters and often catering for owners of particular types of computers. The majority were local clubs, sometimes in universities or companies, but mostly open to anyone with an interest. Among them was Cambridge University Processor Group (CUPG), a bunch of student hobbyists who met up to build computers for fun, listened to lectures on electronics and showed off their machines to each other. 'The real men used TTL chips and built their computers from logic gates, and the wimps like me used these new-fangled microprocessor things,' recalls Steve Furber, an aeronautical engineering student who originally joined the club with ideas of learning to build a flight simulator.[4] Hobbyists could make a functional computer from integrated circuits without even needing a microprocessor, but it was akin to designing and building an engine to put in a car. And it probably would not go as fast anyway.

The microprocessor was a ready-built engine, but still needed the rest of the computer to be built around it, a rather involved process that benefited from bouncing ideas off others. 'You talk to people a lot and you scratch your head and you think about it,' explains Furber. 'The engine itself is a microprocessor and there were a number of 8-bit micros available in the late'70s. You'd look at their specs and pick one.' To the untrained eye, most microprocessors of the time, be they MOS 6502, Motorola 6800, Nat-Semi SC/MP, Intel 8080, Zilog Z80 or whatever, looked rather like each other. On the inside the architecture was quite different, leaving hobbyists to judge the comparative merits of speeds, the numbers of registers, the sizes of address or data buses, and how sophisticated the instruction sets to control them were. Despite the dry technicalities it inflamed the passions of computer hobbyists. 'There was a 6502 versus 6800 war going on in the microprocessor society at the time,' recalls Sophie Wilson, another club member from the 1970s. 'The differences may seem small, but if you think about the wars that people have over different songs, different football teams, etc., it's like that, amongst fans of microprocessor design.'

With the basic parts selected, hobbyists would have to translate their understanding of how the computer might work into detailed plans. 'You have to understand how the microprocessor interfaces to the things you want it to talk to,' explains Steve Furber. 'You have to come up with a circuit diagram that connects the processor's address bus to the memory address pins, and the processor's data bus to the memory data pins.' Add a few components to generate timing strobes for the memory and a clock signal to step the processor along, and with plans complete the building began. And so began the work of soldering sockets and components to breadboards or home-made circuit boards, and wiring connections between different parts of the machine, gradually building up into something that could compute. Assuming it all worked, the result was typically a fairly simple machine with switches for entering data and instructions, and lights for reading off the results. If the builder got that far they probably had the skills to expand it, but if they did not British kit computers were on the horizon.

'Learn about microcomputers by owning one!'

Compared to his American counterpart, the British computer amateur was hard done by, complained a prominent article in the first edition of *Personal Computer World* in 1978. In Britain the personal computer scene was less organised, individual hobbyists had less money to spend on their enthusiasms and the electronics industry was doing little to introduce computer products. The British hobbyist was forced to build their own machine from scratch or to import a kit from the USA at great expense. However, that was about to change, thanks to a kit computer, the NASCOM-1, manufactured by Lynx, a company based north of London.

Lynx was the hobbyist subsidiary of electronic component seller North American Semiconductor, NASCO, run by John Marshall, a frequent visitor to the electronics industry in the United States. Impressed by the well-organised and well-supplied amateur computing scene on the West Coast, Marshall wondered if it would be possible to produce a kit computer within the reach of the British enthusiast, while also boosting his business's electronic component sales. 'He had a warehouse full of TTL* essentially, and he thought, "I've got enough stuff here that I'm sure I could make a computer,"' recalls Chris Shelton, the consultant electronics engineer approached to design the machine in 1977. 'He saw a computer as being a way of shifting some of the silicon that was in his warehouse.' To run the machine Shelton selected the Z80 microprocessor, whose built-in features meant fewer other components would be needed to support it, simplifying the design and reducing the cost.

'Marshall insisted on two things in the design,' recalls Shelton. 'He wanted a cracking keyboard and he sourced a quite big and cumbersome Cherry keyboard, a real, proper long travel electric keyboard.' Full-sized electric keyboards were a premium item for hobbyist computers and added to the expense of a machine, but this was a major selling point compared to the fiddly switches used as input on many home-built hobbyist machines. For output, the NASCOM had a television display adaptor built in, raising the machine's usability even higher. 'The second thing was he wanted to see home construction,' continues Shelton. 'That meant a hell of a lot of soldered joints, and indeed the board ended about A4 sized. Also due, in part, to his insistence that it had a CAD layout.'

While hobbyists were hand-sketching plans for their machines, the NASCOM-1's component and connecting circuitry were laid out using autorouted computer-aided design

---

*TTL, transistor–transistor logic, refers to a widespread family of integrated circuits, different sorts of chips that were often used as the building blocks of more sophisticated electronic devices.

(CAD), but with some rather unexpected consequences. 'I was not familiar with autorouting and it never occurred to me how awful it could be,' explains Shelton. 'Placement is the secret of success of an autoroute, and unless you've got a very cunning algorithm for your component placement the autoroute ends up running tracks everywhere.' The circuit board design that emerged from the CAD system was perfectly functional, but far larger and a bit more expensive than it should have been thanks to the quirks of autorouting. However, with the design money already spent it would have to do.

The resulting machine, an ungainly circuit board of components plugged into a large keyboard and television, was far from elegant, but it worked perfectly well and tapped an unmet demand for computer kits. At a little over £200 in basic form, it was far more affordable than American imports and a range of upgrades was soon available. 'It was very popular in its way,' recalls Shelton. 'Marshall thought it might sell one or two thousand and it rapidly got to five.' As many as 15,000 NASCOM-1s were eventually sold and according to Shelton, its success became a problem. 'It was so sudden. It was not what they had ever done before and was not what they were expecting.'

The problem was not just the scale of the machine's success, but the fact that it was a kit. While it may have been easier than designing a computer from scratch, building a machine from a kit of parts was a complicated business. There were 55 different integrated circuits and dozen of diodes, resistors and other components that needed to be attached to the board without damaging the delicate electronics. There were 1,300 joints to carefully solder on the NASCOM, and the construction notes warned against rushing the exercise and cautioned that it might take as long as 40 hours to build the machine. In practice, some people took months and even then it might not work. Among the few shops to sell NASCOM computers at first was Microdigital, which soon set up a mail-order sideline repairing kit computers, where Bruce Everiss recalls 'piles of dead NASCOMs arriving every day and going away fixed in the evening'. Patience, skill and perhaps a bit of obsession were needed to build a computer kit, attributes not always possessed by the prospective NASCOM user. For a company used to supplying electronics components, it became difficult to deal with the number of returns of wrongly assembled computers, and the later NASCOM-2 was shipped ready-built, not only in kit form.

NASCOM was far from the only British company with an eye on the hobbyist computer market, and £200 was still more than many hobbyists could afford. Near Cambridge, in the small town of St Ives, the innovative electronics maker Sinclair Radionics was also looking at a computer project. Founded in 1962 by Clive Sinclair, a former electronics writer and journalist, Radionics had produced a varied line of kits for the hobbyist and ready-made goods for the consumer, including amplifiers, hi-fi stereos, miniature radios and calculators. By the late 1970s, Radionics, like many other companies, was in financial trouble as the calculator market was flooded by cheap Japanese imports. Bailed out by the Government's National Enterprise Board (NEB), at the cost of a controlling stake in the firm, Radionics was in a poor position to pursue an innovative computer project. However, Clive Sinclair had also set up another small company, Science of Cambridge, under the management of right-hand man Chris Curry.

Science of Cambridge's first product, a kit for a wrist calculator, was by most accounts a disaster, but then an electronics engineer named Ian Williamson approached them with the idea for a computer kit. Williamson's idea was to use a cheap National Semiconductor SC/MP microprocessor along with calculator parts to make a very cheap computer kit. After a bit of toing and froing, and a redesign to make more use of National Semiconductor parts, adverts for the Science of Cambridge MK14 microcomputer kit began appearing in the electronics press. To look at it was simply a circuit board studded with chips and fitted with a small keypad and calculator display. It was a very basic machine, programmed by typing in a list of arcane hexadecimal instructions, like 3A0F60, then looking at the result on the display. The manual included a variety of programs to try out, simple mathematical functions, electronics utilities, and even moonlander and duck-shooting games, all squeezed into the 256-byte memory and played out on the glowing 8-digit display. It could not do very much without expansion, but at £39.95 it was about the cheapest way to own a computer that did not have to be built from scratch and was soon selling very well.

Inspired by the machine's success, Curry parted ways with Sinclair to found a computer consultancy firm with Hermann Hauser, an Austrian physics graduate from the prestigious Cavendish Laboratory at the university. Initially their company was called Cambridge Processor Unit (CPU), but was soon trading under the name Acorn. With few people around who knew that much about microprocessors, the University Processor Group was a handy source of recruits for the new company. Among them was Steve Furber, who, as he tells it, found Hauser in his office one day with an offer: '"We're thinking of starting this company. Are you interested?" And I said, "Well, I've only ever done this as a hobby… but if you think I can help I'm happy to come and talk."' Typical of the early days of new companies with uncertain futures and novel products, it was an informal sort of arrangement at first. 'In general Acorn did not pay me. The quid pro quo was I did this stuff for fun. I gave them the results when they were interested in them and they gave me bits to play with,' remembers Furber. CPU's earliest jobs included work on microprocessor-controlled fruit machines, fixing an unfortunate tendency of the machines to pay out when someone flicked an electrical cigarette lighter nearby. Another job was assisting the development of the MK14 for Science of Cambridge – ironic given the companies' later rivalry. 'Because of my connection with Chris through the embryonic CPU Limited, I actually did some prototyping of the MK14 and wired one together in my front room at home and debugged it,' says Furber, who also recalled that the two companies actually shared office space for a time.

Another recruit to the fledgling company was Sophie Wilson. She had already built several microprocessor-controlled devices, including an automated cow feeder during a holiday job, and was planning a new computer. 'The MK14 had been launched and there were magazine articles about it, and I was designing a single-board computer,' she recalls. 'It would become two boards, but at the time it was a single-board computer that would be much much better than the MK14.' At about this time, Hermann Hauser came up with the idea of a battery-powered 'electronic pocketbook' to remind him to go to meetings and asked Wilson to design it. She turned up with a portfolio of other schemes as well as the pocketbook plans to prove her design would work. Among the papers was a plan for a 6502 processor computer, then called the Hawk, which Wilson showed to Hauser as an example of how the pocketbook display could work. 'So that sort of ended with Hermann challenging me to build that machine rather than his pocketbook.'

With a few improvements, the Hawk became the basis for the Acorn Microcomputer System 1. When it was released in 1979 the little machine, a calculator-style display and keypad mounted atop a pair of circuit boards, was a perfectly respectable hobbyist computer kit. However, the enthusiasts were not exclusively the market it was aimed at. CPU had been founded as a technology consultancy with an emphasis on applications of microprocessors in control systems, such as fruit machines. The System 1 began a series of more capable rack-mounted systems aimed at controlling electronic equipment and use in laboratories. According to Wilson, catering to the hobbyist market was more of a sideline at first: 'The Acorn System range – there was a nod to the fact that people could build System range stuff for their own amusement, but the purpose of a lot of it was to be an electronic controller.' Probably the most famous use of the System 1 as an electronic controller was in the control panel of a spaceship in the BBC science fiction television series *Blake's Seven*. 'This was around the time that Clive Sinclair was boasting that his ZX80 could be used to run a nuclear power station, which is something of an exaggeration,'* recalls Steve Furber. 'Our counter to this was, well, this is nothing, you know the Acorn System 1 can be used to control a twenty-second century intergalactic spaceship.'

Computing for its own sake?

Making a modern PC do something requires little understanding of how the machine works. Users are insulated from the underlying hardware by layers of software that silently automate much of what the computer does, but disguise the complexity of what is going on within the machine. Hobbyist machines demanded that users had an intimate relationship with the computer's operations, unfiltered by user-friendly operating systems. The line between software and hardware became blurred when users had to understand so much about the underlying machine to use a computer. At its most primitive, low-level programming could be a rather manual business of ordering data around the machine, and required a fundamental understanding of what was happening within the computer.

For those with the technical nous it was all great fun – a sort of puzzle game played in the logic of the machine, where finding the bugs in programs and hardware was part of the challenge. Yet beyond the technicalities of the hobby, just what were hobbyists using their machines for? 'I never thought of that,' recalls Chris Shelton of the NASCOM's design phase. 'Never crossed my mind what people would use it for.' To those building their own computers, either from kits or to their own designs, much of the attraction was simply getting the machine to do something. 'You did not use it necessarily for anything; you're possessing a computer and that's an end in itself,' explains Sophie Wilson. A joy for its practitioners, early microcomputing was a niche activity far too complicated for everyone. 'I think we probably still felt that computers were for

*The ZX80 computer was the successor to the Science of Cambridge MK14, launched in 1980.

people like us, right? Enthusiasts, hobbyists, people who were interested in computers for their own sake,' recalls Steve Furber of the end of the 1970s. 'People who'd be prepared to solder things together to connect them or write assembly code.'

The enthusiasts had invented the personal computer, but they had built it in their own image. The problem with microcomputers, mused *Practical Computing* late in 1979, was that they were too fragile for the real world. The small population of 'micro-freaks' may have delighted in the quirks of their machines, but for a larger industry to develop it needed to involve people who wanted computers for practical ends, not just for their own sake. That was never going to happen when computing required hexadecimal and soldering. Hobbyist computing was a movement rather than a mass activity, a loose grouping of enthusiasts, entrepreneurs and technical journalists. Being a part of it required mastering some arcane technical rituals, attractive to the micro-freak, but not to the man in the street. However, things were beginning to change. Over in the US a new concept of the personal computer as a more accessible machine had started to emerge, which would open up microcomputing to the masses.

The trinity

In 1977, three American companies, Commodore, Apple and Tandy, each launched a ready-made personal computer targeted at a wider market than just hobbyists. The Commodore PET 2001, Apple II and Tandy TRS-80 all looked rather different, but all shared a similar design philosophy. They were complete factory-built computers, shipped as boxes, not just bare circuitry. They allowed people to become computer users without having to become computer builders. Each had a keyboard and video-display output, elevating its user-friendliness above the toggle switches, calculator keypads and hexadecimal displays typical of kit machines. On each, the easy-to-use BASIC language was built in. They were ready-built appliance computers that just needed to be plugged in and switched on for their buyers to begin computing. The trinity did not just make computing more accessible to a technically unskilled audience; they made it more convenient than ever before too.

Of the three, the Apple II is by far the best known. Its great success established Apple firmly in the consumer market, and updated versions were still being produced in the early 1990s. The Apple II established a common form followed by many other personal computers in the following years. The keyboard and computer were built into the same case, to be connected to a television set or monitor, along with disc drives, cassette recorders and other peripherals. Its place in the home was made clear by adverts that placed the computer on a kitchen table, with a wife gazing over from her chores at a husband engrossed in his new obsession. The hobbyist lineage was clear in the great expandability of the machine, and the top opened up to allow a range of expansion cards to be plugged in. It also offered the novelty of a colour display at a time when such things were rare, a boon for entertainment use and games. Its popularity benefited from a good supply of software. In particular, the first spreadsheet, *VisiCalc*, was initially only available on the Apple II, lending it some legitimacy as a business tool. Anecdotes abound of accountants and businessmen buying an Apple II just to run the spreadsheet. With prices starting from $1,298, the Apple II was the most expensive of the trinity. Even then there was a certain prestige attached to Apple's product, it set a standard to which other machines were compared. Even if many prospective computer users could not afford an Apple, many aspired to do so.

The Tandy TRS-80 was the most underrated. Its lower build quality and design economics, such as using simplified Tiny BASIC as its built-in language, earned it the unfortunate nickname 'Trash 80' from its detractors.* Apple may have grown from small beginnings as a hobbyist company, but

---

*However, the improved Level II BASIC, available later as an upgrade, was a great improvement and among the better BASICs available for a home computer.

Tandy was already a major electronics business with a huge chain of Radio Shack electronics stores across the United States. However, the TRS-80 designers struggled to convince Tandy management of the potential for their idea, which at $399 or $599 with a black and white display screen was far more than most of their products. The cautious initial plan to provide a single machine for each of the 3,500 Radio Shack stores proved to be woefully inadequate. Tandy found its switchboards jammed with callers requesting one of the computers. As with Apple, Tandy's marketing presented the TRS-80 as a complete domestic appliance. 'NOT a kit', declared Tandy's adverts, which featured a family clustered around the TRS-80 looking delighted at all they could make it do. The TRS-80 was the first of a series of Tandy personal computers, largely sold through mail order and through its Radio Shack stores.

Although Apple stole much of the attention, the first of the trinity was actually the Commodore PET 2001, launched in January 1977. Established in 1954 by Polish-born Auschwitz survivor Jack Tramiel, a legendarily tough businessman and hands-on manager, Commodore was an established international producer of office equipment and calculators. Already a presence in Britain, it became the most significant American microcomputer company to operate in the British market over the 1970s and '80s. Tramiel's strategy stressed vertical integration, but Commodore's reliance on other firms for microchips left the company in serious difficulties in the mid-1970s as the calculator market became more cut-throat. In 1976, Commodore took over over the struggling chip maker MOS Technology, a major supplier of calculator components. As Brian Bagnell's history of Commodore details, Tramiel's takeover of MOS was a brilliantly ruthless business manoeuvre.[5] At the time MOS was heavily dependent on orders from Commodore and embroiled in an expensive legal battle over patent infringement with the far larger Motorola. Tramiel took advantage of the situation to purchase MOS for a mere three quarters of a million dollars, yet such were Commodore's parlous finances that he had to scrape together funding from wherever he could. 'I remember him calling me up late one night saying, "Kit, I need to get half a million dollars by the end of the month." We were in horrible state, the company was struggling,' recalls Kit Spencer a marketing manager at Commodore UK at the time. '"I don't care what you do," he says. "We've got a chance to buy a chip company; there'll never be a chance like this again…" I remember going up to Boots when we had about 20,000 watches in stock, saying, "Have I got a deal for you!"'

Tramiel's search for funding to purchase MOS not only secured a degree of component self-sufficiency for Commodore's calculator business, but also the services of a first-rate chip-development team lead by Chuck Peddle. He had already led the design of the ubiquitous MOS 6502 microprocessor used in several hobbyist machines, not least MOS's own KIM-1 computer kit. By 1976 he had his sights set on making a very different sort of machine from both hobbyist kit computers and the versatile but essentially limited programmable calculators. 'I remember being over in Palo Alto saying, "When are we going to be able to get something like HP have got?"' recalls Kit Spencer, referring to Hewlett Packard's line of programmable calculators, which included magnetic cards for data storage. 'And Chuck says "We're going to go one stage further, we're going to use a VDU for a display, and a tape deck for the input." It was the Commodore PET.'

Initially priced at $495 for the basic version, with 4k of RAM, the PET 2001 was a strikingly futuristic-looking machine. An angular all-in-one case contained the computer, keyboard and tape recorder, topped with a black and white display screen. The PET was developed in much haste, and Commodore wielded its vertical integration to keep the costs down by using things close to hand. The PET had a metal case because Commodore owned a filing cabinet factory. It used a 'chiclet' keyboard fitted with calculator-type keys, rather than a typewriter-style unit, because Commodore could already make such calculator keyboards cheaply. The name PET 2001 was a portmanteau of the friendly and the futuristic: PET, officially an acronym for Personal Electronic Transactor, but originally a nod to the 1970s fad for pet rocks; 2001, inspired by *2001: A Space Odyssey*. Making its futuristic nature clear, William Shatner, better known as Captain Kirk from *Star Trek*, even fronted the PET's advertising campaign.

The PET was as wildly successful as the other machines of the trinity, and helped to propel Commodore out of its financial troubles. Selling at around £695 at first, the PET did better in the British market than the expensive Apple II or the TRS-80. Much of this success was down to the comprehensive marketing and support effort devised by Kit Spencer, now head of Commodore UK's computer division. 'It had no manuals, no nothing, no software – a pretty bare bones machine,' recalls Spencer of the PET's arrival in the UK. Spencer hired a pair of computer hobbyists to prepare a manual and software, built up a network of dealers and started a magazine, giving the PET the support it needed to flourish. By 1980 over 10,000 units had been sold and Commodore's adverts declared it Britain's 'best-selling microcomputer'.

With the trinity the computer became an appliance for the first time, accessible to people who did not have a detailed understanding of electronics or how a computer worked. Yet it was not quite the start of computing for the masses. Much of the appeal of computing was still among technically curious enthusiasts or people with a need for a computer, rather than the public at large. 'They tended to be quite a lot of technical people. Quite a lot of universities starting small computer departments. They actually used it as scientific controller,' recalls Kit Spencer of the sorts of people who became PET users. 'Simple little payroll packages… and hobbyists who just wanted one, everybody was pretty enthusiastic. And not just being users, they tended to be evangelists for it.'

As the 1970s, ended personal computing was still a movement rather than a mass activity. Computing was now technically accessible to a larger market than ever before, but it had only just started to become culturally accessible, as marketing targeted home users, professionals and small businessmen rather than just hobbyists. Most importantly, its uptake was limited by cost, especially in Britain. Not only were the trinity more expensive than typical hobbyist machines, but imported computers were often sold at a premium on their prices in the US. 1979 prices for the trinity began at around £380 for a TRS-80, £550 for a PET and £810 for an Apple II. With Britain suffering from a recession and with the average household income about £6,000, such computers were expensive luxuries. As 1980 dawned, personal computing was just on the cusp of becoming a mainstream activity. To increase its appeal would require a dramatic gesture to increase its affordability.

CHAPTER THREE

Computers for the Man in the Street

Early in 1980, adverts began appearing in British newspapers for something rather unusual. Sandwiched between pages of economic and social troubles, Thatcherite politics and Cold War paranoia was an advert for a small white box. It looked a little like an overgrown calculator, but declared itself to be the Sinclair ZX80 Personal Computer, and could be bought, ready made, for just £99.95. Despite the implausibly low price, the ZX80 was not only a 'real computer', but one that cut through computer 'mystique' to teach programming, and was so easy to use that 'inside a day you'll be talking to it like an old friend', or so the advert said. It was an impressively crafted piece of marketing, creating an impression of affordability and accessibility, ideas hitherto rarely associated with computers. The little white box, and the bold claims that sold it, marked the beginning of a redefinition of computers as affordable and everyday appliances for the masses.

At the time microcomputers were broadly split between two basic types. The first were do-it-yourself machines, typically *hobbyist computers* that were cobbled together from kits of electronic components. They were often quite cheap, but required an intricate understanding of how computers and electronics worked, and an owner who was not put off by the complications. The second type were more user-friendly *personal computers*, machines that arrived ready-built in a neat case, which simply needed to be plugged in to start computing with. There were still technicalities to be grasped, but the machines were much easier to use and more like appliances than hobbyist machines. A few of them were even being spoken of by their manufacturers and journalists as computers for the home, but for the British market these American domestic machines were far too expensive. Such computers were too complicated, or too expensive, to become common household items, but what if they could be user-friendly *and* affordable? Ready-built for under £100, the ZX80 offered just the right combination of user-friendliness and affordability to open up computing to a mass market in Britain for the first time

Owned by Clive Sinclair, Sinclair was well placed to take the conceptual leaps needed to make the computer suitable for everyday use. Sinclair's earlier company Sinclair Radionics had a track record in innovative and low-cost electronics devices, in both enthusiast and consumer electronics markets, and a talent for eye-catching marketing, with bold claims for product performance and value. The thing that stood the company apart, however, was a streak of inventive minimalism to its design philosophy, a harnessing of innovative ideas to do more with less, and to produce ever smaller, lower cost and more capable devices. In 1972, Sinclair used this approach to introduce the first popular pocket calculator, the £79.95 Sinclair Executive. Before the invention of liquid crystal displays, calculators had a fearsome appetite for electricity, limiting them to mains power or bulky batteries. Sinclair's designers discovered that rapidly pulsing the power on and off, rather than leaving it on continuously, made no difference to the display or the operations of the calculator circuitry. However, it reduced the power consumption to the point where the calculator could run on tiny hearing aid batteries. It was the sort of neat technical trick that brought about savings in components, size and cost. Not only was the Executive a huge success, but it was swiftly followed by even smaller, cheaper and more advanced calculators. The company was not without its critics, who pointed to extravagant advertising claims, reliability problems and occasionally eccentric products. For example, the Black Watch of 1975, one of the earliest low-cost digital watches, could have its circuitry scrambled by the static of a synthetic fibre shirt and ran at different speeds depending on the temperature. Sinclair would never quite manage to shake off its critics, but the products and unquestionably inventive approach won millions of admirers too. 'You're really pushing the frontiers of technology,' explains Rick Dickinson, who joined the firm in late 1979 as its industrial designer. 'You're creating the future here, you're evolving things, you're absolutely cutting, leading edge in every way with Sinclair.'

Sinclair had become involved with personal computing in the 1970s, firstly with an unrealised computer project at Radionics, then with the Science of Cambridge MK14 hobbyist computer kit. Financial problems and the collapse of the calculator market brought financial assistance to Radionics from the Government's National Enterprise Board (NEB), but the eventual NEB takeover of the innovative Radionics did not make for a happy marriage. Clive Sinclair resigned to take up at Science of Cambridge full time, at this point it was a tiny electronics company with offices above a parade of shops. Within a few years, renamed Sinclair Research, it was producing more computers than almost anyone else in the world. The company did not invent the personal computer, but the cost reductions it achieved through innovation and design economies made complete computers more widely affordable than the American machines had been. There were 'some very good machines, but they were very expensive,' recalled Sir Clive Sinclair in a 2008 interview. 'My idea was, that if we could get the price way, way down, five times down, to £100, we could aim straight at the general public, by saying, "Here you are, here's a computer, you can learn about computers at home."' The result was a machine with the complete and user-friendly nature of the expensive American imports, but at a fraction of the price, and well suited for a country that was becoming interested in understanding computers.

Like previous Sinclair devices, the ZX80 was a tiny machine, little larger than a desktop calculator. Designed to a price point, its capabilities were quite basic. Within the white case was a machine with just 1k of RAM, enough memory for little more than simple programs. It had no sound,* limited interfacing abilities and a blocky monochrome display. Set against more expensive contemporaries, such as the Apple II, which had more memory, colour graphics and sound, it is tempting to see the little ZX80 as primitive, yet there were many innovations in its minimalist design. 'Of course you can't just suddenly make something for £100 that other people have to charge £500 for. We did a complete redesign,' remarks Sir Clive. 'There were a lot of radical ideas in the thing to get the cost down.' There were just 21 chips inside the ZX80, dozens less than in other computers on the market – the NASCOM-1, for example, had used 55. The way its display flickered whenever the machine had to divert its attention to processing data was another sign of cost-reduction innovations. To avoid the expense of dedicated video circuitry, the machine used the main processor to drive the display, and employed the same memory bank for display and program storage.

By using a domestic television for the display and a tape recorder for data storage, the ZX80 saved the cost of specialist equipment. This also had the side effect of associating the unfamiliar computer with common household items. Rather than go to the expense of a typewriter-style keyboard, where each moveable key was mounted onto an individual switch, the ZX80 keyboard was a flat plastic panel, with the 'keys' simply printed onto it, overlaying a layer of electrical contacts. The small, unmoving keys of the 'membrane keyboard' would be criticised by many users, but at a time when the keyboard was a major part of the cost of a computer it was a large saving. An evolution of the same basic idea is in use in most computer keyboards today. With hardly any parts it also appealed to Sinclair's minimalistic design philosophy. The original conception for the ZX80 was that it would be used for learning

---

*However, inventive users soon discovered that they could make the machine produce sound of sort by programming the display to make the television produce a buzzing noise.

about programming, and the membrane keyboard was intended less for typing than for tapping in programming commands. Another user-friendly innovation was that the built-in BASIC computer language allowed whole commands to be entered at the press of a single button. Rather than type out the command GOTO letter by letter, users simply pressed the G key and GOTO appeared on screen. Even if a wrong key was pressed, a syntax-checking system identified errors as they were typed, helping out beginners with their programming efforts.

The low price of the ZX80, the first complete computer for under £100, attracted much press attention, but it was still on the borderline between personal computing's hobbyist roots and the mass market of everyday consumer appliances. It was still marketed heavily at hobbyists as well as the 'man in the street', and while £99.95 bought a complete ZX80, a kit was available at £79.95. Indeed, in technical respects the ZX80 was little advance on many hobbyist computers, sharing many of the technical quirks of hobbyist computing. Yet through wrapping its complexities in a plastic case, adding user-friendly BASIC and some clever marketing, the ZX80 was made complete and appliance-like in a way that hobbyist machines could never be. In any case, to many people who bought one with little expectation of what a personal computer was, the ZX80's deficiencies mattered little. Over 50,000 machines departed Sinclair into the hands of consumers, many of whom would never have even seen a real computer before, let alone thought about owning one.

The little black box

In 1981 the little white box of the ZX80 and 'old friend' slogan disappeared from Sinclair's computer adverts, to be replaced by a little black box, the ZX81, with the promise that buyers would soon be talking to it like a 'new friend'. The ZX81 was a refinement of the ZX80, advancing the concept with a host of incremental improvements to create a machine that was both better and cheaper, at just £69.95 ready-built. *Personal Computer World*'s reviewer David Tebbutt was full of praise for 'Uncle Clive' and his new machine: 'producing a superior machine to the ZX80 and selling it for a lower price is absolutely wonderful. I'm full of admiration for the man.' One of the most startling claims made about the microprocessor back in the 1970s was that new and better devices would be cheaper than the ones they replaced. With inflation running rampant, anything better costing less in the future must have seemed a little far-fetched, but the ZX81 vindicated the idea. 'Higher specification, lower price', pondered one of the machine's adverts, 'how's it done?'

Many electronic products are made by cobbling together standard components. This saves time and development costs, but creates an end product with many parts. The alternative was the expense of designing a specialist microchip that integrated the logic of several components onto a single chip. Using standard parts pushed up production costs, but saved on design costs, the approach used with the ZX80. 'We hadn't got a lot of capital available so we used quite a lot of standard gates,' recalled Sir Clive of the ZX80 design. 'Because money poured in, we very quickly went to the ZX81, where we mopped up all the random logic on a single chip from Ferranti. And so that computer, amazing really, only had four chips… It was a very, very neat little design.' The new Ferranti chip, called an Uncommitted Logic Array (ULA), was itself a novel technology. Developing custom microchips for commercial products was generally a lengthy and expensive business, costing as much as $250,000 and taking as long as a year. Ferranti's single ULA provided a way of producing a custom-designed chip in mere months at perhaps a tenth of the cost of a dedicated new chip. The ULA was akin to an electronic join-the-dots puzzle, a layer of unconnected logic gates that designers could make connections between to form a specialist chip, but without the cost of a purpose design. Ferranti and Sinclair squeezed the functionality of 18 of the 21 chips of the ZX80 onto the single chip, slashing costs and even adding improvements. The microprocessor made the personal computer possible, but the ULA was essential in making it affordable in Britain, and would be at the heart of many later home computers.

The ZX81's technical specifications were similar to those of the ZX80: 1k of RAM, black and white display, no sound and Z80 processor. However, the machine had a number of refinements. A new mode was added to stop the display flickering whenever the machine was processing, and there were improvements in the BASIC and mathematical abilities. Moreover, the changes outside the box were at least as significant as those inside it. The ZX80 may have been a complete computer, but its form was unappealing and unrefined. The thin white case was compared to plastic egg cartons by one reviewer, and the 'cooling vents' on its case were just black stickers. Although still available as a kit as well as complete, the ZX81 was a much neater and more consumer-friendly package, as its industrial designer Rick Dickinson recalled: 'The product I think Clive was pushing me towards was much more of a consumer product and I found that very difficult because there were no home computers in the shops. What is a home computer? You know, how would people relate to it? How do you identify it? What should it look like? Should it have a feel of Dictaphone or tape recorder, or a feel of television about it? Where will it sit in the home?'

Desktop PC, laptop computer, tablet; today we are used to the forms personal computers commonly take. They differ in the details, but are familiar shapes and sizes that have become established by decades of gradual evolution and use. Back in 1980 there was little precedent for what a home computer should look like. Industrial designers, those responsible for the look and feel of products, had to consider some quite fundamental questions about the nature of the home computer. 'It had to reflect some level of high-tech, it had to be elegant, well considered in its design and its detail,' explains Dickinson. 'It certainly wasn't hi-fi but it certainly would live in the bedroom or in the lounge, certainly not in the kitchen or the bathroom or the garage… it had to look high-tech and desirable.' Using sturdy ABS plastic, Dickinson's design of the ZX81 created a neat device well suited to the home environment. Like most Sinclair machines it was small and economic, but the sleek, angular case, with its black, white and red colour scheme, could have come from the future.

Selling the future

Alongside low-cost circuitry and accessibly user-friendly design, there was a third magic ingredient in the success of Sinclair's early machines. A clever marketing campaign encouraged not just a few thousand enthusiasts to buy the computers, but hundreds of thousands of 'normal' people too. Highlighting just what a crossover product the ZX80 was, it was presented quite differently to the two audiences. Jargon-filled adverts in *Practical Wireless* and other enthusiast magazines listed technical features at length, complete with pictures of circuitry to tantalise the hobbyist and lured them with such phrases as 'you've heard the excitement… now make the kit!' Meanwhile, in the pages of national newspapers large adverts targeted a new mass market of computer illiterates. Not for this audience of novices detailed technical notes, but rather soothing promises of how easy the machine was to use and how it 'cuts away computer jargon and mystique'. Whatever the market, the low cost featured prominently, presented as the outcome of smart design rather than simply being cheap.

Outside the small handful of dedicated computer shops, there were few places where people could just walk in and buy a computer in 1980. Prospective computer owners typically had to send off a cheque to the manufacturer and patiently await the arrival of a box in the post, frequently weeks later than the advert promised. The personal computer was in the same bracket as X-ray spectacles and miniature radio watch kits, a gadget too fanciful or technical to be sold on the high street. This changed in Christmas 1981, when the bookseller WH Smith began to sell the ZX81 through its stores. 'What would I do with a computer?' Smith's bold adverts asked of its customers as it began a major drive to sell the machines. The highly profitable experiment took personal computers out of the realm of the hobbyist and put them on the high street for everyone, legitimising the idea of computers as consumer appliances.

Despite the growing buzz about the threats and opportunities of the microprocessor revolution, computers were still a largely unfamiliar technology to most people.

Sinclair pitched the ZX machines perfectly at a new audience of beginners who wanted to learn about them. They were presented as powerful tools to help the novice master this incredible new technology, a 'passport to the future'. Yet although powerful, they were promoted as easy to use and to understand. As the marketing matured, the promises of the information technology revolution were invoked to encourage people to buy computers to prepare for the profound changes about to sweep society. Buying a Sinclair computer 'represents a firmer grip on the way the world works, an opportunity to join what is certain to be a British way of life', claimed one later ZX81 advert. Clever design may have made the ZX80 and ZX81 easy to use and affordable, but marketing added a gloss of accessibility, with the promise that learning about computers was essential for the future.

The ZX80 may have been the first complete computer for under £100, but the ZX81 rivals it for historical significance. In later adverts the ZX81 was presented as the 'Model T-Ford of computers', in homage to Henry Ford's first mass-produced motor car, the affordable vehicle that introduced America to the automobile age. It was an apt comparison. Not only were both black, but both redefined technology into a more accessible form that opened it up to a mass market. The ZX81 was hugely significant in redefining computers as accessible appliances for all. Placed alongside more expensive machines like the PET and Apple II, the small size of the ZX machines led some to dismiss them as mere toys. However, with little for most people to compare them to in 1980 and 1981, this did nothing to dent their appeal. Their enormous popularity spearheaded the computer's invasion of British homes.

By December 1981, a quarter of a million ZX81s had been sold, and the demand overwhelmed Sinclair and led to lengthy waits before many customers received their machines. Quite apart from the sheer numbers sold, Sinclair become something of a cultural phenomenon. Thousands of people queued to get into the ZX Microfairs, where exhibitors sold programs and hardware upgrades for the Sinclair machines. Part archetypical

British inventor, part entrepreneur, Clive Sinclair himself
became a figurehead for the whole computer boom. While his
critics played on the quirks of some of Sinclair's products to
suggest he was some sort of mad scientist or more marketing
than substance, he was also widely respected as a technological
guru and admired for making computers affordable for
everyone. As he would frequently tell journalists, he preferred
inventing things to running a big business, but the success of
the ZX computers exemplified the sort of entrepreneurship
that appealed to the Thatcher government; he was knighted in
1983 for services to industry and won *Guardian* Young
Businessman of the Year. The computers themselves became
popular culture icons too. 'People would write about it, they
would include it in lyrics of their songs. I remember going to
a theatre production in Cambridge and someone was singing
in a song, "and I've even got a ZX81!"' recalls Rick Dickinson.

Atomic theory and American invaders

Sinclair was far from the only company working towards a
cheap and accessible home computer. Mere months after the
ZX80, Sinclair's Cambridge-based rival Acorn launched the
Acorn Atom. 'Chris Curry decided that he wanted a better
home computer. Home computers had remained in the pretty
techie horrible thing area,' recalls Sophie Wilson. 'And then
you had the Apple II. And Chris wanted something that had
that sort of ergonomics but much cheaper.' The Atom was
more expensive than the ZX80 and ZX81, £170 ready-built or
£120 as a kit, but rather more upmarket, with a typewriter-
style keyboard and sound. It could also display colour and
high-resolution graphics, albeit not at the same time. Although
still available as a kit, signs were emerging that there were more
people interested in owning a computer than there were
people capable of building one. 'We were fed up with receiving
phone calls from people who had misassembled the machine,'
remembers Wilson, who recalls particularly the return of one
faulty Atom assembled by a novice with an aversion to
soldering. 'He'd sent it back to us and we discovered that he'd

glued everything together, knowing that heat could damage the integrated circuits, which was written in the instructions… So he glued it together and nothing worked.'

With the hardware principally designed by Nick Toop, the Atom was affordable, but not cheap, and lacked the minimalism of Sinclair's products. Like Acorn's earlier machines it was built with expansion in mind, and marketed as user-friendly enough for a beginner, but expandable as their knowledge grew. On the other hand, the compromises to keep the cost down were evident too. The mounting of the chips on the underside of the keyboard sometimes led to components falling out of sockets as the machine was used. The display controller components were designed to the 60Hz frequency of American televisions rather than the 50Hz used by British ones, meaning the Atom would not work properly on some televisions. Just like Sinclair's machines, the Atom was on the cusp between hobbyist and home computer, but still sold by the thousand.

Imported American home computers started arriving around the same time. Atari, already a successful maker of video games consoles, a major market in 1970s America but far less so in Britain, launched its first home computers in 1979, the Atari 400 and 800. The video games lineage was obvious, with joystick ports, cartridge slots and bright graphics. Compared to the simplicity of the ZX81 or workmanlike Atom, they were solidly built and positively elaborate in construction. This was reflected in their prices, £345 for an Atari 400, with a flat membrane keyboard, and £695 for an Atari 800 in 1980. Expense was also the failing of another 1979 home computer, the TI-99/4 from semiconductor and calculator manufacturer Texas Instruments, priced at £695, plus the cost of a monitor or modification to work with a British television. 'Are people in the UK ready to spend this sort of money on a home computer?' sceptically asked David Tebbutt in *Personal Computer World*'s review. In Britain, these machines only became more viable as mass-market home computers when their prices dropped.

By far the most successful American invader was a new offering from Commodore, the VIC-20. 'Jack Tramiel, the founder of Commodore was always wanting the mass market, that's what his aim became in computers. The Commodore PET wasn't going to be that,' explains Kit Spencer, of Commodore UK. The threat of Japanese imports was also significantly on Tramiel's mind after the calculator wars of the 1970s. At a strategy meeting in London in early 1980, Tramiel declared 'the Japanese are coming, we will become the Japanese', and redirected the company towards a cheap colour computer. Commodore were already very familiar with the mass market, but the recent launch of the low-cost Sinclair computers also served as an example. 'Sinclair I think demonstrated the potential for a home computer,' explains Kit Spencer. 'I think that probably convinced Jack to push much harder in a direction he already wanted to go in anyway.'

Commodore's chip-development company, MOS Technology, had already developed the Video Interface Chip, VIC, as an integrated sound and video chip, intended for video-games consoles and embedded applications. As luck would have it, an inventive MOS engineer named Robert Yannes had already designed a prototype 'MicroPET' using VIC and the 6502 microprocessor, also developed by MOS. The concept was engineered into a neat $300 personal computer with colour, 5k of memory, sound and a full-size keyboard. Called the VIC-20, it was a simple but attractive package for the novice home computer user and well supported by Commodore. 'You moved it towards the home market and home distribution, you made sure you had good games, software, packaging, you stood it out and showed what it did, not just in a box with nothing round it,' recalls Kit Spencer. 'You had to get a bit of sizzle as well as sausage, but you made sure there was sausage by getting software, manuals, everything else with it.' The VIC was launched in Japan in late 1980, and in the US and Britain in 1981, where it initially retailed for £190. With sales better in Europe than the US initially, Spencer found himself moving to reorient the marketing effort in the US to bring similar success. 'We aimed it at the video-game market,' explains Spencer. Commodore's approach was to emphasise the machine's entertainment capabilities, while simultaneously using its educational merits against the limitations of Atari's games consoles. American television advertising fronted by William Shatner promoted both the fun and learning aspects of the 'wonder computer of the 1980s'. '"Why buy just a video game when your kids can learn about computers too?" So that sold in pretty big numbers,' recalls Spencer. Cheaper than the TI/99 or Atari computers, the VIC-20 came to occupy a similar breakthrough position in the US market as the ZX81 in Britain. Worldwide, the VIC-20 became the first computer to sell a million units.

These quite different designs by different companies all used similar means to reach towards the same basic concept of a computer that was more accessible to the general public than ever before. They all strived towards some sort of user-friendliness, and were available as complete machines, ready to plug in and go. Increasingly, the machines were marketed and sold through non-technical adverts in national newspapers and sales displays in high-street stores. Design cost reductions made them more affordable, even in Britain. The magic ingredients of ease of use, persuasive marketing and affordable price redefined the computer into a machine for the masses. But as manufacturers began selling home computers by the thousand, one question remained largely unanswered. Now that they had computers for the first time, just what would all those hundreds of thousands of people actually do with them? Just what was a computer in the home actually for?

What was a home computer for?
Previously, computers in universities and businesses had tended to be used for things like payroll, stock control and data analysis; tasks that few people would ever need to do at home. The main things personal computers are used for today took years to become established. In the 1980s uses were mainly untried possibilities. 'Everybody always *said* recipes, and nobody ever *did*. I did suggest word processing and I was told by all the established people that I was wasting my time thinking about it,' recalled Guy Kewney of the late 1970s. 'People said "Guy,

no male executive is ever going to type, and to operate a computer you're going to need a keyboard, and it's not going to happen is it?'" Even computer designers had undefined ideas about the use of their creations. 'I'm not sure who the user was at the time,' remarks Sinclair industrial designer Rick Dickinson, 'I'm not sure anybody was.' Other than a commonly understood idea that people would use computers to learn about them and a range of vague possibilities, the specifics of computer use seem surprisingly undefined. 'I think we principally thought people would use them for learning about computers and for doing a little bit of programming – finding out what programming was,' explained Acorn computer designer Steve Furber. 'I was on the technical side, making these machines work. It was really somebody else's problem to work out why anybody would buy one.'

Adverts tended to reel off dozens of ideas for what a computer might conceivably be used for rather than specifying any one 'killer application'. Learning languages, cataloguing stamp collections, address book, calculations, finances, recipe books, controlling a train set or learning about computers – the home micro was portrayed as able to do all of this and more. Few adverts were quite as sweeping as Sinclair's famous boast that a ZX80 could do anything from playing chess to running a power station, but there is a feeling sometimes of a machine with a lot of potential searching for a purpose. 'I did think that word processing would be useful. I did think that coms would be useful,' recalls Guy Kewney, 'but I think I was as vague as anybody else about the specifics. I just had this instinctive feeling that nothing this cool could be useless.'

First contact

Memories of first encounters with home computers are widely revealing. The circumstance of these first meetings and the mix of emotions they stir up tell us much about how the novel machines were seen: unfamiliar, potentially threatening, but exciting and full of promise. For many people, buying a home computer was an introduction to a futuristic technology and a way of not being left behind by it. 'It's really important that we have a computer,' recalled teacher Jean Farrington of how her husband convinced her they needed a home micro, 'I'm really interested in it, I want to learn more about them and I think they are here to stay and they are the future, so we must get involved.' The future opportunities for people willing to update their skill set were one of the central promises of the information technology revolution. 'It was a bit of a miracle to me. It was my first computer,' recalls Jon Ritman, a television repair man who bought a ZX81 to learn about computers. His employer, Radio Rentals, was considering branching out into renting home computers. 'A fellow engineer had become the VHS expert, and he was earning more money than me as he was the only one who'd been on the training course. I thought maybe I can become an expert on computers?' Rather than becoming a computer repair man, Ritman left a few years later to become a games programmer, just one of the many people who found a new career from knowing about computing.

For others, there was an attraction to the technology and what could be done with it. 'You've got to bear in mind that in those days, the 1970s, the idea of having a computer at home was considered to be not only weirdly nerdy but actually morally suspect,' remarks Simon Goodwin, who first encountered computers through an Apple II at school in the late 1970s. 'Computers were seen as things that were demanding, that couldn't be argued with and were very, very inhuman. But that was not how I experienced them. I experienced the computer as a kind of infinite Lego set.' This isn't to say that everyone was wildly enthusiastic. 'The reaction at home was that it was completely barmy,' recalled chemical engineer Steve Higham, after taking home a £600 PET. 'You've got this? What the hell are you going to do with it?'

Whatever they did with their computer, chances are they had to make them do it themselves. There was little in the way of ready-to-run software available at first, but most home computers came with a thick guide to BASIC programming masquerading as the instruction manual. The first experience many people had of computing was just typing something in and watching it magically appear on screen, or using the PRINT command to display a message. In a country of three television channels[*] and few domestic video machines, there was a curious novelty in something that could be plugged into the television and made to do things. Working through the manual was a gradual process of learning the machine's vocabulary and figuring out how to make it do something new. Popular legend has it that for most people, home computer programming began with:

```
10 PRINT "HELLO"
20 GOTO 10
RUN
```

And like magic the screen would be filled with endlessly repeating 'HELLO' messages. In reality, the first programming example to follow in the ZX81 manual was PRINT 2 + 2, highlighting its mathematical capabilities. With a few more commands the machine could be instructed to ask questions, add numbers or display patterns, building up to complex programs for solving mathematical problems or cataloguing stamp collections. For many people programming was hands-on learning about computers through doing, a gradual, practical exploration of what their computers could do. Aptly, there is often a subtext of discovery and exploration in memories of early programming experiences. 'With amateur astronomy,' suggests Simon Goodwin, 'you could get yourself a telescope and armed with nothing other than time, diligence and the ability not to repeat yourself, you could find things out that nobody knows, with nothing but the telescope and effort. And the same was true of a computer.'

More than that, programming could be fun and intellectually engaging too. 'Great fun. It made you think in a different way. You had to start thinking in a very logical manner, it made you

[*]Channel 4 was launched in late 1982.

think very clearly about what you were trying to define and the steps to get there,' recalls journalist David Babsky of learning to program the ZX81. 'Then you got a great big kick at the end if you got something right.' Programming made the home computer not just a tool, like a calculator, or a toy, like an arcade machine, but a logical puzzle that was solved in the process of creating something. 'I'd always made things when I was very young, and progressed through electronics when I was a teenager, and the problem with making things is that you need parts,' remarks Jon Ritman, noting that electronics needed money for parts and time to go to the shops. 'When you've got a computer and you want to make something, you can do it. You've got everything there. And I loved the fact that I could have an idea and I could immediately put it into action.'

Far from killing the printed word, the popularity of home computers instigated a minor publishing boom of cheaply printed introductory books on programming and type-in programs, with titles such as *30 Programs for the Sinclair ZX80 1K* and *The Acorn Atom Magic Book*. Much of the software on offer did little more than act as a demonstration of what a computer could do, such as programs to display patterns or calculate future calendars. The most clichéd examples were 'biorhythms' generators that plotted users' emotional, intellectual and physical well-being cycles on a graph, but were probably most interesting as a pretty demonstration of the computer's trigonometry functions. Computer magazines also bulked out with pages of program listings to be tapped in and run. Yet they were often so buggy, poorly printed or badly typeset, that figuring out how to get them to work was a learning exercise in itself. 'You wouldn't necessarily expect a magazine listing to work but it was a source of ideas,' notes Simon Goodwin, a prolific writer of magazine type-in programs. 'Listings in computer magazines weren't necessarily there to be typed in. They were there to be to be looked at and thought about and have little bits taken out of,' explains Goodwin.

Looking back from an age when hardly anyone knows what happens inside their computer to make it do things, it is amazing that everyday people were expected to become programmers. It is even more amazing that so many of them tried to do so. The sheer number of introductory books on BASIC, letters to magazines about programming and magazine pages of software listings all point to its widespread nature and how many people were at least trying their hands at BASIC. A 1981 survey by consumer guide *Which?* found that programming and learning about computers were the most important motivations for buying a micro, far ahead of calculating accounts and playing video games.[1] Against a backdrop of worries over the information technology revolution we can see programming as an act of empowerment to control the computer, rather than be controlled by it. Yet apart from the intellectual exercise involved, programming explains more about *how* people were going to use computers rather than it answers *what* they were going to do with them.

Electronic homes?

One possible outcome of home computers, eagerly foretold in the media at the time, was the electronic home. Many predicted that the ubiquity of the microprocessor would bring about a long-promised age of home automation. In innumerable 1980s sketches of houses of the future, the micro was entrusted with such tasks as controlling lighting, central heating, coffee machines, cookers and other appliances. An 'information technology house' was even built in Milton Keynes in 1982 with a household management system that could babysit, pay bills and run baths to the perfect temperature. The quixotic 1980s house of the future is an artefact of a society negotiating how the computer would fit into the home. While few people used their micro for household automation, many more did try to employ the computer as a domestic aid to assist with chores and problems.

Alongside programs for the predicted uses of cataloguing collections, storing recipes and doing the household accounts, software was available for all manner of unforeseen uses: Rubik's cube solvers, knitting pattern printers, horse racing analysers, diet planners, fertility plotters and such curios as *Decision Maker*, advertised as being able to help decide which car to buy or which woman to marry. People were using the computer to *compute*, in a very literal sense. They were applying its mathematical and logical capabilities to see if it could automate things they might have worked out by hand. How useful it was seems questionable: switching on the computer to load a shopping list, then print it out, seems rather less efficient than just jotting it down on paper. Every so often a letter would appear in a computer magazine from a reader delighted that their computerised football pools predictor had paid off with a cash prize, but generally it is hard to tell just how much use the computer was as a household aide. Aside from the odd programs that had some demonstrable value to their users, it is likely that much of this software was quickly relegated to gather dust on a shelf after the novelty had worn off.

Most early machines were underpowered for more complex programs, or hobbled by design economies that made them awkward to use for applications like word processing. Only the more expensive machines had full-sized typewriter-style keyboards, many made do with flat-membrane or calculator style 'chiclet' keyboards. These were adequate for programming but unsuited for touch typing without making many mistakes. Small RAM capacity limited the size of documents that could be created, and loading and saving data from cassette tapes (disc drives were an expensive luxury at first) was slow and unreliable. Home-computer displays tended towards big and bold letters, easier to read on the low-resolution televisions commonly used as monitors, but seriously limiting how many words could fit on screen at once. A standard typewritten page was 80 characters wide, yet few computer displays approached this. On a machine like the VIC-20, with a 22-column display, or the 32-column display of the ZX81, the whole screen could be taken up by a single paragraph of text. Some people found it easier to physically cut and paste printouts together with scissors and glue rather than attempt to edit documents on screen, assuming of course they could afford a printer.

Full-sized printers started in the £200–£300 range, frequently costing more than the computers they were bought to be plugged into. They were so noisy that magazines warned they could be disruptive to family life and cautioned against using them late at night. Dot matrix printers hammered an array of pins against an ink ribbon to leave a trail of spotty characters in the wake of the print head. For letter-quality text people were advised to purchase a daisy wheel printer instead, essentially an electric typewriter under computer control. Manufacturers offered a range of ingenious mini printers as cheaper alternatives to fit their machines. The output of many of them was like a shop till roll, thermal printed on heat sensitive paper. As this had a habit of blackening if left too close to a heat source, users were advised to make photocopies if they wanted a lasting version. Other devices avoided complicated printing mechanisms altogether by using coloured pens controlled by the computer to draw onto a roll of paper. Such was the novelty of colour printing that promotional pictures inevitably showed them sketching attractive multicolour graphs. Sinclair produced the tiny ZX Printer for their machines, which formed characters by using electric current to vaporise the coating on a roll of metal-coated paper. Fans would later fable the ZX Printer as the 'silver bog roll burner', but at £49.95 it was cheap and sold well. The tiny rolls of paper and poor print quality of these devices made them unsuited to formal outputs, but mini printers were a cheap way of getting a BASIC listing when the only alternative was to write it out by hand.

There were many things other than printers available to plug into home computers. A cottage industry of small electronics companies and kitchen table businesses emerged to supply add-ons and upgrades. Many, such as speech boxes, sound synthesisers and high resolution graphics upgrades, were probably of most appeal to hobbyists, for whom tinkering with the hardware was part of the fun. However, the most popular devices remedied the worst deficiencies of cheap machines to make them much more useful. A huge range of replacement keyboards were produced to replace the membrane or calculator-style keyboards on cheaper machines, including everything from stick-on keys for the ZX81 to fully fledged typewriter-style keyboards. Plug-in memory upgrades, 'RAM packs', were virtually standard issue on machines like the VIC-20 and ZX81, which had particularly small memories. Sinclair's RAM Pack, a box that simply slotted into a ZX81's expansion port, was infamous for wiping its contents if it wobbled and severed the connection to the computer. With many people making do with Sellotape or Blu-Tack to hold it firmly in place, other manufacturers quickly saw an opportunity, and began marketing their own RAM packs with the boast that they were immune to 'RAM pack wobble'. With upgrades such as these, computers grew with their users' experience, as people learned to make the most of their micro.

If people were prepared to put the effort in, spend some money on upgrades and accepted a few limitations, it was perfectly possible to use a VIC-20 as a word processor or computerise a small business with a ZX81. In the absence of anything better suited, people began experimenting with putting cheap computers to work. Over 1983 and 1984, *Sinclair User* magazine ran a delightfully twee series of features called 'User of the Month', which chronicled what people were up to with their Sinclairs. The results were far more than learning to program and playing *Space Invaders*. Alongside families learning about computers, a military memorabilia collector cataloguing their helmet collection and a computer cookbook writer were small businesses and professionals. An engineer running stressing calculations, a small business running its payroll, an archaeologist planning digs, a Methodist minister matching preachers with parishes, all had written programs to use these simple computers in their work. None were using a ZX80 to run a power station, but most seem amazed at how their machines could do jobs in minutes that would have taken hours before and did not make the same sort of errors that people did. In countless little stories like these, the cheap home microcomputer acted as an introduction to what computers could do in working lives as well as domestic ones. Even big businesses with a central computer department for payroll and stock control only started to get office computers in the 1980s. For smaller businesses, nominally home microcomputers were a cheap way of getting started with computerisation and experimenting with possible things the machines might do. One 1984 survey of computers in small businesses found that as many were using cheap Sinclair computers as were using the upmarket Apple II.[2] For those who were willing to build up their machine or learn to work within its boundaries, the cheap home computer could be a useful tool at home or in a small business. For those who tired of such worthy efforts there was always the distraction of games.

Leisure software

The use of home computers for games was not, as is sometimes suggested, unforeseen. Games were commonly listed as among the interesting things to try out on home computers from the earliest adverts, and designers were quite aware that games would be among the uses of their machines. 'I knew that games would be a part of it, but it became a bigger portion than I'd expected,' recalled Sir Clive Sinclair. The surprise was less that people were playing games, but the *extent* to which they came to do so, and the way that gaming became an activity in its own right, rather than just one of the many things doable with a computer.

As we shall see in later chapters, the growth of games had a major impact on home computing, but home computing made an impact on games too, freeing them from the restrictions that had previously been placed on them. Curious academics had written games since the earliest electronic brains had been turned to OXO and chess in the 1950s. The first action game, *Space War*, was created on a DEC PDP1 minicomputer at MIT in 1962. DEC started using the game as a demonstration of the PDP's capabilities, but with a basic PDP1 priced at around $120,000, it was a privileged form of entertainment for a small number of people. Video games reached the general public in the 1970s on amusement arcade cabinets, home games consoles and *Pong* machines, but the experiences they offered were limited. Arcade games had to be simple, quick to grasp and quick to play, not least to efficiently encourage punters to part with their coinage. *Pong* machines did nothing but offer games that involved hitting a square ball with a rectangular bat. Consoles with games on cartridges, such as those of Atari and Magnavox, were more flexible, but generally limited by the rudimentary controls of joysticks, paddles or tracker balls.* Before personal computers, home video games were a packaged entertainment experience, diverting but fundamentally closed to further experimentation.

Home computers freed video games from these constraints and gave them the space to grow into new forms. In late 1977, Radio Victory, a local radio station in the south of England, started broadcasting simple quiz computer games over the airwaves. 'I just assumed there were some people around the South Coast within radio range,' explains Mel Croucher, a former architect, musician, guidebook publisher and PET computer owner, who was branching out into producing leisure software. 'I used radio distribution methods because I had no idea where anybody was who owned a home computer.'

The incomprehensible electronic squealing transmitted through Radio Victory may have sounded like a faulty radio to casual listeners, but to home computer users it had another significance. The noise could be recorded and fed into a computer, at which point it would become a quiz game with puzzles to solve and prizes to win from the radio station. 'Dead easy to win. It had to be, we had an audience of about ten to start with,' remarks Croucher. 'After a few months it increased to a hundred or so, then we got sponsored by a brewery, which

---

*Keyboards and programming cartridges were also released for a few consoles, such as the Atari 2600, but they were uncommon, and the very small RAM of consoles, just 128 bytes on the Atari 2600, made them rather rudimentary as programming tools.

was a dream come true.' Radio broadcasting of software was widely experimented with over the following years, but it never became a standard practice. Nevertheless, the radio computer quiz game is an interesting example of how computers started to be used for entertainment in ways never before considered.

For most people, software arrived in the form of a type-in listing or a tape, but these were open to experimentation too. Through PEEK and POKE commands in BASIC, gamers could look around inside the memory locations occupied by games, and modify what they found to enable ways to cheat and work out how the games worked. Type-in games could be easily modified into something a bit different or learned from to create new games. Games were there to be played with, not just played on. In the exploratory home-computing culture of the time, their creation was often the result of people just seeing what their computers could do. 'Each game I saw visually, without considering its feasibility. Hence I was learning to solve software problems, not just produce a game,' reflects Malcolm Evans, an early ZX81 games programmer. At first, computer games were products of the imagination, an organic outgrowth of programmers being creative, exploring their machines and expressing themselves in this new medium. 'Writing a game was a way of expressing your personality in a way where idiosyncrasy is considered good. If you're programming a cash machine you don't really want to express your personality,' suggests games writer Simon Goodwin. 'Games were simply a quick way of getting something meaningful to me and meaningful to others.'

Imagination was essential on the playing side of the experience too, as most of the games on offer at first were fairly basic. Programmers had to fit their creations into tight memory restrictions, limiting their size and complexity. Often the games world was nothing more than a single screen, such as a *Pac-Man* maze or a screen of attacking *Space Invaders*, where the action would be repeated over again with minor differences. Graphics were often extremely basic. Rather than attempt high resolution images, many programmers simply used the letters and the ready-drawn graphics characters that most computers included in their character sets. Programmers could type pictures with the right combinations of boxes, lines, corners and other shapes, but it was like creating a sculpture out of building blocks. On the original *Pac-Man* arcade game, players raced an open-mouthed yellow *Pac-Man* around a maze, dodging different-coloured ghosts and guzzling pellets and fruit. On a ZX81 version of *Pac-Man* they might guide a letter C around a maze, pursued by hostile black squares, as they tried to eat full stops and asterisks. Gaming needed a bit of imagination, but it could be thrilling stuff when there was little better to compare it to.

At first home computer games took inspiration from existing forms, both traditional and electronic: chess, blackjack, reversi, Scrabble, bridge, and other board and card games aplenty. Home computer versions of games originally created on university mainframes quickly appeared, notably text adventures following the example of *Adventure*, which had been created in the 1970s for PDP minicomputers. Classically players found themselves on a quest in some sort of dungeon or fantasy world, reading textual descriptions and messages off the screen, and used typed commands like 'GO NORTH' or 'SAY TO BARD "SHOOT THE DRAGON"'. Versions of popular arcade games quickly appeared too, and most home micros boasted several different interpretations of games like *Pac-Man*, *Breakout*, *Frogger*, and *Space Invaders*. TV repair man Jon Ritman wrote his first ZX81 game, *Namtir Raiders*, after encountering a pub arcade machine while camping in Wales. 'I was never very good at it, but I had this vague memory in my head so I kind of very vaguely copied it. Very vaguely because it had been about six months and I'd only played it about five times.' Saving money otherwise wasted on arcade machines was even suggested as another benefit of buying a microcomputer. Just because they borrowed from existing forms of game did not mean there was not innovation and exploring going on at the same time. 'In those early days, you have to remember that none of us knew how to do anything,' explains Jon Ritman. 'I'd played *Battlezone*, which was an arcade 3D tank game, and I thought I'd love to do something like that. I wanted to find out how to do 3D, and trying to find that sort of stuff out was a nightmare.' Magazines and books could only supply some basic concepts, and recreating a fast-moving arcade experience on a home computer was a learning exercise in the trigonometry behind wire-frame graphics.* 'Finding out how to do stuff was often an everyday journey of discovery in those early days,' sums up Ritman, who recalls spending hours staring at the magical sight of his first rotating cube as he wrote 3D *Combat Zone*, his own three-dimensional tank game.

The creative freedom of home computers allowed programmers to create games that would have been unlikely on arcade machines or university mainframes. A good example is *Shop Steward*, written by Simon Goodwin on the Video Genie, a TRS80 clone, as a type-in for *Computing Today* in 1980. Fittingly enough for the time, *Shop Steward* was a trade union activity simulator based around making labour relations decisions. 'The management would make various offers to you about what they were going to pay you, whether they were going to hire more people, whether they wanted to get rid of people and bring in new technologies,' explains Goodwin. 'You would respond by what your demands were going to be, whether you were going to have a work to rule, wildcat strike, all out comrades, that sort of thing. And then the management would respond with a lockout or something along those lines.' In home-grown games like *Shop Steward*, home programmers often took things that mattered to them to create quite different types of gameplay experience from the instant gratification of consoles and arcade machine games. 'I tried to avoid twitch games, of the *Space Invaders* kind,' remarks

---

*In wire-frame graphics – commonly used in design or in drawing three-dimensional shapes – only the outer lines of a solid shape are drawn without filling in the surfaces between them.

Goodwin. 'They were technically difficult to do, clones of arcade games. They also didn't seem to be terribly creative and at the time I was being taught economics and politics in A-levels, and what seemed to me interesting was to try to make games that were satirical in that kind of way.'

As well as innumerable *Pac-Man* and *Space Invaders* clones, a few programmers created some surprisingly innovative action games. Among the best was 1982's 3D *Monster Maze,* one of the first three-dimensional games for a home computer, and developed simply because a programmer started experimenting to see what he could do with his new machine. 'My wife bought me a ZX81 for my birthday and I thought, what the hell do I do with this?' recalls its creator, Malcolm Evans, an engineer who worked on spacecraft electronics in his day job. 'My first task was to see if I could write an algorithm to compute a maze, so that's what I did, a 2D maze. It was a natural step then to see what it would look like in 3D when one walked through it. So the next task was to devise a method to give that impression.' Evans created a striking visual effect, the illusion of walking through a maze of corridors in first person, 'as you would see them in real life', wowed a later review in *Home Computer Weekly.* 'I mentioned to John Greye that I had this 3D maze and he suggested I put a monster in it and turn it into a game,' recalled Evans of the chance encounter at a musical society that suggested the next step.

Evans added a Tyrannosaurus rex, turning a stroll through a maze into a tense cat-and-mouse game, as the player tried to escape being eaten alive by the dinosaur stalking them. There were only three controls, turn left or right, or move forwards, yet it offered surprising moments of drama as the tension built, added to by messages of 'HE IS HUNTING FOR YOU' or 'RUN HE IS BEHIND YOU'. 'I didn't realise how realistic it was going to be,' chuckles Evans. 'I was testing the game before adding text when suddenly I jumped out my skin, and I thought if someone had a heart attack would I be responsible for it?' Just in case, Evans added an introductory warning to those with a 'nervous disposition'. The culmination of the

game began with the alarming moment when the lumpy
something spotted at the end of the corridor advanced to
become a recognisable dinosaur, in spite of being created from
blocky graphics characters. 'With the ZX81's low-resolution
graphics it had to be something bulky,' explains Evans.
'Something that could walk towards you getting bigger, and
yet still be recognisable further away with very few pixels. The
image of T-Rex was simply superimposed over the computed
background.' The T-Rex could be outrun, but hurriedly
fumbling the controls on the ZX81's tiny keyboard meant
players would have to be lucky. All too often the game ended
with dinosaur teeth filling the screen. After completing his
game independently, Evans showed it to Greye, and the two
began selling it. They soon parted ways, with Evans founding
the successful New Generation Software company in 1982. 3D
Monster Maze's adverts promised that 'you've never seen
anything like this before' and they were probably right. Just like
so much else in the home computer world, it was new and
being done for the first time.

Whatever they did with their home computer, whether it
was learning to program, calculating tax returns or shooting
down alien invaders, all of the early home computer users were
pioneers in their own right. They were all doing something
new, by taking a much-hyped but little-understood technology
and exploring what it was capable of. Manufacturers may have
created home computers as affordable and accessible machines
for learning about computing, but they only gave them a
vague purpose at the start. It would be largely down to
computer users to explore the machines' capabilities and
determine what they could do. However, there were other
powers at work when it came to defining what the home
computer would mean to 1980s Britain.

CHAPTER FOUR

Computer Literacy

In January 1982, millions of people across Britain tuned in to watch the first episode of a new BBC television series: *The Computer Programme*. What was this thing called information technology, why was it suddenly important and what should people know about it? asked presenter Chris Serle as the show began. For the next 25 minutes viewers found out, through an eclectic mix of material that included everything from data processing centres and online booking of plane tickets to Stonehenge and an old lady's computerised sweet shop. In the best traditions of the BBC it was informative, entertaining, educational and very much intended as a public service.

Back in 1978 the stark warnings of the BBC documentary 'Now the Chips Are Down' had helped to start a debate on what microprocessors and widespread use of information technology would mean to Britain. It had also raised awareness of how limited understanding of these new technologies was and how unready the nation was to make the most of their opportunities. *The Computer Programme* was part of the BBC's answer to the 'challenge of the chip', but it was just one element of a much grander plan. The BBC's Computer Literacy Project was a far-reaching scheme of television and radio programmes, books, a BASIC programming course and even a tie-in home computer. The idea behind this comprehensive effort was to demystify information technology for the public and to encourage people to have a go at computers for themselves.

The Computer Literacy Project was wide ranging, but was just part of an even larger campaign waged by the British state to cajole Britain into the computer age. As we will see several times in this story, information technology held ideological attractions to the Conservative government of the day. When

Margaret Thatcher came to power in 1979, large parts of British industry were still owned and run by the state, such as British Leyland, British Coal and British Aerospace. To critics on the right wing of politics, state industries were bloated bureaucracies, dominated by unions, unproductive and unable to adapt to new conditions. By contrast, many of the companies making the information technology revolution happen were innovative and enterprising small firms, run by entrepreneurs. Clive Sinclair's business success over the early 1980s was all the more marked because the demise of Sinclair Radionics in the 1970s was associated, to an extent, with the heavy hand of state control via the National Enterprise Board. 'Let the vision of the inventor, and the flair of the businessman, create the wealth and jobs of tomorrow,' declared Thatcher in a 1982 speech on information technology, in which she praised home computers as an innovation stemming from personal initiative.[1] The sudden success of entrepreneurial British computer companies was symbolic of the prosperity claimed to be achievable for the enterprising and technology-savvy in Thatcher's Britain. Yet there was more to this interest in information technology than mere political spin.

Just as *The Mighty Micro* and 'Now the Chips Are Down' had brought the microprocessor revolution to public attention at the end of the 1970s, various advisory bodies were reporting to the government on the subject. Of particular concern were the economic effects of computerisation and that British businesses and workers were unprepared for the mass use of information technology and automation. In the wake of 'Now the Chips Are Down' the Manpower Services Commission, responsible for employment and training across Britain, asked the BBC to report on the impact of information technology and microelectronics. 'A couple of us went round looking at various countries and what they were doing about micro electronics,' recalls David Allen of the BBC's Continuing Education Department. 'Around the world there were a lot of people, especially in education and in trade unions, who were really worried about computing. They were worried about what it was going to do to employment – particularly to middle-ranking white collar jobs, such as clerks. They were worried it was going to be in the hands of an elite and imposed on people. The Germans were calling the chip the job killer.' While there were opportunities for new industries and services built on the new technologies, travelling around other developed nations, such as Japan, Sweden and Germany, it was clear that Britain had fallen behind in adopting microelectronics. 'We had some interesting visits to Japanese factories that were absolutely terrifying,' remembers Allen. 'You could see massive factories full of computer-controlled machine tools being used to speed up and improve production, and being exported to every other country in the world rather than here. There were ubiquitous robots when we had almost no robots in British industry at all.'

The BBC report painted a worrying picture of the microelectronic future.[2] In the paperless office a few electronic word processors might replace the typing pool, data banks reduce the need for filing clerks and information systems strip out layers of middle managers. Manufacturing jobs that required experienced craftsmen could be deskilled by computer-controlled tools. Traditional jobs would be lost on a large scale and workplaces disrupted by the shift to a more efficient and faster moving economy. The sum of all these changes might be a polarising effect. Society could become split between a prosperous and technology-literate, elite and the second class citizens who were left behind. At the extreme, information technology threatened to turn Britain into a dystopian society of technological haves and have-nots. The best way of avoiding it was seen to be making people aware of the opportunities of new information technology and educating them in its use.

Meeting the challenge of the chip
From the late 1970s, policymakers were advised that people needed to be taught not to fear information technology, but to understand and exploit it.[3] With a suitably skilled workforce,

the potential microprocessor crisis could become a chance for national economic renewal; Britain could benefit from this new industrial revolution rather than be overwhelmed by it. Before the 1970s were out the Labour government had already started to lay the groundwork for the first technology literacy schemes. The effort started from the top, with the Microelectronics Application Programme (MAP) aimed at alerting business and industry leaders to the possibilities of microprocessor technologies. After Margaret Thatcher's election in 1979, the scope was widened and the profile raised as schemes targeted groups across society. Headlining the Conservative government's commitment to making the nation computer literate was the creation of a minister for information technology, initially Kenneth Baker, to show that the government was taking the challenge of the chip seriously. Baker, occasionally referred to as 'Mr Chips' in the press, became the public face of a wide-ranging set of information technology education schemes and a dedicated supporter of computer literacy.

The political and economic backdrop to the computer boom was a concerted effort by the state to convince the British public to stop worrying and love information technology. Highest in profile of the government's efforts was declaring 1982 as Information Technology Year. IT82 was marked by events across the country to promote appreciation of information technology's benefits and possibilities. Conferences were arranged for targeted audiences on such subjects as business efficiency and computer-aided design. Exhibitions showcased computing in different environments, such as the home, health care, banks and offices. There were even IT82 commemorative stamps featuring past information technologies, such as hieroglyphics, alongside such modern wonders as electronic bar code readers and personal computers. Much of the effort of IT82 was aimed at businesses and industry, but its value was probably in fuelling a wider feeling that information technology was the next big thing and in raising awareness. At the start of 1982, only two in ten people had even heard of information technology, according to a Margaret Thatcher speech at the end of IT82. That IT82 raised this figure to six out of ten was presented as a great success.

While IT82 was largely a flag-waving exercise, more comprehensive and systematic computer literacy efforts were directed at other groups in society, especially at children. In particular, the Microelectronics Education Programme provided the resources and expertise to equip schoolchildren with the skills widely thought needed for future workplaces where microelectronic devices were widespread. Yet few schools actually had computers to instruct pupils with. To meet the shortfall, the Department of Industry ran Micros in Schools, a scheme to pay half the cost of computers for schools, provided they chose a machine from an approved list. As the only computers on the list were from British companies, it was also used as a way of boosting British industry. The original aim was to provide a micro in every secondary school, a rather symbolic political gesture given the dozens of pupils who would need to share it, but it still gave many children their first glimpse of a real computer.

While the schools schemes safeguarded a computer-skilled workforce for the future, other programmes addressed more immediate skills shortages. The Manpower Services Commission, for instance, helped to set up 170 Information Technology Education Centres (ITEC) by 1986 to retrain people to get computing jobs.[4] It was no coincidence that many were located in areas of high unemployment. Media reports of the ITECs invariably seemed to feature unemployed teenagers making good, emphasising how they had secured better futures by learning about computers.[5] To a large extent, the government's support for encouraging understanding of computers was motivated by a view of information technology as a driving force of future economic prosperity. Computer literate youngsters would become productive future workers in the new high-tech society brought about by the information technology revolution. However, most of the population fell outside the direct reach of the government's schemes. With a revolution imminent, Britain at large needed to be educated too. 'There is a much bigger problem of trying to familiarise people in their twenties and thirties with all this,' lamented Kenneth Baker to the Parliamentary Education, Science and Arts Committee in 1981, 'how do you reach them?' The task of educating the British population at large about information technology would fall chiefly to the BBC's Computer Literacy Project.

Computer programs on television programmes

The Computer Literacy Project fitted well with the government's plans, but it began as a largely independent initiative within BBC Education. The BBC was in a uniquely qualified position to encourage Britain into the information age. Foremost, it was a public service organisation with worthy aims to educate and inform the British public. After stirring interest with 'Now the Chips Are Down', and advising the Manpower Services Commission on microelectronics, groups within the BBC were well aware of the issues raised by information technology. 'There was a feeling that this was something important that was coming along which might effect everybody,' remembers David Allen, project editor of the Computer Literacy Programme. 'We ought to do something about it, and we ought to do something systematic about it for the public as a whole.' The BBC also had a strong background in educational broadcasting. Most pertinently, in the 1970s the BBC Adult Literacy Programme had provided a model for how a nationwide education scheme could work. This combination of learning materials, helpline and television, including a motivational drama staring Bob Hoskins as a removal man who was learning to read, had proved an effective way of encouraging illiterate adults to overcome their frustrations and fears. The Computer Literacy Project aimed to do the same for computing.

The BBC was well positioned for a nationwide educational scheme, but computer education was a new and unfamiliar topic. 'We were starting from absolute scratch,' explains Allen.

'We knew nothing about the subject, but some of us had got
hold of early home computers and started to learn to use
them. We were just reasonably intelligent graduates working as
producers, so we were dependent on the people we could find
to advise us.' As a precursor to the project, the 1980 awareness
raising series *The Silicon Factor* and 1981's *Managing The Micro*
helped producers start to understand the new subject. However,
they also consulted widely, discussing their ideas with experts
from the computer industry, government departments,
universities, schools and elsewhere. As well as pulling together
ideas from this web of experts about what people *should* know
about computers, the BBC set out to discover what the public
actually wanted to know about them. A pilot episode was
screened to potential viewers, who were extensively questioned
about their attitudes and knowledge of computers. The
potential audience was revealed to be anxious about computers,
but could also see their advantages and wanted to learn more.
Some were technically engaged and wanted detailed
information, but the majority just wanted a general introduction
to what computers were and what they could do. Accordingly,
the tone of *The Computer Programme*, the television series at the
heart of the project, was set as a gentle introduction to take the
mystery out of the machine.

Explaining the technical subject of computing to millions
of computer illiterates was not going to be easy. The archetypal
education programmes of the time were the *Open University*
lectures, broadcast at obscure hours on BBC2 and typically
featuring bearded academics trying to explain complex subjects
with the aid of stock footage and diagrams. BBC Education
also produced programming for more general audiences,
broadcast in a variety of time slots on both BBC1 and BBC2,
The Computer Programme was more in this mould, and had to
reach out to much wider audiences than those typical for
educational programming. It could not just be informative. It
had to be engaging and accessible too.

The Computer Programme's creators went to great and
sometimes unusual lengths to catch viewers' attention. Each

episode focused on a particular topic, such as computer programming or data storage, but was far from a lecture. Viewers were led step by step through an extended montage of sequences that explored and explained the week's topic in entertaining fashion. How computers followed instructions, for example, was explained via a tooting Victorian steam organ, a beeping 1960s mainframe computer, soldiers on parade, computerised machine tools and studio discussions between the presenters. It was varied and entertaining, using familiar and old-fashioned technologies to explain very new ones. In spite of the importance and urgency of its message, the programme did not take itself too seriously. One episode features a presenter dressed as a cowboy, moseying through a fake Wild West town explaining the impact of the telegraph, as a lead-in to explaining networking. In another we see the show from the point of view of the computer as it looks out of its screen at the presenters as they explain how it works. This light touch was key to *The Computer Programme*'s appeal, particularly the interaction between the main presenters: computer expert Ian 'Mac' McNaught-Davis and curious novice Chris Serle. Each week the slightly confused looking Serle asked questions it was thought the audience wanted answered, and the sage-like Mac patiently answered them. It was a simple but effective double act, which used good-humoured banter to make computing less threatening.

Gentle though its explanations were, *The Computer Programme* did not shy away from the impact computerisation would have on the world, showcasing the use of computers in workplaces. It was often cutting edge material at the time. 'In each programme we went out to try and find people using machines to show the way they were using them in their business or in all sorts of things, and not just personal computers,' recalls David Allen. 'There weren't necessarily that number of people out there using personal computers already, so it was quite difficult to find interesting stories.' At least part of each episode would feature Mac and Serle sitting at a computer in the studio trying something related to the week's topic. Behind the scenes, it took much effort to get the computers working properly amid the stray electromagnetic fields and hot lights of the studio. However, it was a useful way of converting abstract concepts into activities that viewers could picture doing themselves, and for relating the wider world of computing to the machines viewers had at home.

Wide ranging in scope, but gently encouraging in its explanations, *The Computer Programme* was a marvellous way to introduce computers to an audience largely made up of computer illiterates. 'Now the Chips Are Down' had unsettled with stark warnings of a microprocessor revolution, but *The Computer Programme* aimed to help viewers come to terms with the changes at hand. About 7 million people watched at least part of the series, which was repeated and widely recorded for use in schools. Its holistic approach to showcasing computers was much praised, but also had critics among people who wanted more technical instruction on how to use computers. However, *The Computer Programme* was only ever intended as the first step on a longer journey to computer literacy.

Alongside *The Computer Programme* the BBC planned an extensive range of other materials and services. The book of the series, *The Computer Book*, quickly became a best-seller as an introductory guide. For the more technically minded there was a course, 30 Hour BASIC, provided by the National Extension College. The numbers of people who took advantage of these opportunities were huge, suggesting the public's great appetite for learning about computers. Before 1982 was over, *The Computer Book* had sold 60,000 copies, and *30 Hour BASIC* over 100,000. For a time the BBC was answering 2,000 letters a week, and 120,000 people used the telephone helpline to find other sources of information, such as colleges and computer clubs.[6] There were further television series too. *Making the Most of the Micro*, the second major series, was more technical and designed to offer more direct help to new computer users. A two-hour live special, *Making the Most of the Micro – Live,* was followed by *MicroLive,* which ran until 1987, covering new developments. There were also more specialist series, such as *The Electronic Office* and *Computers in Control,* about robotics. Yet the most important additional element of the project was not a programme or a book, but a computer.

Other brands of microcomputer are available

Encouraging people to give computing a try was crucial to the Computer Literacy Project. 'It's not like an Open University series. It's general programmes that create a general interest, and associated with them you have things that you can do,' explains the BBC's David Allen. 'We thought we must have course material and so on and so forth, so that people could learn to actually do things. This hands-on philosophy was very strong.' The practical philosophy led, via a rather roundabout route, to one of the most influential parts of the whole endeavour. Many television series are accompanied by books and merchandising, but *The Computer Programme* was probably unique in having a branded computer to accompany it. However, at the start the plan was not to develop a computer, but just to provide a standard way of teaching programming.

Because programming was widely seen as key to developing a working knowledge of computers, the BBC was naturally keen to include it. The beginners' language BASIC was the obvious choice to use, but many educationalists and professional programmers hated it for being unstructured. The commands available in a structured programming language, such as Pascal, imposed a certain style on how people could write programs. They were restricted to arranging their code in neat blocks of subroutines and procedures, and to following logical paths. Due to a lack of alternatives to the GOTO command, frequently the flow of BASIC programs jumped around all over the place. Educationalists claimed that BASIC lured people into the sins of bad programming habits and badly structured code. To make matters worse, different computers commonly used different dialects of BASIC. While the principles were similar, the differences in implementation meant a program written on one machine might not work on another – not ideal for teaching programming consistently and systematically.

The solution was for the BBC to try and specify its own version of BASIC, as close to a standard as it could be when there was no actual standard, but also to include features more commonly found in structured languages. This widened its educational value by adding features to teach good programming practice, but retained the essential ease of use of BASIC. 'We came up with this thing called Adopted BASIC for Computers, ABC,' recalls David Allen. 'We had a meeting with all the manufacturers that we could find and the DTI (Department of Trade and Industry), and we tried to persuade them to implement this ABC on their machines.' When it was not possible to reach an agreement with the manufacturers, the BBC began to consider other options for getting the computer language it needed to support the series. 'We were really stuck,' recalls David Allen. 'This is why we got the germ of the idea of getting a computer that we could use systematically for the series and for people who wanted to follow the series seriously.'

In typically thorough fashion, the BBC consulted widely on what sort of features its computer should have, but the necessity of having a specific machine to go with the series put the corporation in a tricky situation. The BBC could not make the machines itself and would need to collaborate with a computer company to get them designed and built. However, at the time the BBC saw itself as a largely non-commercial and impartial organisation that tried to avoid endorsing specific brands of product. If the machine did well the BBC could be accused of interfering in the computer market, while profiting from royalty payments. No matter how many other brands of computer were available, the company selected would gain a major stamp of approval and much free publicity from the partnership. But what if the computer were made by the government, not by a private company? As luck would have it, in a Britain where the state still owned large parts of industry, there was just such a machine under development, the Newbury Newbrain.

The Newbrain had its origins somewhere in an early computer project at Sinclair Radionics in the late 1970s, long before the ZX80 had been conceived. After Clive Sinclair parted company with Radionics when the company was taken over by the National Enterprise Board, the project continued at the government-owned Newbury Laboratories. When first announced in 1980 the Newbrain was quite an advanced machine. It had generous provision for plugging in peripheral devices, a key concern to the BBC, and its small built-in display made it easily portable. Suitably modified with ABC, the Newbrain could have been the technical fix to the BBC's problems. Just as importantly, Newbury's government backing dodged the problem of endorsing one commercial rival over another by matching a publicly funded computer with a public service broadcaster. However, like many other computer schemes of the time, it ran into technical problems that delayed it until after the BBC needed it, by which time it was arguably a dated design anyway.

With pressing deadlines overcoming commercial concerns, the BBC started the search for a new machine already under development, which could be adapted to meet its unique needs. 'Newbury having failed to come up with anything, John Coll* and I sat in an office between Christmas and the New Year, that funny week when nothing much happens,' recalls David Allen of late 1980. 'We drew up a specification. It was only two or three pages: we want colour, we want sound, we want graphics, we want a fully positive keyboard, we want this that and the other, we want ABC on it.' The specification was

*John Coll was a member of MUSE (Micro Users in Secondary Education), a user group for teachers, which was one of the advisers to the Computer Literacy Project, and he later became a presenter on subsequent series.

sent out to British computer manufacturers, and an increasingly desperate BBC waited to see what they had to offer.

The machine with two brains

After months wasted waiting for the Newbrain, a small team from the BBC Computer Literacy Project set out to visit Cambridge in early 1981. There had already been some preliminary discussion with manufacturers, but they were going to see for themselves what the British computer industry had to offer. The Cambridge area was home to several microcomputer companies at the time, of which three were in the running to supply the BBC. Out in nearby St Ives was Tangerine Computer Systems, producer of the hobbyist Microtan 65 computer, and with other projects in the works. Sinclair Research, with a prototype of the new ZX81 to show, could be found above a parade of shops. And tucked away in shabby offices above the Eastern Electricity Board showroom was Acorn, whose computer designers had just had a remarkably busy week.

Acorn had dabbled in a range of computer market sectors by 1981. The System 1, a cheap kit computer, had found favour with hobbyists; the more expensive and more versatile System 2 and System 3 rack-mounted computers had been aimed at industrial and laboratory users; the appliance-like Atom had broken Acorn into the home computer market, but they had problems deciding what to do next. 'The Atom was a modest success so the company determined that they'd like to do something better and we had a long argument over many months over what it would be – practically everybody wanted something different,' recalls Sophie Wilson. Would the successor machine be a home computer a scientific computing workstation, a control computer or something else entirely? 'Steve and I wanted something we could be proud of,' remarks Wilson. 'Nobody could decide what to build next. Obviously we kept working, churning out things for the System range and writing new software for the Atom. It wasn't a period of stasis, but in terms of design forward motion we had nothing.'

And then they hit upon the idea of a machine that could do it all, the Acorn Proton.

The original scheme for the Acorn Proton was essentially two computers in one. Acorn would build a professional version of the Atom, running a faster version of the tried and trusted 6502. This machine would then be used as an input/output (I/O) interface to control a more powerful machine containing a *second* processor. As a whole it could be a powerful scientific computer, or the I/O unit could be sold on its own as a basic home micro or as a controller. 'So with that Frankenstein mash-up compromise we had a forward strategy,' recalls Wilson, 'when Chris Curry discovered the BBC computer Literacy Project. And jointly Hermann and Chris sprang on Steve and myself the notion that the BBC would come and look at our prototype. The prototype we hadn't got.'

It was an extraordinary situation. The biggest, most prestigious microcomputer contract in Britain was open to anyone who could satisfy a desperate, but somewhat particular, customer. The cheaper half of the Proton design was a reasonable fit for the BBC's needs, but Acorn did not have anything like an actual computer to show them. 'We only had skeleton ideas in our heads,' recalls Wilson. 'There wasn't even a line on a piece of paper saying what we were going to do and how we were going to do it.' With time short, Acorn's management turned to rather unconventional means to motivate its designers. The weekend before the BBC was due to visit, Hermann Hauser rang up Steve Furber with the proposition that Wilson thought it was possible to show the BBC a prototype by Friday. 'Hermann rang me and said "the BBC are coming on Friday, Sophie thinks we should show them a prototype. What do you think?"' recalls Furber. 'And I said, "well, it's a bit unlikely, but if Sophie's willing to have a go I will."'

Unbeknownst to Furber at the time, Hauser's conversation with Wilson had been just the same. 'No we can't do that, it's impossible,' answered Wilson, only to be told, '"Well, I've been talking to Steve, and Steve thinks it can be done." "Oh, well, I think it's impossible, but if Steve thinks it can be done we can give it a go."' It was the start of a busy week for all involved. 'We turned up at the office on Monday morning, discovered the deception really quickly, but decided to go on anyway,' explains Wilson. They began sketching out circuit plans while Acorn's chief engineer Chris Turner searched for the parts to build it, not a trivial task given the fact that some of the components had to be imported specially. With no time to create a printed circuit board for the prototype, Ramanuj Banerjee, 'the fastest wire gun in the west', was borrowed from the university computer laboratory to connect the board-mounted components together using a wire wrapping gun. From then on it was an all-out effort to get the thing working, with the team gradually working its way across the prototype fixing its bugs.

By 2am Friday morning, with the BBC only hours away, the machine was still confounding efforts to make it work. Wilson escaped to snatch a few hours sleep in optimistic preparation for programming the prototype for the BBC demonstration. The others carried on working through the night in an increasingly frustrating search for the problem, but then they had a stroke of luck. Connected to the prototype was an Acorn System series computer to aid the testing and development process. 'There was a big earth cable to try and keep the [electronic] noise down and Hermann said, "Why don't you just disconnect that?" And the machine annoyingly sprang into life,' recalls Furber. 'We were very tired and very, very much out of ideas, and this one just happened to work.' In a timescale that Furber describes as 'basically silly' Acorn delivered, more or less, just what the BBC was looking for. 'They were all asleep under the benches and the machine was working,' recalls Wilson, who arrived in the morning to set up the software for demonstration to the BBC. 'It was clearly impossible,' explains Wilson. 'You don't build in five days a working thing with five circuits in it that you haven't even envisaged. It was a massive piece of luck that it did work.'

The Beeb

The prototype Proton became the basis for a collaborative effort to develop what became known as the BBC Microcomputer, better known simply as the BBC Micro or 'the Beeb'. Most of the direct development was the responsibility of Acorn, but with ongoing input and monitoring by various BBC experts throughout the process, such as BASIC expert Richard Russell and BBC Engineering Designs engineer David Kitson. Almost all early 1980s home computers were designed and marketed with learning about information technology in mind, but none had so much thought put into its educational value as the BBC Micro. Acorn BASIC and the ideas for ABC were adapted by Sophie Wilson to produce BBC BASIC, rich in features, easy to learn and structured to encourage good programming discipline. In a subtly user-friendly touch, the machine printed MISTAKE messages instead of ERROR when something went wrong. Ready-built, user-friendly and supplied with a well-written manual* and welcome tape of introductory software, the Beeb was easy to use for beginners and potentially very powerful too.

The hardware was impressive. It had a full-sized keyboard, sound and a colour display, with several different modes to display text or high-resolution graphics. Cheaper computers were very limited in what devices could be plugged into them,† but the BBC Micro was endowed with an array of

---

*However, presumably because of the hasty development of the machine, some early users would be frustrated by a lack of information as the first 6,000 BBC Micros were shipped with provisional manuals and a postcard to request a free upgrade to the final manual when it was ready.

†The ZX81, for example, had connectors for a television, a cassette recorder and a single 'user port' into which anything else you wanted to plug in had to be connected. The BBC Micro had a serial interface, user port, analogue interface, 1MHz bus, the Tube, Econet, printer port, disc drive connector, cassette recorder connector, auxiliary power output, television connector and two different sorts of video output.

different sockets for just about anything it was possible to think of plugging into a computer at the time. 'We wanted a machine that could control equipment, that had A to D [analogue to digital] conversion, that could produce sound,' recalls the BBC's David Allen. 'We were interested in versatility, that was the whole point, teaching people that computers could do a whole range of things.' There were also a couple of unique Acorn features that were far ahead of most other machines on the market. Acorn benefited much from its links to Cambridge University, particularly through Andy Hopper, one of Acorn's directors and also a lecturer with research expertise in networks. As the rest of the industry was only just getting tooled up to make small stand-alone computers, the BBC Micro had the option of networking. Through 'Econet', BBC computers could connect together onto a local network to share files and printers, a very useful feature in a school environment. The second unique feature, the Tube, went back to Acorn's original scheme for the dual processor Proton, by allowing a second processor to be attached. The Tube turned the BBC Micro into the front end of a more powerful computer better suited for specific tasks, like business computing or laboratory work. The BBC Micro emerged as an astonishingly versatile machine, but it came at a premium price.

The machine was released in two versions, £235 for the Model A, with only 16k of RAM and a cut-down range of interfaces, or £325 for the fully featured 32k Model B. Shortly after launch the prices were increased to £299 and £399, expensive for a time when several manufacturers were working on machines for under £200, but further marking it as premium product. Price aside, the Acorn and BBC collaboration produced a computer that was widely seen as outstanding. Guy Kewney declared it the nicest machine he had seen, in his review for *Personal Computer World*, praising its graphics, ease of programming and expandability. Initially Acorn was briefed that the Micro would probably sell around 12,000 machines. They took that many orders by Christmas 1981, before the first episode of *The Computer Programme* had even aired. 'The success of the BBC Micro astonished everybody involved,' recalls Steve Furber. 'Once the BBC Micro was out there, Acorn's only problem for two or three years was making enough of them.'

Not only was the demand huge but technical problems caused delays. To reduce the cost of the machine, Acorn used Ferranti ULAs to mop up the logic from several chips onto just one. The problem was that the ULA used for the video display, the video processor or VID PROC, kept failing as the machine got warmer, killing the display. It was a particular problem for the machines being filmed under studio lighting by the BBC for *The Computer Programme.* 'The first ones were shot with Steve in the wings with a can of cooler,' recalls Sophie Wilson. 'Every time the director said "cut" he'd dash onto the set and spray the VID PROC with the cooler for the next shot.' It was typical of the sort of problems which many computer manufacturers would experience in getting their machines to market in the early 1980s, and took Acorn some months to rectify. Problems with the system software, leading to errors saving and loading data, would also frustrate users of early machines, many of whom thought it outrageous that Acorn charged £10 for a ROM change to fix the problem. For a few companies such problems would have serious financial consequences, but such was the demand for the BBC Micro, and the gold standard of the BBC brand, that the issues did little to dampen enthusiasm for the machine.

One thousand machines came off the production line as *The Computer Programme* was first broadcast in January 1982. By March it was 5,000 a month, still not enough to meet demand. By the end of April the backlog of orders was over 20,000.[7] The machine was a runaway success, for both the BBC and Acorn. Before the BBC, Acorn was just one of many small computer companies, but after the success of the BBC Micro it became one of the best known. Some of the trust people had in the BBC brand rubbed off on Acorn, suggesting that it was a safe bet to buy a £400 computer from. The BBC's selection of Acorn attracted some controversy among other computer manufacturers who saw the market upset by a competitor given an unfair advantage. Clive Sinclair claimed that his company could have built a machine that matched the BBC's needs for half the price. The BBC, he complained in a 1982 interview to *Practical Computing*, had no more place making BBC computers than it did BBC branded toothpaste or cars. For its part, the BBC saw Sinclair's machines as too limited to provide the wider education it had in mind. *Computer Programme* producer Paul Kriwaczek called the ZX81 a 'throwaway' product in a *Practical Computing* interview in which he criticised the limitations of the machine. Sinclair was already a well-established player with a particular way of doing things. In Acorn, the BBC found a company at a more formative stage, with an expansive design philosophy that matched its wide-ranging vision for showing people what computers could do.

Just as the BBC had hoped, the sheer adaptability of the Micro meant it found many uses. Thanks to its good quality keyboard it was a solid basis for an office system. The multitude of ways to plug things into it made it useful for running laboratory sensors. Acorn itself used it in the development of advanced microprocessors. There was an additional adaptor for Teletext, which allowed 'telesoftware' to be broadcast to the computer, via the BBC's Ceefax servive. The BBC Micro would also become common around the BBC itself, where it was useful for generating graphics and text for television programmes. As we shall see in a later chapter, it was even used to create some innovative games. As home computers went, the BBC Micro was a machine that was suited to almost anything its users could ask of it, but its major impact was in education.

Programming children

In 1986 Acorn celebrated the production of the 500,000th BBC Micro. Impressive though this was, several other machines far outsold it, Sinclair had sold about 2.5 million ZX Spectrums by this point. However, the BBC Micro had an influence out of all proportion to its numbers due to its popularity in the education market. The connection to the BBC's Computer Literacy Project already gave the machine a sort of official approval as an educational device. This was furthered by the Department of Industry's much trumpeted Micros in Schools scheme, which gave schools half the cost of an approved computer, the other half often met by local authorities or parent-teacher associations. When first announced in 1981, the only two machines on the approved list were the BBC Micro and the Research Machines RM380Z, which was little competition to Acorn's computer.

The RM380Z dated from 1977 and had had some success when there were few other educational computers available. It was big and so robustly heavily engineered that it was popular with the Ministry of Defence as well as schools and laboratories, but with prices starting at around £1,000 the 380Z was even more expensive than the BBC Micro. By 1981 it already looked quite old-fashioned, and did badly against its cheaper and BBC-approved rival. Despite being cut out of Micros in Schools, Sinclair's ZX81 did quite well in the educational market at first, thanks to the company heavily discounting the machines for educational customers. The more advanced ZX Spectrum was later added to the list of approved computers when Micros in Schools was expanded to primary schools. However, Acorn's lead was unassailable in the education market. By 1985 the BBC B was used by around three-quarters of schools. For most of a generation of children the BBC was effectively *the* school computer. It was so robust and well provisioned with educational software that many were still chugging away in school computer rooms well into the 1990s, if not beyond.

Just having machines there for children to use was helpful for familiarising them to computers, but what would computers in schools actually be used for? Educationalists debated at length what place computers had in schools. Should pupils be taught how they worked or just the skills to use them? Or should they be educational tools for computer-assisted learning, particularly for those with special needs? To the most forward thinking, the computer might dramatically change the way that children were educated, an individual electronic teacher attuned to the needs of each child and causing a classroom revolution. Clive Sinclair's 1982 prediction that computers would replace schools rather than just encyclopedias was not uncharacteristic of the time. Others, however, were more cautious, concerned that unimaginative teaching machines would program children by rote, treating them as empty vessels to be filled with computer-delivered facts to the detriment of a more rounded education.

In the short run, the more dramatic visions of 'schools of the future' where every child had an individual computer tutor were unrealistic given how few computers most schools had, how little software was available and how few teachers understood them. By 1984 the average school had nine machines shared between hundreds of pupils and often living a nomadic existence trundling between classrooms on trolleys. Children would have to wait to take their turn with the machine or crowd around it watching demonstrations. At first, computer education was often left up to maths and science teachers, seen as the natural keepers of a technology long associated with science and numbers, but who were also learning themselves. With little educational software available, teachers often wrote their own programs, with varying degrees of success.

In common with microcomputing in general, programming was an important part of school computing in the 1980s. Educational computing articles of the time have an underlying rational of empowering children, an idea that they should program computers rather than be programmed *by* computers. However, school computing was not as novel as we may suspect. As early as the 1960s, a few secondary schools had got their pupils to punch out programs on computer cards, then posted them off to a university computing department for processing. A few weeks later printouts would return, bringing results for pupils whose programs had worked and disappointing error messages for those whose did not. 1980s school computing was more hands on, with pupils able to learn programming directly and see the result of their efforts on screen, or even moving around the classroom. Alongside computers, robots began appearing in the 1980s classroom too, such as robotic arms and floor turtles. The floor turtle typically looked a little like an inverted goldfish bowl with a robotic buggy trapped inside it, and was an eye-catching way of demonstrating programming. Commonly programmed through the beginners' language Logo, the floor turtle was armed with a pen and could be instructed to draw pictures on the floor as it trundled along. They were a simple and fun way to introduce computing concepts to children expected to live in a future here robots and computers were commonplace, but far more important than classroom robots was educational software.

Down in *Granny's Garden*

There was little good-quality educational software available when computers first entered schools. A common complaint at the time was that computer-aided learning programs were drilling rather than skilling pupils. Children were subjected to a range of programs that did little more than pose multiple choice questions or order them to solve arithmetic problems, then beep at them in a disappointed tone when they made mistakes. The computer risked being relegated to the role of educational inquisitor, but fortunately some had more creative ideas about how computers could be used in classrooms. Among them was teacher Mike Matson, who found his initial disinterest in computers overturned after losing a weekend to playing *Adventure* on a friend's machine. 'As a primary school teacher it occurred to me that if something could grab me like that for a whole weekend, could motivate me, then the potential there for kids had to be enormous,' explains Matson. However, after convincing his school's parent-teacher association to buy a computer he found his colleagues less enamoured with the idea. 'When I mentioned it to the staff I couldn't believe the reaction; it was just unbelievable,' recalls

Matson. "'What the hell is this all about? Do you know how many football shirts we could have bought with that money?" Anyway, I now had a PR job to do. I had to convince all these staff that this computer, that was going to cost £400, a lot of money then, was going to be worthwhile.'

Matson began learning to program and to write educational software, eventually becoming a computer advisory teacher. Uninspired by other schools software, he created something rather different, an educational adventure game, *Granny's Garden*. The game sent players off on a quest to find the children of the king and queen of the mountains, who had been kidnapped by a wicked witch. Along the way they explored a colourful fairytale world, completing tasks such as solving logic puzzles about feeding dragons, searching for keys and answering questions set by a talking Mushroom, while trying to avoid the attention of the Wicked Witch. The frisson of panic at the appearance of the Witch when they made a critical mistake, complete with purple hat, green hair and blue skin (the BBC's pallet was limited to eight colours), was a shared experience for a generation of schoolchildren. The worst that could happen was that the Witch would 'send them home', but this not only marked game over but could mean having to pass the computer to a classmate to have a turn. However, faced with a small number of computers, one of Matson's motivations for the game was that it could be used with a whole class. 'The main concern was that if you have got one machine in a school, how can everybody use it? Answer: they can't. So what I wanted to do was write something that would allow everybody to participate.'

A turn playing *Granny's Garden* was used as a way of stimulating pupils in other educational activities, like writing a story about the Witch or doing arts and crafts projects. Teachers could use the game to tell a story to the whole class and spark discussion about the various puzzles it posed. *Granny's Garden* provided a far more stimulating way of using computers to teach than using the machine to interrogate children with maths problems and questions. Buoyed by positive reactions to the game, Matson left teaching to start an educational software company, 4Mation, with a friend. As of 2015, 4Mation is still selling *Granny's Garden* to the education market, albeit no longer for the BBC Micro, a remarkable longevity given that the schoolchildren for whom it was originally written are now approaching middle age.

Learning the language of the future

If Sinclair's machines were the Model T Ford of computers, then the BBC Microcomputer was, if not quite a Rolls-Royce, then certainly a trusty family car. The £400 price tag and BBC approval lent it a certain middle-class respectability, and the Beeb was a solidly built, reliable family computer, with an abundance of features for users to explore. Just as Sinclair's machines exemplified the populist mass market end of the British home computer scene, Acorn's marked the respectable upper bounds of it. While many other computers appeared on the market over 1982 and 1983, they tended to be considered between the yardsticks already set out by these two companies and their very different approaches. Yet despite their many differences both machines shared a common idea of being educational, and they were far from alone in this.

Computer design varied widely over the early 1980s. There was no fixed idea of what a computer should look like, what technical specifications it should have, or how it should behave, but most shared a common educational posture. While few designers put quite so much care as the BBC had into making their BASIC educational, they were all designed to make programming easily accessible. The user interface on switching on the machine was normally just a BASIC prompt inviting the user to start entering commands. The pages of any early 1980s home computer manual were mostly taken up by an extensive guide in how to program in BASIC.

Design and instruction were reinforced by marketing. Alongside the inevitable claims of low cost and high capability, the educational value of a home computer was strongly emphasised.

Computer advertising explained that the information technology age was coming and that people risked being left behind if they did not adapt. 'We live in an age of computers. Coming to terms with them is part of coming to terms with the twentieth century,' declared one Commodore VIC-20 advert. 'To you computers are a mystery from the future,' taunted a Dragon 32 computer advert that cautioned parents that their computer literate children were smarter than they were. Unsurprisingly, most adverts suggested that the solution to impending personal obsolescence was buying that particular brand of computer and learning to program it; 'I AM GOING TO TEACH YOU THE LANGUAGE OF THE FUTURE', as one Acorn BBC Micro advert rather forcibly put it. The skills and knowledge that these machines promised to bring were often touted as a route to future prosperity. One Acorn advert even featured a group of formerly unemployed teenagers with the news that 'they didn't have to burden the state much longer', after finding brighter futures through computer education. Yet at the same time as portraying computing as something important whose complications had to be mastered, marketeers had to play down complexities to avoid scaring buyers off and to present computers as accessible. A common advertising cliché was the picture of a family posed with their new computer in a cosy household setting as they learned together. With so much emphasis on computers in schools, manufacturers presented their machines as important for children's futures, almost emotionally blackmailing parents into buying them.

The technical magazines that had nurtured hobbyist computing in the 1970s were joined by new publications aimed at a less skilled audience that wanted to know about computers. By 1984, there were around 115 different computer magazines vying for shelf space in newsagents, several with weekly or monthly circulations of over 100,000.[8] Alongside general magazines like *Personal Computer World* and *Your Computer* were specialist magazines for particular brands of computer, such as *Sinclair User* and *Acorn User*, with the most popular machines supported by several titles. As well as news, adverts and product reviews, early 1980s computer magazines often had considerable educational content, such as sections for beginners and introductory articles on programming or computer science concepts. They also helped normalise the computer with features about how the general public was using computers. For a time, pictures of 'everyday' people using computers were commonplace on computer magazine covers. Over 1982 and 1983, the covers of *Sinclair User* featured ZX computers in the hands of everyone from schoolchildren and businessmen to a knight in shining armour and a traditional Morris dancer, suggesting that computing was now accessible to anybody, even Morris dancers. Probably the most explicitly educational magazines were *The Home Computer Course*, a general guide to 'mastering your home computer', and *Input*, an extensive guide to learning programming 'for fun and the future'. Partwork publications to be collected on a weekly basis and stored in matching binders, they were intended to build up into definitive guides to their topics. The final issue of *The Home Computer Course* even came with a certificate to certify that the reader had completed the 'course' of education the magazine had provided.

The interaction of computer producers, the BBC, high-profile government information technology schemes, magazine publishers and educationalists in pushing the computer literacy agenda had a profound effect on the first years of British popular computing. Whatever else it could and would be, the British home computer was originally cast in a way that emphasised its educational value and encouraged people to explore what it could do. Behind this was a hope that computer literacy would have beneficial effects in the long term, be it for individuals or for the national economy. Combined with a growing interest in video gaming and the allure of an exciting and much-hyped new technology, computer literacy was an important force in pushing the British public into an unprecedented home computer buying spree. By the end of 1982 home computing was booming.

CHAPTER FIVE
The Boom

Buying from a computer shop could be a bewildering experience in 1983. You enter in search of expert help, tentatively move your way past the screens flashing with the newest games, racks of computer magazines and programming books, and find a pale teenager who seems to work here. 'You want to buy your first computer?' he asks 'Well, let's see what we've got in stock... want to learn about computers? How about trying a ZX81? A bit old, and black and white, and the keyboard is a piece of plastic, but it's cheap and there's lots of software for it... Perhaps a BBC Micro? It's the one the kids use at school, and it's been on television a lot, and its got Econet, the Tube, a printer port, ah but it's £400... maybe something cheaper? The Oric's quite nice if you like a 6502 machine, but there's loads more games for the Spectrum... You don't like the rubber keyboard? I'd offer you an Electron but we've got none in, so try a good old VIC-20, it's only got 5k of RAM but we sell an expansion pack. Maybe a Commodore 64 instead? It can do sprites and the sound is fantastic! Or we've got a Jupiter Ace, Dragon 32, TI99/4A, Atari 800? There's a special offer on the Mattel Aquarius, but between you and me, nobody seems to want one...'

The early years of new technologies tend to be messy periods of divergent philosophies, experimental ideas, emerging standards, and technical and commercial failures. In the early days of flight, designers flew, and frequently crashed, all sorts of unlikely looking contraptions. There was no generally accepted right way for designing an aeroplane, so different ideas were tried out until it was discovered what worked best. Much the same could be said of home computers in the early 1980s. With few firm ideas of what a micro should look like, what it should do and how it should do it, computer manufacturers came up with a wide variety of designs. In late 1983, *PCW* listed some 26 different home computers available for under £500, and even more would follow the year after. The diversity of design bred impassioned debate over which machine was best, but there could never be a clear winner in this technological game of Top Trumps, as all of them had their strengths and weaknesses to play off against each other.

Quite apart from the variety, the sheer numbers sold were amazing. By the end of 1983, a home computer seemed to be at the top of every Christmas list. By December, major retailers were reporting a surge in demand for computers far beyond their expectations and the plans of the manufacturers, who struggled to meet the huge number of orders. Retailers ordered 200,000 of Acorn's new Electron, a 'ridiculous' figure complained one Acorn marketing manager to the press. Sinclair, after stockpiling 100,000 machines over the quiet summer months, reported to have received orders for 200,000 in one week of November alone. Manufacturers of less popular machines were reckoned to be benefiting from the shortages, as people bought whatever they could find rather than go home empty-handed. It was an extraordinary end to a year that saw an estimated 1.1–1.8 million home computers sold in Britain.[1]

There is no neat narrative through the boom years. Too much was happening at once in too many companies, yet some salient themes stand out. As well as a sales bonanza and a carnival of technical diversity, the home computer boom was a cultural event. Most of those computers were going to people who had no experience of what a computer was and what it could do. In homes across Britain, millions of people experienced that strange first moment of making a computer do something, an experience for which the magic has been lost for every generation that followed. Better still, so many of the machines they were using were designed and made in Britain, albeit normally assembled from chips made in the Far East. Nonetheless, the boom had an element of patriotism to it, as British ingenuity was celebrated. After years of industrial decline, the invention of these fantastic new devices, the opening of new computer factories and the export of British computers around the world was presented as a national success story.

In 1983 Britain proudly boasted the highest level of computer ownership in the world. About one in ten British homes had a computer, ahead even of the USA and technologically advanced Japan. A tiny percentage by today's saturated standards, it was seen as a triumph at the time. The claim even found its way into the 1983 Conservative Party manifesto, which was anxious to take some credit for it, declaring, 'we have speeded this progress by supporting research and spreading knowledge of the technologies of tomorrow'. In 1982 Margaret Thatcher, a science graduate as well as a free-market thinker, proudly presented a Sinclair ZX Spectrum computer to the Japanese Prime Minister. For a Britain in recession, the home computer boom and the accompanying growth of the microcomputer industry were touted as a sign of economic progress and of national inventiveness.

A distinct type of home computer emerged from Britain in the boom years. As we have seen already, the influence of computer literacy was strong, and ensured that programming and education were prominent features in design and marketing. Simultaneously, the emergence of games as a major use meant that designs came to be optimised more for entertainment than they had been before. All of this had to be achieved at a low cost. The most vibrant sector of the market was in cheaper machines costing under £200. Design to such a price point necessitated design economies and led to simpler machines than those generally favoured in the USA or Japan, the other major microcomputer-developing nations of the day. The result was a series of comparatively simple and low-cost machines, which mashed education and exploring the computer with entertainment and fun.

The Speccy

Several companies dabbled in making low-cost computers in the early 1980s, but the most influential in establishing the concept was undoubtedly Sinclair. Having already introduced Britain to the affordable home computer with the ZX80 and ZX81, Sinclair extended the concept in 1982 with a colour successor, the ZX Spectrum, arguably the most famous British home computer of all. With the loss of the BBC contract a recent memory, Clive Sinclair joked that the Spectrum could have been called 'Not the BBC Micro', when announcing the machine. But while the Beeb was a hefty piece of electronic engineering with everything but the kitchen sink built in, the Spectrum was small and sleek, a masterclass in inventive minimalism, and on sale at less than half the price.

Known before release as the ZX82, the Spectrum took the ZX81 as its starting point. 'To the extent that there was a specification, the guidance was we should improve the graphics and we should add colour. That was about it,' recalls Richard Altwasser, the Spectrum's hardware designer, who began by drawing up a specification: 'Defined the graphics system, the rest of the hardware features, worked hard with Nine Tiles, mostly Steve Vickers, to define further extension to Sinclair BASIC. And that became the specification. The whole thing was done really rather quickly.' The Spectrum emerged as a much more capable design than the ZX81, not only with colour graphics, but with many other improvements, such as more memory, extended BASIC, sound and an improved keyboard. The whole thing was wrapped up in another distinctive black case from Rick Dickinson, and the thought put into the choice of textures, colours and shape created a design classic. At the bargain price of just £125 for the 16k version or £175 for the 48k version, the Spectrum was the cheapest colour computer on the market when it was released, and soon became a firm favourite of games programmers and players.

When the ZX80 and the ZX81 had been released there had been little experience with what people would actually use computers for in the home. However, the Spectrum's designers had more of an idea of what people would use their machines for than before. 'By that time we had some experience with the ZX80 and we knew that people were doing programming and that quite a lot of people were playing games,' recalls Richard Altwasser. The use and reception of the earlier machines, including their use for entertainment software, was accordingly factored in to the design of the Spectrum. 'Because of the games development, the Spectrum was a logical next step,' remarks Sir Clive Sinclair. 'We improved the keyboard and we put in colour.' It would be a stretch to say that the Spectrum was designed as a games computer, but it certainly seems to have been intended to have more potential as an entertainment device. 'I don't recall the design brief would have said games, except in as much as saying it needed to have high-resolution colour graphics,' explains Altwasser. 'Which is obviously something that would make games very much more attractive.'[*]

Despite games being considered more in its design, in most other respects the Spectrum was as much a machine for exploring computing as the ZX81 had been before it, but with increased potential as a general-purpose computer too. Early Spectrum adverts mentioned business software about as much as they did entertainment, and described the machine as suitable for 'professional-level computing', as well as learning to program. 'I imagined that the computer would be used for practical purposes in peoples' homes as well,' explains Richard Altwasser, 'without at that time perhaps having too clear an idea, or too close a constriction, of what those practical applications might be.'

The machine took shape quite quickly over 1981 and 1982, with software development led by Steve Vickers at Nine Tiles software consultants, and the hardware largely the responsibility

---

[*]Colour was not universally thought necessary for a microcomputer in the early 1980s. With limited memory and processing power available, monochrome displays offered higher resolution, allowing for more detailed graphics or clearer text for productive purposes. Some machines offered different screen modes, where the number of colours available could be traded off against the screen resolution, from low-resolution colour to high-resolution monochrome.

of Richard Altwasser, working in Sinclair's cramped Cambridge offices. 'In one sense that was quite simple because all you needed was a sharp pencil and a drawing board, and a notepad to do some calculations on,' recalls Altwasser. 'The circuit board layout was done with little bits of black tape sticking on a light box. The whole thing was done manually. In one sense it was simple, crude you might say, in another sense it was very time consuming and quite risky.' While the Spectrum's development proceeded quite smoothly, such simple working methods could lead to problems. One issue, recalled by Altwasser, occurred when Ferranti in Manchester missed out a single connection on the ULA physical layout, the mask of the chip used to produce silicon wafers packed with numerous individual chips. With a connection missing none of the initial batch worked, bar one. 'On the mask that they used to produce the wafer, there was a little bit of dust, and that little bit of dust fell in exactly the place that the engineer who did the track layout forgot to put the aluminium connection,' chuckles Altwasser. 'We found out of all the chips on the initial wafer, that there was only one that actually worked.'

Colour was one of the defining features of the Spectrum, but for technical and economic reasons, it used a rather distinctive means to achieve it. The Spectrum was intended to use a television for its display, but the limitations of the PAL system used in British colour televisions were problematic for displaying high-resolution colour computer graphics. 'You haven't got a high-resolution colour monitor to display high-resolution colour graphics, so I decided to adopt some of the principles that had been used on TVs for graphics on Ceefax and teletext,' explains Richard Altwasser. 'That is to say, have a block of pixels in a character block, but have one or two colours, a foreground and background colour associated with that.' A computer display is made up of thousands of individual dots, or pixels. A conventional colour image would require colour information to be stored for each individual pixel. Instead, the Spectrum stored a simple monochrome bitmap image, then split the screen into a number of different colour blocks. Each block could be assigned a foreground and a background colour, or INK and PAPER in the Spectrum's BASIC. Essentially, the screen was colourful but the graphic was not, it just happened to appear in a part of the display that was colourful. 'It certainly is cheaper, of course. If you have to have every single pixel where you have to have a byte or more for colour that would be a huge amount of memory,' remarks Altwasser. As the Spectrum relied on the same memory bank for video information and program storage, another way of saving costs, this method was also more efficient for getting data out of the memory quickly enough to provide a television signal. Looking at the Spectrum's display is a bit like viewing a black and white picture through a multicolour overlay. It could lead to 'colour clash', an odd effect when the underlying graphic moved between blocks assigned to different colours. For example, a red figure walking across the screen would appear to be half blue as it crossed from a red block to a blue block. In practice programmers found ways to mitigate the problem, and it contributed to the distinct graphical style of many Spectrum games.

The keyboard was another design economy. After the criticism of the flat-membrane keypad of the ZX80 and ZX81, it was an obvious target for improvement, but cost and company style dictated another inventive improvement. 'It's part of the company culture we weren't going to simply buy one off the shelf,' remarks Rick Dickinson, invoking the firm's innovative approach. 'You're not going to take some bog-standard keyboard off some steam-powered computer and slap it on as the starting point; it was the first thing you'd throw out. Can't put that in, it's like having a steam engine in a modern car.' The solution was an enlarged membrane keyboard overlaid with a sheet of rubber 'dead-flesh' keys that moved when they were pressed. The new keyboard was a bit spongy to type on, but addressed the fundamental criticism about tactile feedback. 'If you distil what differentiates a Sinclair computer keyboard from other computer keyboards at the time, it was moving keys,' explains Dickinson. 'We needed to create the impression of when you press the thing that's supposed to be the key top, it goes down and you can feel it'. Providing a whole 40 moving key keyboard with just four parts had a neat efficiency too. The BASIC, largely developed by Steven Vickers, was an expanded version of that on the ZX81. As the number of commands increased, some keys had as many six different functions, and it would take users some time to get used to the various combinations of shift keys used to access them all.

The Spectrum met with a positive response from the computer press. Aside from minor niggles, such as judgements that the BASIC was slower than the BBC Micro, that the sound was a bit quiet, and some people disliking the keyboard, most reviewers seemed to find far more to love than to hate. *Personal Computer World*'s reviewer David Tebbutt declared that Sinclair had set an example of how to produce a decent colour computer at a uniquely low price. *Your Computer*'s reviewer Tim Hartnell judged that 'despite minor faults, the Spectrum is way ahead of its competitors'. The response from the public was highly enthusiastic. Sinclair's stand at the *Personal Computer World* show in 1982 was mobbed by a crowd several people deep trying to place orders. After escaping the hubbub, Richard Altwasser found himself listening to a pair of teenagers discussing the machine. 'They were enthusing about the ZX Spectrum, the features of it, they'd been on the stand, read the literature,' remembers Altwasser. 'Listening to these two going on about what a wonderful machine it was, it sort of made all the late evenings, all the travel up to Manchester and back, well worth it.' Although it held general appeal, the Spectrum became particularly popular with the youths who saved pocket money or nagged parents to get their hands on one. The Spectrum was exciting and, despite its compact size, offered a lot of computer for not a lot of money. Once again, Sinclair was overwhelmed by the heavy demand. Despite taking criticism for how long it took to fulfil orders, it still managed to sell 200,000 units by the end of 1982. 'The response was incredible, it was mind blowing, everybody wanted one. Christmas was the time, the classic Christmas gift and they were sold out,' recalls Rick Dickinson. 'It was an incredible time, despite the criticism. But you can criticise away, people wanted them.'

The Spectrum had the same basic interface port as the ZX81, non-standard but easily open to exploitation by the many kitchen table inventors and small electronics firms that developed peripherals for it. Sinclair itself also launched a series of devices to plug into it. The company's normal genius for inventive product names fell somewhat short with the ZX Interface 1 and ZX Interface 2, but it showed the intent for the Spectrum to be at the heart of an expanded system. The £19.95 Interface 2 enhanced the Spectrum's entertainment capacity by adding a slot for game cartridges, and joystick ports. Unfortunately, there were cheaper joystick interfaces on the market, and the expensive £14.95 cartridges were little used. The £29.95 Interface 1 was rather more interesting, adding a standard RS232 interface to link to other peripherals, or network up to 64 Spectrums together, useful for the schools market. Its other use was to connect the Spectrum to another of the company's inventions, the ZX Microdrive.

One of the things that marked out a home micro from a serious business computer by this point was the use of floppy disc drives. Discs offered far faster and more reliable data storage than cassette tapes, but they were very expensive, something home users might aspire to own but few could afford. Announced at the Spectrum's launch, but only vaguely described on advertising that noted it was 'coming soon', there was some mystery to the ZX Microdrive at first. Rumoured to be some sort of cheap miniature floppy disc drive, it was widely seen as the device that could transform the Spectrum into a professional machine. When it finally went on sale in 1983, after many delays, there was some surprise when the Microdrive turned out not to be a disc drive at all.

The Microdrive was a wonder of miniaturised mechanical engineering, a whirring little black box that read tiny cartridges packed with a continuous loop of nearly five metres of cassette tape that whizzed through it at high speed. The so-called 'stringy-floppy' was far slower than a disc for accessing data, but compared to the endless wait watching a colourful loading screen as a cassette loaded, the Microdrive was blindingly fast. Adverts boasted that it could load a 48k program in just nine seconds. Despite a certain amount of tutting in the press that it was not the anticipated disc drive, the device was well received. *What Micro* even reckoned it might be more significant than the Spectrum if other companies started taking up the idea. However, with use the tape stretched, causing reliability problems, but the real killer of its commercial fortunes was the delay in producing it. In the year and a half between the Spectrum's debut and the first Microdrive shipping, hundreds of Spectrum programs were released on cassette tape. At an initial price of £4.95 per Microdrive cartridge, software houses were reluctant to support the new format, and cassettes remained the default option for Spectrum data storage.

With its extra features, the Spectrum finally cracked the schools market for Sinclair by being included in the government's new Micros in Primary Schools scheme. It was too late to stop the BBC Micro dominating the education market, but it was a stamp of approval for the machine nonetheless. Although many people would find serious uses for the Spectrum as they learned what computers could do, the Microdrive delays dealt a blow to its fortunes in the professional market. Instead, as we shall see, the Spectrum's reputation would be made as a games computer, arguably one of the most influential games computers of all time.

The sawn-off BBC Micro

If imitation is the sincerest form of flattery, then one of the biggest compliments paid to the Spectrum was in its influence on competitors. Sinclair's formula for a low-cost computer was widely influential and several manufacturers introduced machines following a similar philosophy to target the same market. On the other side of Cambridge, Acorn began developing a machine to compete with the ZX Spectrum to give it a bite at the booming market for cheaper computers.

'It was a market-driven initiative,' recalls Steve Furber, who did much of the Electron's hardware design. 'The BBC Micro had been hugely successful, but if only we could engineer the cost down a bit, there was potentially an even bigger market, particularly in the home.'

Compared to the BBC Micro, the Electron had fewer interfaces, simplified sound and fewer screen modes, and performed a little more sluggishly too. Perhaps most important were the features that were retained, with many of the Beeb's admired capabilities shoehorned into a box half the size and cost. 'We actually built a cardboard mock-up of what we thought the Electron should look like,' recalls Steve Furber, 'it was basically shrunk down to the size of the keyboard.' The Electron had the same 6502 processor, the same size 32k RAM, and the same fully featured BASIC as the BBC Micro, and had a typewriter-style keyboard. Advertising emphasised its similarity to the machine children used at school, and it was compatible with much BBC Micro software. The Electron was essentially a sawn-off BBC Micro, but with a price of just £199. At only £24 more than a 48k Spectrum, and with several refinements Sinclair's machine lacked, the Electron was a serious contender to it.

It took considerable ingenuity to squeeze so much of the BBC Micro's capability into a package half the price, but the Electron still represented a retrograde step for Acorn. If the BBC Micro had been an innovative top-of-the-range product that led the market, the Electron unashamedly followed the market. It was an uncomfortable move for a company more culturally attuned to advancing technology. 'We felt the market was moving forwards, that the way to go was to higher capability,' explains Steve Furber. 'So building this product, which was going the opposite way, to compete more directly with Sinclair, we were not very enthusiastic about. But technically it was very challenging.'

The trick to the Electron was again a ULA, probably the largest then fitted to a home computer, combining such functions as sound, internal timing and display control in a single chip. Acorn's previous ULA were designed by hand on a big sheet of translucent paper on a glass office wall. Such was the size of the Electron ULA and all that it had to do that, according to Steve Furber, 'the glass wall would have been too big.' Instead, ULA development tools were written on the BBC Micro; the older machine quite literally gave birth to its diminutive successor. There were over 100 chips on the BBC Micro circuit board, but the Electron had about 14. The enormous ULA was the making of the Electron, but also contributed to its downfall. Christmas 1983 should have established the machine as a market leader, but ULA problems meant there were nowhere near enough Electrons to meet the huge demand. Acorn missed out on a sales bonanza, as people bought whatever micro they could find. The Electron would come back to haunt Acorn, but fortunately enough for the consumers there were plenty of other machines to choose from, some of them even supplied by other companies from Cambridge.

The Cambridge connection

Acorn and Sinclair were but the best known of a cluster of computer companies around Cambridge in the early 1980s, including Camputers, Jupiter Cantab, Tangerine and their subsidiary Oric. To the press of the time it was Britain's very own Silicon Valley, or Silicon Fen at least – another shining example of the sorts of high-tech knowledge industries that would pull the nation out of recession and into a more prosperous future. Silicon Fen itself was just one aspect of a larger scene of scientific and technical industries developing around the university town, sometimes referred to as the Cambridge Phenomenon. Between the mid-1970s and mid-1980s, over 200 high-tech businesses were formed in the Cambridge area, many connected with electronics, software or computing in some way or another.[2] For budding high-tech entrepreneurs it was a good place to set up shop. The surrounding businesses offered both potential customers, and consultants to advise on all manner of specialist and obscure technical issues.

Cambridge University was another factor in the growth of the phenomenon. This source of ideas, academics turned entrepreneurs and skilled personnel was particularly important to Acorn. 'Most of the staff of Acorn in the early days came from Cambridge University,' reflects Sophie Wilson. Over half of the hundred-odd graduates employed by Acorn by 1985 had studied at Cambridge. Among them were Wilson, Hermann Hauser, Steve Furber and Andy Hopper, one of the company's directors and also a lecturer at the university. From Hopper's academic research and connections came the inspiration for Acorn's Econet network and, later, the revolutionary ARM microprocessor.

The mobility of ideas and people is key to the growth of high-technology clusters. Entrepreneurial individuals with an idea often outgrow the companies that employ them and split off to found new firms. Through its co-founder Chris Curry, Acorn was partly an offshoot of Sinclair. So too was Jupiter Cantab, founded in 1982 by former ZX Spectrum designers Richard Altwasser and Steven Vickers, who had the idea of producing a computer of their own, the Jupiter Ace. 'We saw a commercial opportunity and took it,' explains Altwasser, whose successful sideline writing programming books had already given him some entrepreneurial experience. The unique selling point of their computer was using FORTH as its programming language instead of the common, but often disparaged, BASIC. 'Steve came up with this idea of FORTH,' recalls Altwasser, 'I played with it and very quickly convinced myself that FORTH was a very much more appropriate language for this type of home computer than BASIC, mainly because it was very much faster and more flexible.'

With the Spectrum complete the pair founded Jupiter Cantab to work on a FORTH computer. That the Jupiter Ace was designed at Richard Altwasser's home says much about how few resources were required to design a viable microcomputer if the designers knew what they were doing. 'Your equipment needs were not great. On the software side we had a Z80 development kit, which was just a small box and a monitor,' recalls Altwasser. 'On the hardware side it was really just a drawing board with a light box.' Their creation looked rather like a white ZX81, with similar specifications – a Z80 processor, monochrome display and just 3k of RAM. However, the hardware was rather different, more expandable, and FORTH made for faster and more efficient programs than BASIC.* Given the many different variants of BASIC used by different computers and the accepted importance of programming at the time, a FORTH computer was not a bad concept. Indeed, the Ace's rejection of BASIC for FORTH generated considerable press attention when it was released. 'I think we thought that for those people interested in programming, the arguments in favour of FORTH, in speed and flexibility, would be attractive,' explains Altwasser. 'Going to FORTH was no greater disadvantage than going to yet another variant of BASIC.' However, as colour graphics and ready-to-play software became more important, the Ace was left as something of a niche product, whose popularity was probably among programming enthusiasts. Selling perhaps 5,000 units in total, it was far overshadowed by Altwasser and Vickers's more famous creation for Sinclair.

Oric

The most significant of the other home computers to emerge from Cambridge in the boom, and perhaps the most serious challenger to the ZX Spectrum, was the Oric-1, the futuristic name simply an anagram of Micro without an M. In another sign of the success of home computers, the industry was starting to interest investors, among them David Wickins, the millionaire owner of British Car Auctions. Wickins got talking to the directors of Tangerine Computer Systems, but preferred not to co-invest in the venture capital funded firm. Accordingly, a new company, Oric, was set up to target the lower end of the market where Sinclair were doing so well. Tangerine had already

*Key differences include a second expansion port, sound and dedicated video circuitry on the Jupiter Ace.

produced the Microtan 65 hobbyist computer, and was working on a professional workstation, the Tangerine Tiger. The Oric-1 would take it into the consumer market and directly into competition with Sinclair's products. 'We were creating a Spectrum type of computer,' explains Oric-1 hardware designer Dr Paul Johnson. 'We knew it had to be under £200 to keep within people's budgets.' Oric's development was contracted out to Tangerine. 'The deal was £100,000 for the design of the machine and 50 pence a unit for the first 100,000 units,' recalls Johnson. 'That was a lot of money then for just designing a computer, when I was churning this stuff out. It didn't take me long to design the Oric.'

A similar size to the Spectrum, the Oric-1 followed the same low-cost colour computer concept, but in a more refined fashion. 'The Spectrum was crap compared to the Oric,' argues Johnson. 'You had that horrible keyboard and little sound chip – it just didn't measure up at all.' The Oric-1 offered yet another variation on how to provide a cheap keyboard, with small plastic keys, and despite not being typewriter style, it was well regarded and well laid out. 'Keyboards were expensive then and the industrial designer came up with this very clever design, he put a cam action on the push-down keys,' recalls Johnson. 'It gave you a nice feel.' One of the most startling features of the Oric-1, and a clear advantage over the Spectrum, was the sound quality, with almost a fifth of the circuit board area taken up by a large speaker. 'We put a General Instruments sound chip into it and the sound out of the Oric was monster,' explains Johnson.

Oric's advertising stressed the machine's suitability for both the home and business, but according to Johnson, the assessment of their target market was realistically more about entertainment: 'You can use it for business, you can use it for this, you can use it for that… We knew what it was going to do – kids were buying them for playing games.' Just as with so many other computers of the time, the Oric-1's launch suffered from technical problems and delivery delays, with some people waiting up to three months for their machines. *PCW*'s reviewer wryly noted that the first two review machines it had received had not worked. Despite the teething problems, the Oric-1 was recognised as generally excellent value for money. In spite of its refinements it managed to briefly undercut the ZX Spectrum when it first appeared. Indeed, at a launch price of £99.95 for the 16k version, or £169.95 for the 48k version, the Oric-1 was the first colour home computer for under £100, although a price cut in the ZX Spectrum gave it only a brief advantage.

'When you design a new computer like the Oric your biggest problem is who's going to supply software for it,' explains Paul Johnson. 'You had to convince the software vendors that this was going to be a big seller, that was the problem.' By the time the Oric-1 was launched in January 1983, Sinclair had already sold 200,000 Spectrums, and there were already around 350 assorted games available for it. Although the Oric-1 attracted the support of several software houses and sold around 160,000 units in Britain, it was never able to challenge the established position of the Spectrum. However, the Oric-1 and the later Oric Atmos would find a ready market in France, largely unintentionally.

As Paul Johnson was finishing the hardware design, he found himself with four unused logic gates. 'I can't waste four gates. I've got to use them for something because otherwise they're doing nothing,' recalls Johnson, who managed to shoehorn the circuitry to drive a monitor into the unused capacity. France and Britain use different standards for television displays, the SECAM and PAL systems, meaning that British computers normally needed special adaptors to work with French televisions and the results were often poor. However, French televisions also had SCART connectors, which turned out to be readily compatible with the Oric's monitor connector. Small technical decisions can sometimes have surprising consequences. Most of the other cheap computers only had an RF television connector. According to Johnson, the Oric's ready suitability for the French market gave it a decisive edge: 'Our major sales were in France. We had 80 per cent of the French computer market with the Oric, and the reason we got that was unintentional.' While it may have been an also-ran in Britain, the Oric-1 occupied a similar niche in France to the ZX Spectrum in Britain.

An industrial rebirth?

We need to leave the cloistered design offices of Cambridge to appreciate another aspect of the microcomputer-driven economic revival. At the height of the boom, home computers were not just being designed in Britain but were also made in Britain, rather than just being outsourced to the Far East. The major ZX81 and ZX Spectrum production line was at Timex in Dundee, a city hit by a decline in traditional industries like shipbuilding, but with a growing high-technology sector. Commodore set up a factory in Corby, promising 1,000 jobs in a town that had a 30 per cent unemployment rate after the closure of the steelworks, and qualifying for hefty government redevelopment grants, naturally announced by Information Technology Minister Kenneth Baker. For a time, computer factories pointed to a brighter, high-tech future for the manufacturing sector.

The Dragon 32, a Welsh home computer backed by the Welsh Development Agency, is perhaps the best example of how computers came to symbolise industrial renewal. The Dragon was the brainchild of Tony Clarke, the managing director of Swansea-based toy company Mettoy. The machine was intended to cash in on children's growing interest in playing with computers instead of Mettoy's traditional lines, which included Corgi die-cast toy cars. The Dragon, produced by Mettoy subsidiary Dragon Data, was something of an oddity among home computers. Rather than the common Z80 or 6502 microprocessors, it used a Motorola 6809. This earned it some interest from people concerned about processor details, but sadly not so much from software companies, whose expertise lay in programming computers with more popular processors. However, some common design heritage shared with the Tandy TRS80 Colour Computer, about the only other 6809-based home computer, meant that some programs written for the 'Co-Co' would work on the Dragon too.

A robust machine with a typewriter-style keyboard, 32k of RAM, colour graphics and good value at £199, the Dragon initially sold quite well, some 32,000 machines by early 1983. Yet at least part of this success was from Mettoy's contacts with major retailers, and the shortages of other brands of computer at the time. Whatever the Dragon 32's technical merits, its fame rested most on the new factory built to produce it in the Welsh steel town of Port Talbot. Journalists could not help but compare the town's declining heavy industry with this futuristic new start-up and the future it represented. Less well publicised was the fact that this proudly Welsh machine was actually designed for Mettoy by PA Technology, yet another Cambridge-based consultancy.

Overseas exports were another aspect of this apparent economic success story. Other European countries were slow to develop their own personal computer industries, and large parts of the continent had their introduction to the microcomputer age through British machines. Indeed, some of the lesser-known computers enjoyed better fortunes overseas than they did at home. Dragon computers would later find a home in Spain, and Oric did well in France. The low cost of Sinclair's machines proved well suited to Communist countries, and cheap Spectrum copies were still being made in Eastern Europe in the 1990s. For a few years it seemed that Britain was not so much leading the rest of Europe in the personal computer race, as helping Europe find the starting blocks in the personal computer race.

There was a steady trickle of optimistic reporting at the start of the 1980s about British computers being exported around the world: trade deals signed to introduce the ZX81 and Spectrum to China; Acorn supplying BBC Micros to Indian schools, after the Queen gave 30 of them to India on a state visit; there was even an Arabic version of the ZX81 with the text on the right-hand side of the screen. The reality behind the headlines was a bit more complicated. A recent report on the legacy of the BBC Micro suggests that, while the machine sold well in Australia, Holland and South Africa, there was actually disappointment that its overseas sales did not match the media hype.[3] The biggest hope of British companies was breaking into the US market. Like a trained Shakespearian British actor dreaming of success in Hollywood, there was something aspirational about British ingenuity making it big in the country that invented the personal computer, but it was also a major market.

The two companies to try hardest to crack the US were Sinclair and Acorn. In a reversal of the normal flow of American ideas and products into Britain, by mid-1981 Sinclair was doing rather well directly supplying American enthusiasts by mail order. Shipping up to 20,000 ZX81s a month, Sinclair was reputed to be outselling Commodore, Apple and Tandy.[4] In 1982, Timex produced a licensed Americanised version with double the memory, named the Timex TS1000. Sold in stores across the USA, the TS1000 was initially something of a sensation. Timex was overwhelmed with queries, and sold over half a million of the little machines in the five months after its launch. Unfortunately the success was short lived. By the following year sales had plummeted, and neither discounting nor the release of the improved TS1500 could stop Timex from pulling out of the computer market in 1983. The $100 computer was an interesting novelty for a time, but there was not the same need for such extreme design economies in the affluent US market as in Britain. Nevertheless, the appearance of the TS1000 was enough to jolt some American computer producers into projects to make even cheaper computers, albeit with limited commercial success.*

*Among these were the Commodore C116, part low-cost successor to the VIC-20, part 'Sinclair killer', launched in 1984; and the Tandy MC10, released in 1983, both distinctly backward steps for the companies involved.

Sinclair's US sideline was not a long-term success. However, it was profitable for a time and Timex's problems did little to harm Sinclair. By comparison with the TS1000, Acorn's attempt to enter the US market was a disaster. In 1983, Acorn tried introducing the BBC Micro into the US, on the back of sponsoring public broadcaster PBS to show *The Computer Programme*. The many expansion opportunities of the BBC Micro were part of its appeal, but unfortunately American consumer products had to comply with strict electronic emissions standards laid down by the Federal Communications Commission (FCC). 'The design of the BBC Micro was really not good for the US market because it had so many ports,' explains Steve Furber. 'When you do the emissions test you have to stick a metre of cable in every port, so the more ports there are, the more wires there are transmitting radio interference.' The machine gained a couple of pounds of shielding to stop it leaking radio waves, but the reworking delayed its official release until after PBS's broadcast of *The Computer Programme*, leaving it as advertising for a product that was unavailable. More fundamentally, the US computer market was a tough environment by 1983. Apple was already entrenched in education establishments, Commodore was battering Atari and Texas Instruments in a vicious price war for domestic customers,* and building a dealer network in the large country was a challenge. 'A glorious failure,' concludes Steve Furber. The venture cost Acorn millions and would have serious consequences for the company's future finances.

---

*Among Commodore's more imaginative marketing strategies was to offer a $100 discount on a Commodore 64 computer if customers traded in an older computer. With Sinclair-Timex TS1000's discounted to around $50 at the time, Commodore found itself inundated with new TS1000's bought purely to apply for the discount.

Keeping up with the Commodore

While British companies were trying to break into the US market, US computer firms were touting their wares in Britain. The price of Atari's home computers dropped considerably after the introduction of the overpriced £395 Atari 400 and £695 Atari 800. By 1983, they were retailing for around £160 and £400 respectively, and new models were starting to appear, such as the £160 600XL and £250 800XL. Texas Instruments had replaced the £750 TI99/4 with the improved TI99/4A, priced at about £200, in 1983. Atari did better than Texas Instruments, but neither company made a great deal of impact on the British market. Domestically produced computers tended to offer more for the money and were better supported by British software producers. By contrast, Commodore became a major player in Britain, not to mention around the world.

While British companies resorted to ULA's as a poor-man's way of producing custom chips, Commodore benefited hugely from its ownership of MOS Technology, with its chip design and fabrication capabilities. The VIC-20 had been made possible thanks to MOS's Video Interface Chip (VIC), providing a cheap means to generate sound and colour graphics on a home computer. History repeated itself with the Commodore 64, which grew out of a new pair of chips originally developed by MOS to provide advanced graphics and sound for a top of the range games system. The first was the VIC-II graphics chip, developed by a team led by Albert Charpentier, which examined the graphics facilities offered by other home computers and video games, then adopted the best features that they found.[*] Simultaneously, Robert Yannes developed the Sound Interface Device (SID) chip. As an electronic music hobbyist, Yannes had been disappointed with

---

[*]One of the most significant features of VIC-II was its sprite capability. Sprites were small graphical objects, which simplified the creation of animations.

the primitive sound of most computers. His design for SID offered sophisticated audio capabilities, more like those found in professional synthesisers than in home computers. VIC-II and SID was a powerful entertainment combination and gave Commodore's engineers the basis for a remarkable machine, developed with much haste.

'I'd worked for Phillips… to bring a product from inception and design to market it would take them at least two years,' remarks Kit Spencer, who led the machine's marketing. 'We effectively did the Commodore 64 in six months. Everything was in parallel. It was crazy times.' Alongside the rapid development of the 64 by a small team of engineers lead by Charles Winterble, Spencer directed a comprehensive marketing effort to support and sell the machine when it was released. 'Previously Commodore had not been very good at launching its products,' recalls Spencer. 'We'd done a better job in the UK on the whole. And I was determined we were going to do that one right.' When the Commodore 64 was released in 1982, there were already manuals, programming guides and a software list to entice people to buy it and encourage others to create software for it.

Priced at $595 on release in 1982, the Commodore 64 was competitively priced and had a major selling point in its 64k memory, which was larger than most competitors. 'I decided it wasn't going to have a name like VIC or PET. I was going to put the biggest sales point right there in the name,' recalls Kit Spencer. With memory probably the only number on a computer that really mattered to consumers at the time, the 64k featured heavily in a major $20 million advertising campaign. As a visual reminder of the 64's memory, many adverts featured elephants, famed for never forgetting anything. It says much for Commodore's confidence in its product that other adverts featured competitors' machines too. One campaign featured a line-up of computers from Apple, IBM and Tandy, each declaring that it had computed that the Commodore 64 was better than it were on price and memory grounds.

Even in a booming market the Commodore 64 was a distinct success. 'When I launched it at CES, one of the headlines of my press conference was "we're going to sell a million of these computers in the next year,"' reminisces Kit Spencer. 'I went back a year later and said, "I'm going to have to apologise. I said we're going to sell a million computers. We didn't. We sold one and a quarter million."' Retailing at around £350 in 1983, the machine was soon one of the top sellers in Britain too, with 240,000 Commodore 64s sold that year. Together with over 410,000 VIC-20s, it was enough to place Commodore in second place for sales after Sinclair in 1983. Estimates vary, but over its long life as many as 17 million Commodore 64s were made, making it the most produced computer model in history.

The good, the bad and the indifferent

In contrast to the superlative power of the Commodore 64, the computer boom also saw a series of cheap and cheerful machines produced to cash in on the huge demand that had been unleashed. Following the success of the innovative ZX81 and Spectrum, several other companies produced low -cost machines. Some, like the Electron and Oric, were perfectly respectable micros by the standards of the time they were released. The same could not be said of some of the others, basic computers with hardly a hint of innovation nor claim to do anything more than play games or be vaguely useful to the beginner, machines whose only redeeming quality was being cheap.

Take, for example, the £89.95 Mattel Aquarius. Mattel may have been a toy company best known for the Barbie doll, but its 1979 Intellivision games console had been quite an innovative design and a great success. The same could not be said of the Aquarius. Seeking a quick way into the home computer market, Mattel bought a design off the shelf from Radofin Electronics, a Hong Kong-based manufacturer of Intellivision components. The result was a cheap Z80-based computer, with a calculator-style keyboard and pitiful 4k of

RAM, less than 2k of which was actually available for BASIC programs. 'Aquarius: System for the Seventies' was the slogan apparently suggested by one of the machine's creators. The tale is possibly apocryphal, but the truth is that the Aquarius was quite an advanced home computer by the standards of about 1980. It was just a shame that it was released in 1983, by which time it was underpowered and seemed like a toy, even set against other games computers.

Much the same could be said of the little Tandy MC10, developed as a low-price alternative to the Tandy Colour Computer, one of Tandy's successors to the TRS-80. Looking rather like an inflated ZX80, albeit with colour graphics, sound, 4k of RAM and a chiclet keyboard, the MC10 was probably intended as Tandy's answer to the Timex-Sinclair TS1000 or TS1500. In the buoyant computer market of 1983, even these stunted creatures were thought to have a chance. Despite struggling to find much nice to say about the MC10 beyond 'average' and 'adequate', *Personal Computer World*'s reviewer was forced to concede that the MC-10 would sell, if only because people trusted the Tandy brand. *PCW* actually gave the Aquarius quite a positive review as a computer for beginners and was optimistic about its future. However, the Aquarius was in production for a mere six months, and the Tandy MC10 for around a year.* At least the old ZX81, often derided as a toy, had dreams of helping with the home accounts or maybe even running a power station someday. Neither the MC10 nor the Aquarius had any such pretentious. They were just cheap computers made to cash in on a booming market.

The Japanese are coming

Amid the baffling diversity of the home computer boom, there was at least one serious attempt at standardisation. In 1983

---

*Unpopular in the USA and Britain, the MC-10 was another machine that found success in less developed markets. In particular, an MC-10 clone, the Matra Alice, achieved some success in France.

the major Japanese computer and electronics companies got together with Microsoft to agree a standard specification for building a computer – MSX.* Essentially, it was a common blueprint that each member of the MSX group could build from, eliminating the confusion and compatibility worries of consumers and software developers alike. The reality was rather messier, as manufacturers were allowed to add extra features around the MSX standards to build machines for different market niches. The result was over 250 different types of MSX computer, retaining a core of compatibility, but offering widely different features, such as light pens, video discs or advanced sound – Yamaha's MSX computers could even be plugged into the company's synthesiser keyboards.

Nevertheless, MSX was a powerful idea and a serious threat to the established home computer producers, not just because it offered the advantages of standardisation, but because it was Japanese. Japan's post-war economic miracle had seen it export masses of cheaply produced cars, televisions, transistor radios, hi-fis, calculators, typewriters and other products. National industries around the world had found that they could not compete with efficient Japanese production methods, supported by protective trade barriers in Japan. To domestic computer companies in the US and in Britain, MSX was the threatening foreign invader they had long expected. Back in 1980, Jack Tramiel had launched Commodore's efforts to build a cheap home computer with a warning that the Japanese were coming. By the time MSX appeared, Commodore, Apple and others had established strong positions in the US market, against which MSX made little headway.

Big in Japan, MSX also achieved some success in such countries as Brazil and Holland, but in Britain MSX was seen as a threat to the burgeoning domestic industry. In 1984, as British computer manufacturers met the government to

*The MSX standard demanded a Z80 microprocessor, at least 8k of RAM, Microsoft MSX BASIC, common video and sound chips, and standard keyboard layouts and expansion connectors.

discuss the implications of MSX for their businesses, Roger Kean in a *Crash* magazine editorial decried MSX as 'selling British innovation down the drain for the sake of a convenient standard'. For all the concern, MSX made little impact in Britain, but it probably said more about the market at large than about any deficiencies in MSX as a technology. As the market had matured, introducing any new computer had become increasingly difficult, even one backed by most of Japan's electronics industry. Buttressed by software houses and relationships with retailers, the established players were in a dominant position.

The maturing market

What had started off as an open market – where seemingly anybody could combine a few chips, a keyboard and a pretty case, and expect it to sell – had evolved quickly into something more restrictive. By about 1983, market conditions favoured established machines, such as the ZX Spectrum, BBC Micro and Commodore 64, over newcomers. Not only were these machines well known, but they were well supported by books, magazines, retailers and software companies. Buyers did not want to be stuck with a machine they could not easily get software for. The well-established machines with their extensive back catalogues were safe bets. A virtuous circle developed. People bought computers that offered a good choice of software, and because these computers sold in the greatest numbers, software companies were motivated to create yet more software for them.

Big chain retailers, the likes of WH Smith, Dixons, Boots and Laskys, had done much to bring the computer out of the shadows of mail order and into the bright lights of high-street sales, but they were selective in what they sold. It was far easier for the big chains to concentrate their efforts on selling a handful of types and the software to go with them, than expect inexpert staff to navigate the technical minutiae of every machine on the market. Once a retailer had put a product onto its shelves, it was in its best interests to get behind it with advertising, giving another advantage to a selected few products.

Not all of the home computers launched in the early 1980s could be successful. The machines that did best in the tumultuous years of the boom were not always the best, or the cheapest or the most technically advanced. They were ones that built up brand recognition, relationships with retailers, software catalogues, shelves of books, magazines and loyal users. For those that did not, some sort of market shake-out was inevitable at some point. Yet as 1983 drew to a close, microcomputing was on an all-time high, and people were finding all sorts of interesting uses for their machines, some of them ahead of their time.

CHAPTER SIX

Two Information Revolutions That Weren't

The home computer was not the only information technology marvel of the 1980s. Imagine having a box of electronics in your home, which connected to a wealth of information and services held on distant computers. At the push of a few buttons it allows you to read the news headlines, send electronic messages, look up train timetables, plan your next holiday, check your bank balance or even do the shopping. Hundreds of thousands of pages of information on all manner of subjects, brought to a screen in the comfort of your living room. After the explosion of Internet devices into every aspect our of lives, this is a familiar scene from the twenty-first century, but it could also have been one from the 1980s. For a few years Britain stood on the brink of an information revolution, as a networking system named Prestel promised to put homes and businesses online and open up electronic communications to the masses. Ultimately, Prestel never lived up to its potential, but even as a failed technology it was ahead of its time, and introduced Britain to another aspect of information technology, one that would only become widespread with the dramatic growth of the Internet from the 1990s.[*]

---

[*]Despite the apparent similarities, Prestel had little direct relationship with the Internet or the World Wide Web. The start of the Internet is generally traced to 1969, when the computers of four US universities were linked through ARPANET, named after its funder,

Before the 1980s liberalisation of the telecoms market, the Post Office virtually had a monopoly on telecommunications in Britain, with responsibility for the network, the phones connected to it and researching future developments. In the early 1970s, a Post Office research engineer named Sam Fedida was investigating a 'viewphone' system for making video calls, along the lines of Picturephone, which had been introduced into the US by AT&T in the 1960s. Picturephone was a flop, expensive to use and crippled by its need for telephone lines to be upgraded to handle the heavy data flows of video calls. However, simple textual information required far lower bandwidth and could be sent down normal phone lines. Rather than *viewphone*, Fedida hit upon the idea of *viewdata*, a system to supply information from a computer databank through the phone network to a customer's television set.

Fedida's idea had similarities with Teletext, a system for transmitting data as part of the television signal and displaying it on a television screen, which was being developed at around the same time by the BBC, Independent Broadcasting Authority and electronics manufacturers. Eventually the two systems adopted the same display standard, using 24 lines of 40 characters and 7 colours, but despite the visual similarities, viewdata was a much more capable system. Teletext offered very little interactivity and a limited size of databank. Viewdata was seemingly unlimited in size and allowed information to be sent through to the databank as well as

the US Department of Defense Advanced Research Projects Agency. Small experimental networks were established in other countries at around the same time, but much of what we regard today as the Internet grew out of the gradual expansion and evolution of protocols of ARPANET. The World Wide Web, the information system behind the Web pages that appear in Web browser windows, was first proposed in 1989 by a British scientist, Tim Berners-Lee, working at CERN.

Above: Early computers, like the 1949 Manchester Mark 1, a development of 'Baby', were large and expensive machines confined to machine rooms.

Below: By the 1980s, computers, such as this ZX Spectrum, were becoming affordable appliances that brought computing to the homes of the masses.

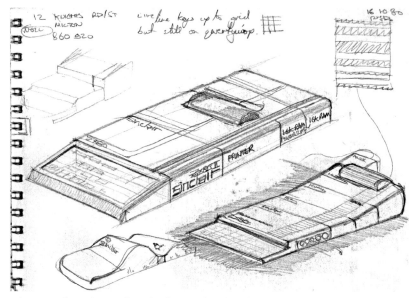

Above: Rick Dickinson's early design sketches for a modular ZX81. Industrial designers were vital in shaping computers into forms suitable for the home.

Above: Computer magazines tied the microcomputing world together with news, reviews, adverts, letters and programming articles. As *Sinclair User* shows, initially home computing was about education and applications as well as gaming.

Above: The ZX81
was amongst the
first machines
aimed at a
mass market.
Its advertising
presented the
computer as
an accessible
introduction
to the wonders
of information
technology.

Right: The endless
creativity of
programmers and
the surreal streak of
early British games
are well illustrated
in this controversial
1981 Automata
advert for 1k ZX81
games.

Left: Programmed through a hexadecimal keypad and built from a kit, the Science of Cambridge MK-14 was one of many hobbyist computers, suitable for the tinkering enthusiast but not the mass market.

Below: The futuristic Commodore PET 2001 was the first of the 1977 Trinity of ready-made appliance computers, and was far more user-friendly than hobbyist machines.

Above: Bundled together with a monitor and built-in cassette recorder, the Amstrad CPC464 looked far more like a serious 'real' computer than most other home micros.

Left: Unique in using FORTH not BASIC as its built-in programming language, the Jupiter Ace was developed by the former designers of the ZX Spectrum, and shared its diminutive size.

Left: Well built, with a typewriter-style keyboard, the Dragon 32 was a large and proudly Welsh computer, which achieved only short term success.

Above: The VIC-20, Commodore's first home computer, offered an attractive combination of sound, colour, and a typewriter style keyboard, but had only a tiny 5k memory.

Above: Although aimed at the games market, the Acorn Electron retained many of the fine qualities of the larger and pricier BBC Micro.

Left: The terrifying T-Rex roaming the corridors of *3D Monster Maze*, one of the most ambitious and tense ZX81 games.

Right: *Elite*'s combination of three-dimensional graphics, open-ended game play, and enormous scope, created a gaming experience like no other before.

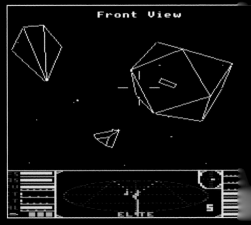

Below: Early home computer games, such as *Namtir Raiders*, were often inspired by arcade games, and despite the basic capabilities of early micros were still great fun.

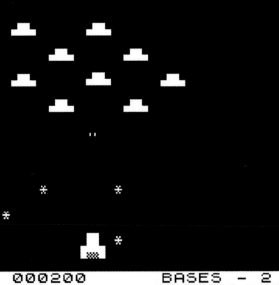

Above: Isometric 3D games, such as *Head Over Heels*, pushed the simple hardware of home computers to create surprisingly detailed graphics and novel gameplay.

Below: Combining a game with music, philosophy and a celebrity cast, the surreal *Deus Ex Machina* was a multi-media work of art to be experienced rather than just played.

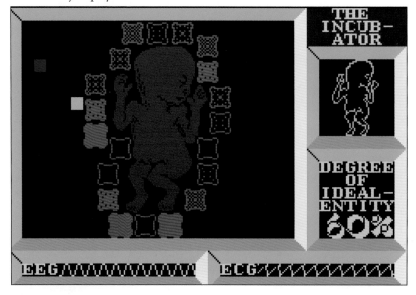

Above: Keyboard design varied enormously, such as the calculator-like buttons of the PET (top left), flat membrane of the ZX81 (top right), rubber keys of the Spectrum (bottom left) and the ideal typewriter-style keyboard of the Electron (bottom right).

Below: Prestel, seen here running on an Acorn BBC Micro connected to the phone by an acoustic coupler, connected home computer users to a huge range of online services and information, long before the World Wide Web.

receiving data from it, opening up the possibility of interactive services.*

By 1972, Fedida had an experimental viewdata system running. As the system developed over the subsequent years, Post Office management saw an opportunity to launch a prestigious and innovative service. 'I think the thought was that if we came up with this thing, almost like the jump jet or Concorde or something, we could be leading the world. It was very appealing,' comments Alex Reid, director of Viewdata in the late 1970s, around the time that the service was renamed Prestel. There was also a serious business case behind the Post Office's interest. 'I think the main thing that interested senior management about this was the potential for traffic generation,' explains Reid. 'The cost of the infrastructure was pretty much fixed. In terms of the financial performance, if you can persuade people to make more calls it's almost all profit.' The Post Office had a promising technology and the infrastructure to make it available across the country, but it was pointless creating an information system that did not have any information on it. Without a mass of interesting content there would be no good reason for customers to sign up to Prestel. With no potential customers there would be no good reason for electronics manufacturers to make Prestel televisions. Content was key to the Post Office's hopes for the system.

*Teletext is essentially a passive, one-way service. All the Teletext pages are broadcast on a repeating cycle. After typing in a page number, viewers have to wait for the page to be broadcast before it appears on the screen. Teletext allows eight 'magazines', each containing up to 256 individual screens listed in hexadecimal. As television remote controls do not have hexadecimal buttons, the full range is not easily available. Another practical limit is that adding more pages to the system slows it down, as all the pages have to be broadcast in each cycle, which takes longer the more pages are in it.

An open medium

Fedida originally envisaged the Post Office playing an active editorial role in the service, but management saw the organisation as being in the business of carrying information rather than creating it. By the late 1970s, thinking had shifted to encouraging other organisations to generate content. However, the underlying structure of the Prestel network placed the Post Office in a powerful gatekeeper position. Unlike the information on today's Internet, which is distributed on computers all over the world and owned by a great variety of individuals and organisations, Prestel was essentially a centralised databank owned by the Post Office. A set of GEC4000 minicomputers holding copies of the databank were dotted around the country to allow people to make local rate telephone calls to access them.[*] The contents of each databank were kept synchronised, more or less, by a central update computer in London named DUKE.[†] This arrangement meant that the Post Office essentially owned Prestel, but it raised questions over what responsibilities it had for the information on its system and what controls it should exercise.

The range of potential options held different pros and cons. At one end of the spectrum the Post Office could vet all of the content on the system. Such tight control might safeguard

---

[*]Almost like the electronic brains of the 1950s, the GEC Prestel computers all carried individual names, often with local significance or named after old telephone exchanges. One of Manchester's two machines was named ARKWRIGHT, like the Industrial Revolution era inventor, while Edinburgh's were named SCOTT and BURNS.

[†]The number and location of Prestel databank computers changed over the life of the system. The first computer was at the research centre at Martlesham, but as the system was rolled out computers were installed in London, Manchester, Leeds, Croydon, Birmingham, Chelmsford and Cardiff. Other towns were served by multiplexers, which connected local users to a Prestel computer located elsewhere. As technology improved, more multiplexers were installed and the number of Prestel computers consequently reduced.

quality, but involved more administrative burden, raised awkward questions of censorship and might limit how much information made it into the system. Granting exclusive licences, so that there could be only one approved provider of financial news, for example, was another alternative. A monopoly on certain types of information may have convinced providers to invest in content development, but could leave the Post Office facing criticism over its selections. A more free-market approach, allowing freedom to a range of information providers, had the risk of leading to poor-quality content that would tarnish the prestige of the service. However, it would be far easier to administrate and keep Post Office management out of messy debates over what was on the system. 'The thought that the minister would ring up and say, "the news report was outrageously biased in favour of X, Y or Z," they just didn't want to cope with that,' suggests Alex Reid. The common carrier approach, where the Post Office was responsible for transporting the message but not concerned with its content, was in line with existing postal and telephone services. For an information system of potentially unlimited size there were philosophical arguments in favour of an open market too. 'Because there was no natural limit to the number of pages of information that could appear on Prestel, it was philosophically right to let everybody have a go. It seemed to me this was quintessentially an open medium,' explains Reid.

Prestel's content would come from a range of media companies and other organisations, but content providers and the television manufacturers would need reassurance that Prestel was going to be enough of a big thing to justify the investment. 'In order to get the participation of the media industry and the television-set makers to incorporate the kit into the backs of their sets… we needed to do the thing in a bold way,' explains Alex Reid. 'It was decided that we would actually roll straight out to essentially national coverage or into the major cities.' Rather than the gradual development of the Internet from an academic system as various people found new uses for it, Prestel was planned to have a critical mass of content from the start and roll out to the public.

   Launching Prestel on a large scale was an ambitious scheme, particularly for an organisation well known for its bureaucratic ways. At the time it could take months to get the Post Office to install a new telephone line, and there were strict regulations on the sorts of devices that were allowed to be connected to the telephone network. Rather than lose time going through the normal channels, a specialist unit was set up under Alex Reid in 1977, with the backing of Post Office Telecommunications managing director Peter Benton, to bring the system to fruition. Thereafter progress was rapid. In early 1978 the decision was taken to launch a public Prestel service. By summer a test service was functioning, in spite of difficulties with the databank computers and with manufacturers struggling to produce enough working Prestel televisions. In 1979, Prestel was being rolled out to the public, with no less than 100,000 pages of information on all manner of subjects.* In just a few years, the Post Office built an electronic information network of unprecedented scope and scale.

Going online

Using Prestel originally required a special Prestel television with a built-in modem connected to a telephone line. Viewers pressed the Prestel button on the television keypad to dial into the service, and from the welcome screen tapped in a page number to go directly to the information provider they wanted: 221 would go to British Rail, 2020 to electronics newspaper *Viewtel 202*, 92 to their Prestel bill. A moment later a page of information would appear, mostly coloured text with a few pictures made up of blocks. The system could also be navigated through a hierarchical series of menus where users would eventually find what they were looking for in one of the listed categories. 'There was no search facility at all. We didn't have the technology to offer a sort of Google-type search. It was a completely hierarchical menu,' explains Alex Reid. Unlike the

---

*Technically speaking, Prestel's 'pages' were referred to as 'frames' at the time.

paid-for search rankings and sophisticated algorithms used by search engines to tailor search results, the Post Office naturally did its best to remain impartial. 'We wanted to keep a completely neutral role', recalls Reid. 'There was no editorial judgement or recommendation.'

The information on the system was wide ranging, including news, business information, sports, film reviews, quizzes, gardening advice and recipes. There were also pages from major retailers, such as WH Smith, Currys and Comet, banks and building societies, travel companies, and organisations as diverse as the RAC and the charity Save the Children. The Ministry of Agriculture, Fisheries and Foods even started using the service to provide up-to-date information to farmers. Previously, if you wanted the news you waited for a radio or television bulletin or bought a newspaper. With Prestel a range of providers was there at the click of a few buttons. Today, with Prestel's central computers long shut down and nothing left but screen shots, videos and paper documents, it is hard to appreciate the enormity of the system or how revolutionary it was at the time. 'I would have these high-powered captains of industry around and I'd say, "Here's a television set," ' remembers Alex Reid, who found himself demonstrating the system to a succession of high-profile figures. ' "We can access 100,000 pages of information that's being constantly updated and supplied by information providers, so if we wanted to know what the weather is in Madrid, I click here and up would come the weather in Madrid." Now, today, people would yawn. Then, these people would be astonished; their jaws would drop.'

The television commercials used to publicise Prestel invoke something of the science fiction nature of the system at the time. They began with a sinister note playing as an animated finger on a display screen beckoned over. Seconds later followed messages explaining the system, punctuated by rapid montages of Prestel pages set to Strauss's *Blue Danube*, the music used to open that most famous of mad-computer films, *2001: A Space Odyssey*. It was a striking display of the overwhelming range of information on offer. *Tomorrow's World*, the BBC's television showcase of new technology, featured Prestel in 1979. According to *Tomorrow's World*, Prestel would a affect the daily lives of everybody, and would be particularly useful if the fuel and job shortages of the 1970s developed into a crisis that confined people to their homes. When the system was launched most commentators presented it as a world leader, a breakthrough in technology with great potential for the future. However, within a surprisingly short time the Post Office's vision of electronic information for the home was in trouble.

The armchair grocer

The Post Office predicted that by the end of 1980 Prestel would have a few tens of thousands of users, with optimistic estimates suggesting as many as a million users after five years. This was not unreasonable given that it already ran most of the nation's telephones. However, uptake of the service was painfully slow. By the end of 1980 there were just 6,000 users. Contrary to the original aim of creating a domestic system, the major users turned out to be businesses. The travel industry was an enthusiastic user of Prestel, and terminals became common in travel agents; indeed, viewdata technology was still in use in this sector in the twenty-first century. A few companies and other organisations, such as British Rail, also used the technology for developing internal information systems. More widely, for a corporate world becoming ever more interested in up-to-the-minute share prices, there was a wealth of financial news and stock market information available. By late 1982 the number of subscribers had increased to about 18,000, all but 2,500 of them businesses.[1]

Home users were the original target, but proved to be the market hardest for Prestel to crack. Much of the problem related to cost. The cheapest Prestel television set available when the service launched was a £650 black and white model, at a time when a normal colour portable television could be bought for around £170, but there were few alternatives. Home computers were too rare to be seriously considered as a way for the general public to access Prestel when the service launched. The introduction of adaptors to fit to existing television sets was hindered by the lengthy approval process before new devices were allowed on the telephone network, and by television companies' opposition to cheaper alternatives. Nevertheless, by 1981 Prestel adaptors were starting to appear, notably the Tantel adaptor manufactured by Tangerine, better known for its role in creating the later Oric-1 home computer.

'Modems were very difficult. Also, you were dealing with the public sector, Post Office Telephones, and there were very strict regulations about wiring anything up to the telephone system,' recalls Tangerine's Paul Johnson. The £170 Tantel adaptor was a neat console containing a modem and a keypad, which plugged into a phone line and television, and almost failed the stringent approval process due to lack of an isolator to protect it from high voltage from the television. 'I said "That wasn't in the spec." He said, "It is now… you'll have to reapply,"' remembers Johnson, who bet a disbelieving Post Office Telephones engineer that he could do the modifications in a week. 'So we turned it round in a week and we got approval,' chuckles Johnson. Thanks to devices like the Tantel, the expense of owning Prestel equipment dropped, but the ongoing running costs were still considerable.

Prestel's subscription charge was £5 a quarter for a home or £15 for a business in 1982. Free to access in the evenings and part of the weekend, there was a 5 pence a minute charge for connecting to the system during the day. Premium content and closed user groups attracted extra fees, with the price noted in the corner of the screen and added straight to Prestel bills. In this respect Prestel was notably in advance of the World Wide Web, providing a straightforward way for information providers to generate revenue long before paywalls or advertising revenue. Given the hefty costs of being a main information provider on the system, £5,500 a year for the basic package, charging by the page did at least provide an incentive for providers. Main information providers could also generate income by renting out pages to smaller sub-providers. Nevertheless, it was a premium service that was most attractive to larger or more forward-thinking organisations.

In 1981, British Telecom (BT), including Prestel, was split off from the Post Office as the telecoms market was liberalised. BT took pains to increase Prestel's appeal to new users by encouraging new interactive services with various partners. 1982 and 1983 saw a renewed effort to widen the uptake of the system with the launch of a range of innovative services, including education, banking and shopping. Among these was Homelink, Britain's first home online banking service, run by the Nottingham Building Society and the Bank of Scotland. Homelink was a premium service, with pricing structures oriented towards attracting wealthier customers, but its uptake was always going to be limited at a time when many people did not have bank accounts. Basic by later standards, it still provided many of the services that are familiar today, such as paying regular credit card and utility bills, and juggling money between accounts. Other banks were slow to follow the example, yet for the Bank of Scotland it was a useful way of reaching customers in England.

Online shopping and ticket booking were much more widely experimented with. In Gateshead, pensioners were offered the chance to order their Tesco shopping using Prestel terminals accessed in local libraries. Catalogue shopping came to Prestel through services like Littlewoods' Shop TV, launched in 1985. One of the biggest experiments in providing two-way services to the public was Club 403, a Prestel service launched in 1982 in the West Midlands with a flat £4 monthly fee and a free terminal to entice users to join. Uptake was slow, as the stores tasked with selling the system did not understand it well enough to perform a convincing sales job. The solution was technological Tupperware-style parties, where free membership was offered to people willing to invite their neighbours over to show them how Club 403 worked.[2]

Club 403 stands as a remarkable demonstration of what Prestel was capable of. Among the most prominent services was the Armchair Grocer, which allowed people to buy their weekly food shop through Prestel, albeit with the aid of a printed catalogue to make a shopping list. They simply keyed in the numbers of the shopping, and a little while later a Club 403 van trundled round from the Carrefour supermarket near Sutton Coldfield with a delivery. A range of other shops and businesses provided services through Club 403, including a master butcher and a Beer at Home service. People could also book seats for shows at local theatres and football matches, gamble, book hotels and access the other Prestel services.

To judge from impressed users quoted in the press, the new interactive services, which touted the convenience of avoiding queues and having to go out in the rain, should have been a hit. In fact, they suffered from the same low uptake problem as Prestel as a whole. Club 403 managed to attract just 1,000 users by late 1984. In spite of hopes that it would expand after the end of the subsidised trial period, by 1987 most of the shopping services had been withdrawn. In the latter half of the 1980s the media moved from marvelling at the novelty and convenience of armchair shopping to discussing why it had not taken off. Other interactive services would be launched through Prestel to mixed success during the 1980s, but outside businessmen and the travel industry the biggest new market for Prestel turned out to be the burgeoning new market of home computer users.

Micronet 800

The idea of using a television as a Prestel terminal was conceived at a time when very few homes had computers. However, family televisions were already a contested space. 'In a sense it was a flawed idea in that the television was already family entertainment territory and it was difficult to capture that for solitary information retrieval,' notes Alex Reid. As many people bought computers and portable televisions to go with them, the possibility opened up of connecting a modem to a home computer and using it as a Prestel terminal. However, the Post Office was protective over what was allowed to be connected to its network. Telephones were normally rented from the Post Office and hardwired onto the network by its engineers. Before market liberalisation and the introduction of the modern telephone socket in 1981, it was unfeasible for people to simply plug a modem into a phone socket. In the meantime, people wanting to go online generally had to resort to the acoustic coupler, a modem fitted with a pair of rubber cups that fitted to a normal telephone handset. A few people were already buying couplers to experiment with connecting their micros to other computers, but outside Prestel, electronic communications was the domain of the enthusiast and on a fairly small scale. The most common systems were bulletin board systems (BBS) for users to connect and leave messages for each other and swap files. Sometimes managed by a computer club, sometimes just a computer run by a hobbyist and online only part of the day, BBSs were a semi-underground world of enthusiasts and people in the know.

Prestel already carried content from computer user groups, but in 1983 East Midland Allied Press (EMAP) began offering a more comprehensive service to computer enthusiasts on Prestel, named Micronet 800. The original idea was 'a computer magazine which came down the phone line, because every ink-on-paper magazine was completely out of date by the time you bought it,' recalls Micronet's founding editor David Babsky. EMAP already owned the Prestel information provider TELEMAP, and had just bought a stable of computer magazines from publisher Richard Hease, and electronic-goods comparison site *Electronic Insight* from its founder Bob Denton. The idea for Micronet built on this, but was more ambitious. 'If we sold programs and provided everyone with an email address and if we gave them news stories, surely this would be a winner,' explains Babsky, who also helped to brand the new service. 'We decided never ever to mention Prestel because Prestel was thought of as a failure. We'd only mention Micronet 800.'

Unlike paper computer magazines, setting up Micronet was not just a matter of recruiting an editorial team and finding some content, but of overcoming some of the technical and financial barriers that had so far held back Prestel. With so many different types of computer on the market, few of which had a screen mode compatible with Prestel, each machine required specially written software to display Prestel pages. Efforts had to be made to keep the price down too. David Babsky sourced a cheap modem. 'If I'd just paid £400 for a BBC Micro,' explains Babsky, 'the most I'd be prepared to pay would be £49 for a modem to give me access to downloadable programs, so we fixed the price at £49 and Richard Hease put together these various subsidies.' With the liberalisation of the telecoms network, Hease negotiated a subsidy from the Department of Trade and Industry to provide Micronet users with a free telephone socket to allow them to directly plug in a modem. Micronet cost £16.50 a quarter for subscribers, with free off-peak calls to access the service. At £52 a year it compared quite favourably with buying a paper computer magazine once a week.

Key to Micronet's offerings was a mix of free and paid for 'telesoftware' downloadable for different microcomputers, a convenient service at a time of lengthy magazine type-in programs. 'It seemed blindingly obvious that there was a market for selling computer programs down the phone lines instead of people sitting at home mistyping,' recalls Babsky. 'When we first launched it we went to [an exhibition at] the NEC in Birmingham and asked people what do you want?' The service offered a mix of games, and business and education software, for several of the most popular machines. Yet just as in microcomputing more widely, one use came to dominate: 'They said education, of course. But no one ever wanted the education programs or business programs; they just wanted entertainment.'

Prestel did not initially offer electronic mail. In part, this was allegedly because the Post Office feared that it would damage its core business of delivering letters, however, such services did not quite fit the original conception of the system as a databank. By the time Prestel's Mailbox feature for sending short messages was widely available, it already faced more sophisticated rivals, such as BT's own Telecom Gold. All the same, it gave another way of interacting and mail was one of the most popular services. Indeed, Micronetters sent twice as many electronic mails as other Prestel users.

Micronet also had games that users could play against each other. These included *StarNet,* a one-turn-a-day space strategy game, and the real-time game *Shades.* This was a multi-user dungeon (MUD), a multiplayer text adventure game with hundreds of rooms to explore. Players could put aside their everyday lives, adopt fantasy identities of knights or wizards, and go adventuring together or fight each other to the death with frantically typed commands. Costing nearly a pound an hour to play was no barrier to *Shades'* popularity and the highly addictive game built up a cult following of people willing to run up large phone bills.[3]

Unlike the static offerings that filled much of the rest of Prestel, Micronet built a community through involving its users in interactive activities. Another popular service was Chatline, online chat rooms where users could discuss anything they liked, subject to moderation. 'Chatline had specific individual chat rooms where you could talk about the price of a bottle of milk or Clive Sinclair, as long as you were careful not to libel him,' recalls David Babsky. Celebrity Chatline brought in well-known figures of the day to answer Micronetters' questions, such as athlete Fatima Whitbread and punk rocker Feargal Sharkey. In another forward-looking move there was a gay Chatline. Individuals in the community who stood out in some way or another might also be offered some pages of their own to fill. 'I spotted people and thought they could do it – they're interesting, so let's give them a page,' explains Babsky.

Micronet gave its users an online space like no other offered to the public before: not just a range of information and software, but a place for all sorts of different people from all over the country to interact as a sort of virtual community. 'There seemed to be no clear demarcation of who they were,' recalls Babsky. 'People doing all sorts of things. The only general coherence that held them all together was that they were all interested to some extent in new technology.' Through

Chatline, Mailbox and games, Micronetters had a space to discuss, argue, explore and maybe even find love through the lonely hearts section. And yet despite all that was on offer, even Micronet never quite matched its original hopes. 'What we found was that there was a high churn rate,' explains David Babsky. 'So we kept getting lots of new people, but at the same time about a third of the people we had disappeared.'

Although it would last until 1991, when BT pulled the plug on its 12,000 users, Micronet never quite managed to attract a sufficiently high number of users. Yet to those who were part of Micronet, it was an exciting place to go when there was nothing else like it. 'The people who used it loved it,' recalls journalist Robert Schifreen, a Micronetter and occasional contributor to the service. 'It was the communication side of things. It was the social side of things because you did chat and email. It was the novelty of being able to log on.' In a sense Micronetters were akin to the computer hobbyists of the 1970s, a gathering of enthusiastic early adopters who cottoned on to what the future might be before everyone else had. 'It was a sense of people don't want to do this stuff in enough numbers to make it pay. But I don't recall anyone saying we really need to go to sleep and come back in 10 years,' recalls Schifreen. 'Because you don't know what's going to happen.'

Good morning Prince Philip
Much like hobbyist computing, Micronet and Prestel fostered a cadre of curious people who were more interested than most in exploring what the technology could do. The meaning of the term computer hacker has shifted over the years. Originally hacker meant someone with a fascination in mastering, modifying, exploring and pushing a technology to do something interesting, without the breaking-and-entering connotations the term later acquired. As one might expect, Prestel and Micronet quickly spawned a community of such enthusiasts fascinated by seeing what they could access on the network. Among them were Micronet contributors Steve Gold and Robert Schifreen. 'It was very much a social thing. We'd get

together and share exploits, and talk about stuff and share passwords,' recalls Schifreen of the sociable group of Micronet hackers. 'We'd generally meet up in a Chinese restaurant in Soho and get through huge amounts of lemon chicken.'

The early 1980s were the formative years of hacking in popular culture. In 1983, *Making the Most of the Micro – Live*, a live television follow-up to *The Computer Programme*, was disrupted when hackers broke into the electronic mail system being demonstrated. The same year, an American teenager almost triggered a pre-emptive nuclear strike on the Soviet Union after hacking into a military computer, in the science fiction film *War Games*. Around the same time, the FBI swooped in on a group of real-life American teenagers charged with breaking into a series of computer systems, including Los Alamos National Laboratory, a major nuclear research centre. The following year, news broke of a quintessentially British equivalent: the hacking of the Duke of Edinburgh's Prestel Mailbox.

It was all rather embarrassing for BT, who declared hackers the electronic equivalent of shoplifters rather than harmless computer buffs. Seemingly to rub it in, the hackers sent a message to Prestel's administrators from the account, expressing their love of solving puzzles and signed 'ta ta! pip pip! HR Hacker'.[4] The incident inspired a spate of hacking stories in the media: hacks carried out on television for journalists, suspicions of electronic spies, rumours of moles in Prestel, concerns over online banking systems, claims that computers at the Atomic Energy Research Establishment at Harwell had been infiltrated and gossip that Prestel had a sinister military dual use that was now compromised. To a general public that was still only learning about computing, hackers were presented as having almost magical powers to manipulate information and get at secrets. Newspapers called those involved 'codebusters' or 'computer snoopers' more than 'hackers' at first, a fumbling for terminology that suggests the novelty of the idea. Behind the moral panic was a story of curiosity overcoming some naive security measures, and a society and its legal system waking up to the new concept of computer crime.

'It was purely by accident. Purely a bit of fun. Just a bit of an obsessive playing about really,' recalls Schifreen, who, with Steve Gold, was responsible for the breach. 'Tapped some random keys, stumbled across some passwords which led me to a closed area that had the telephone numbers of the test mainframes.' The staff member's account number was 2222222222 and their password was set to 1234. Unforgivably lax today, but in 1984 computer security was a rather new concept that perhaps was not taken as seriously as it would be later, and BT was much criticised over its handling of security in the wake of the incident.

With the list of test mainframe telephone numbers from the closed group, the hackers could dial in and connect to the machines used by BT for system development, but not normally accessible to the general public. They got no further than the login pages of the test computers at first, but curiosity kept taking them back, until another security lapse opened a door. 'Eventually I found that someone had left, on the login screen of one of the test mainframes, the system manager's ID and password,' recalled Schifreen. 'Turned out the data on the test computer had been published on the live system, so I now had all the user files and everyone's user name and password.' With a bit of curiosity and some security lapses from BT, the hackers had the keys to the entire network. They could access any Prestel computer and login as anyone: as a top-level system administrator, a member of a paid closed user group or even the Duke of Edinburgh.

'When you got to the little personalised screen you got "Good Morning HRH The Duke of Edinburgh, Welcome to Prestel,"' recalls Schifreen. Apart from birthday messages to Princess Diana, another service recently offered by Micronet, there was, according to Schifreen, 'nothing terribly exciting. Nothing of security value. But it was interesting to say that I've logged into Prestel as Prince Philip.' Through Micronet, Schifreen and Gold informed a disbelieving Prestel of the hole in its system. 'Prestel said there was no way someone could be system manager of Prestel,' recalls Schifreen. To prove their point, the hackers changed Prestel's top-level page 1 to read IDNEX instead of INDEX. 'I was expecting them to say, "Come and tell us how you did it, because this is important,"' recalls Schifreen. 'Rather than that, they phoned Scotland Yard and got the computer crime unit involved.'

But what to charge them with? There was no such crime as computer hacking in 1984. The Metropolitan Police Computer Crime Unit was not set up until 1982. Most of its early trade was in fraud among bank clerks and computer operators, and there were no laws relating specifically to computer crime at the time. Real-world hacking was a novel concept, and Schifreen and Gold's activities were in a legal grey area. Probably the closest thing to the specifics of the case was 'phreaking'. From the late 1960s, telephone networks had been infiltrated by enthusiasts using electronic 'blue boxes' and 'bleepers' to control automatic switching systems to get free calls and access to exotic locations. In one case from 1971, a London student made a free phone call to a Bethlehem hospital on Christmas Day to give his best wishes to the babies born that day. For the phreaks it was less for the free calls and more for the intellectual challenge, but if caught they could still be prosecuted for abstracting the electricity used to make the calls. 'They could have done that with me and Steve,' explains Schifreen, 'but they decided not to because they wanted a precedent for a better piece of legislation that they could use against computer crime in the future.'

Instead of abstracting electricity, Schifreen and Gold were prosecuted for forgery. The case of Bug Hunter and Squeaky Mouse, the 'code names' of the two according to the press that seemed to find something sinister in people having online identities, came to trial in 1985. The prosecution hinged on the idea that entering login details that were not theirs amounted to forging the contents of the Prestel computer's memory, akin to using a fake identity card. The defence made much of how Prestel's security was ridden with holes, and how the hackers' activities had done a public service by bringing the deficiencies to light. It was a bit of a legal stretch, but the pair was found guilty of forgery and each was fined several hundred pounds.

The convictions were overturned on appeal in 1988. Concluded by the failure of BT's subsequent appeal against the verdict, the case revealed the limits of the law as it stood to address hacking. The hackers had not benefited financially, save for avoiding some trifling access charges. 'What I actually cost paying customers of Prestel was about £11,' recalls Schifreen. The episode was just a bit of fun that occurred in uncharted legal waters. 'I never set out to cause any damage or do anything malicious. I didn't steal any data or anything like that. I was doing it out of fun and to show how insecure this was,' explains Schifreen. 'Nobody ever tried to give the impression that what we'd done was serious. But it was potentially important for the future, a test case to be sorted out one way or the other.' The case was foundational in the formulation of *The Computer Misuse Act 1990*, which explicitly made it illegal to gain unauthorised access to computers. With a few amendments, *The Computer Misuse Act* is still with us today, an underlying piece of British computer law that has far outlived both Micronet and Prestel.

A failed technology?

At its peak, Prestel attracted about 90,000 users, but it was widely considered something of an expensive failure.[5] The network limped on into the 1990s, increasingly targeted at businesses rather than the general public, only to be run down by BT, who eventually sold its remains in 1994, by which time the Internet was rapidly expanding. Despite its demise, we cannot simply write off Prestel as a failure, nor should we casually dismiss it with the cliché of being ahead of its time. The technology worked satisfactorily enough for tens of thousands of people to make use of it; indeed, Prestel was adopted, with mixed success, in several other countries, and the massive success of the World Wide Web proves that the basic concept was sound. 'In many ways Prestel was a sort of precursor, a prototype,' suggests Alex Reid. 'The idea that the public could at the touch of a button get access to hundreds of thousands of pages of information over the telephone network.' From the connected world of the twenty-first century it is hard to see why people would not want online access to something like Prestel. So why did Prestel not take off?

The basic nature of the information Prestel could display was a limitation on its uptake. Each frame could only display a few hundred characters of text and some blocky low-resolution pictures. It offered no sound, no photographs and no video. In this respect, Prestel suffered from being a pioneer. As more advanced viewdata systems with better graphics were launched in other countries, such as the Canadian Telidon system, unfavourable comparisons began to be drawn. Placed alongside the more dynamic entertainment capabilities of home computers, Prestel's static pages also looked staid. Even in the early 1980s, journalists complained that they lacked excitement and emotion. A high-resolution 'Picture Prestel' capable of displaying more realistic images was developed, but not rolled out to the public due to the limited uptake of the original.

Almost any contemporary press article about Prestel gives the impression that it was a costly service, and the expense involved in using the system was undoubtedly a major factor in limiting its uptake. The 5 pence a minute daytime connection charge meant it was all too easy to rack up large phone bills, even without adding the costs of any paid for frames. As a system intended to challenge traditional media it seemed expensive in a period of recession, when a daily newspaper cost about 15 pence. At a time before multiple contracts for broadband, mobile phones and satellite television packages, the very idea of paying for extra services was fairly novel too. Despite BT's best efforts, the pricing and business model was not quite right for the time.

Prestel did not have to be a failure, as the experience of Minitel, its French equivalent, demonstrated abundantly.

Launched across France in 1982, Minitel was of a similar level of technology to Prestel, but was massively supported by the French state. Free terminals were handed out to businesses to automate communications with the government, and to home users to replace telephone directories, at the rate of 10,000 a week by 1984. At its high point in the late 1990s, there were nine million Minitel terminals installed across France. Giving away free Prestel terminals was discussed several times in the 1980s, but never came to anything. The British telecoms industry was going through a profound change with liberalisation and privatisation, but old reservations about a public utility indulging in commercial activities probably played a part in limiting the options. 'We said to BT, instead of spending £6 million on an advertising campaign, why don't you spend £3 million on an advertising campaign and buy £3-million worth of Tantel adaptors and give them away?' recalls Paul Johnson of one attempt to convince BT to offer free Prestel adaptors. 'Oh, they couldn't do that because "it's commercial".'

Alongside French government support, at least part of Minitel's success is often attributed to its highly popular sex chat lines, or 'Minitel Rose'. In 1980, not long after Prestel was launched, there was a minor tabloid scandal over it carrying a service called 'A Buyers' Guide to Dirty Books', authored by the implausibly named Rupert Street-Walker. A Conservative MP went so far as to demand a government inquiry, but the allegations generated a robust response from Prestel's managers that it was not their role to act as a censor and the service was a parody anyway. Aside from the illicit activities of individual users messaging each other, sex was never a major feature of what Prestel had to offer. Minitel may have benefited from a bit of titillation, but it probably did not fit the Post Office and BT's vision for their prestige system, not to mention the legal issues involved in a less liberal-minded time.

Prestel was not the only online service available to home computer users in 1980s Britain, but it was the most extensive, the highest profile and the most ambitious.* The failure of this flagship project says much about how communications was only a minority interest among home computer users. In the short-term communications would have little influence in shaping the development of home computing in Britain. The technology, infrastructure and services were there for it to have grown into a major application of home computers in the 1980s, but compared to the giants of educational computing and gaming it never hit the mainstream. For a few years, computer magazines often carried a few pages of news on 'comms' to cater to the enthusiast community that was interested. However, for most people there would be no going online until the Internet explosion of the 1990s, when the network was opened up to commercial interests rather than just academics.

'Vision of the future' is a term thrown around far too easily and thoughtlessly, but it genuinely applies to Prestel. For a few years it gave a few tens of thousands of people a glimpse of the sort of online world that would become common in the twenty-first century. Then it was gone, only to reappear over the subsequent years in a much slicker form in the Web browsers of many hundreds of millions of people. 'It's not like some perpetual motion machine that never worked and never would work,' sums up Alex Reid. 'It's more like the Wright brothers' aeroplane. Our one crashed, but air travel later became universal, so I think we were the harbinger of something.'

An electronic *Domesday Book*
The 1980s was a period rich in experiments to find out what computers could do. Prestel was far from the only 'ahead of its

---

*One other online service that deserves a mention is Compunet, or CNet to the several thousand Commodore computer users who enjoyed it. Started in 1984, when it grew out of the earlier PETNET service for teachers, CNet provided chat, gaming, email and other services. It also gave users the space to upload and share programming efforts, and supported a lively community of hobbyist developers before its demise in 1993.

time' application to be developed, or the only system to try to make vast amounts of information available through computers. Among the most ambitious use of computers as a way to provide information was the creation of an up-to-date version of the *Domesday Book*, the great survey of the realm ordered by William the Conqueror after his invasion of England. With the 900th anniversary of the *Domesday Book* approaching, a BBC producer by the name of Peter Armstrong was asked to consider doing a special programme to mark it. 'Thinking about it, I thought, well, that's all very well, we could do a standard documentary, but what about doing it again?' wondered Armstrong. 'Wouldn't, that be more fun to see what King William could have done if he'd had the kind of opportunities we have today?'

Like Prestel, the notion of a high-technology *Domesday Book* touched on one of the fundamental ideas of the information technology revolution; the expectation that computing would make large volumes of information more easily accessible and bring conceptually new ways of interacting with it. By 1984 this was one aspect of the revolution that had not reached the typical microcomputer user to any great extent. Reference works for home computers were little more sophisticated than small databases on various subjects, such as fact files about countries of the world. The common cassette tape was too slow for effective data retrieval, and faster floppy discs were too small for anything ambitiously encyclopedic. Yet on the horizon were new data-storage technologies that offered new opportunities. Among these was the LaserVision disc, a shiny 12-inch predecessor of the compact disc, which was finding favour among film buffs as a premium home video format. 'If we're hooking up a BBC Micro to all kinds of devices, then how about a LaserVision disc?' pondered Peter Armstrong. 'And if we did that what kind of coverage could we get on it about Britain today?'

LaserVision, developed by the electronics company Philips, was one of a number of formats of laser disc to emerge onto the market in the late 1970s as home video players gained in popularity. LaserVision offered superior picture quality compared to the tape-based Betamax and VHS systems, but without the ability to record programmes at home, and only storing about 30 or 60 minutes of video, depending on mode used, on each side of the disc. The ability to quickly jump around the data on the LaserVision disc led to much discussion about interactive books, exhibitions, education systems and catalogues, but few actual substantive uses. A rare exception was *The BBC Videobook of British Garden Birds*. This included video, selectable audio tracks of birdsong or narration by David Attenborough and, in a novel step, teletext pages of information about the birds. 'In order to put the teletext magazine onto the disc master we had to take BBC2 off the air over lunch time, because there were only two teletext inserters in the BBC,' chuckles Andy Finney, then of BBC Video, who developed the idea of adding teletext to the *Videobook* and software to allow it to run on the BBC Micro. 'And then one day a guy knocked on my office door and said he'd heard I was the person who knew about video discs. He'd got this idea for something to celebrate the *Domesday Book* anniversary,' recalls Finney, who explained to Armstrong the severe limitations of the technology for developing an interactive documentary. 'As far as my memory goes, he went away and came back the next day with this idea for doing it all using still frames and maps and photographs and so on,' recalls Finney. 'That was it really. It didn't seem too difficult to get the BBC behind the idea.'

Pulling in expertise from various departments across the BBC, and partnering with Acorn, Philips, software firm Logica, professional geographers, universities and others, the project took shape between 1984 and 1986. The result was a *Domesday Book* for the electronic age. The two discs of the project contained not only statistical data, text and maps, but also photographs and videos startlingly more realistic than the blocky graphics seen on computers of the time. *The National Disc* was a wealth of professionally created content on the economy, culture, society and the environment. It included the 1981 census, newspaper stories, commissioned essays, video clips and a mass of survey data with analysis tools. Complementing this top-down perspective on life in Britain was the grass-roots view offered by *The Community Disc*'s 150,000 pages of text and 20,000 photographs created by ordinary people around the country. It was nothing less than a multimedia encyclopedia of Britain in the 1980s with a scope far beyond anything achieved using computer technology before.

Other than its 900-year-old inspiration, pretty much everything about *Domesday* was novel and pushing the edge of current technology. 'That helped a lot because it meant that all the broadcast engineers at the BBC were fascinated and we got lots of cooperation,' recalls Andy Finney. 'We really could get our teeth into something that hadn't been done before and I think that's what it made it really exciting.' *Domesday* ran on a Philips LaserVision player connected to a specially adapted AIV (Advanced Interactive Video) BBC Master computer, the more powerful successor to the original BBC Micro. 'We were pushing it to its absolute limits,' recalls Peter Armstrong. 'It was only an 8-bit machine. It only had eight colours. So everything was extremely tight.'

Realistic colour photographs and video were technically beyond the capabilities of even the adaptable BBC Master, but they were not actually displayed by the computer as such. In fact they were not digital computer files in the sense understood today. LaserVision discs were originally intended to store analogue video, meaning each photograph stored on *Domesday* was an individual video frame, and each video was a stream of such frames. The *Domesday* software displayed the BBC Master's computer graphics and text over the top of video and photographs generated by the LaserVision player; the slightly jarring contrast between blocky 1980s computer graphics sharing a screen with realistic photographs hints at the mix of technologies brought to work together. To allow the discs to work with digital computer data for other sorts of information, Philips replaced the soundtrack on the LaserVision disc with a data track, creating the LV-ROM disc. At a time when a standard floppy disc was perhaps a few hundred kilobytes, each LV-ROM disc could store 324 megabytes of computer data per side, as well as up to 54,000 video frames, quite sufficient for the task at hand.

The novelty of *Domesday* was not just its sheer amount of data, or the variety of different formats it was in, but how it was accessed. Most computer-user interfaces of the time were text based, relying on typed commands to make things happen. Graphical user interfaces (GUI), based on moving a pointer around a screen of windows, icons and menus, were in their infancy at the time. The $9,995 Apple Lisa, the first commercially available personal computer with a GUI, was only launched in 1983, and the high price limited its impact and influence. The scope and variety of *Domesday*'s content necessitated a fresh approach to the user interface. 'First of all, what was it like to design a multimedia interface? Because that was completely new,' remarks Peter Armstrong.

A good example of the innovation put into the user interface is *The Community Disc*'s use of maps for navigating through the data. 'I started sketching it on pieces of idea and trying to work out if you start with maps and you wanted to zoom down how many levels of maps would you need?' recalls Peter Armstrong. 'I did some calculations and it was clear you could do a very creditable zoom that would end up with a block of 4 kilometres by 3, due to the 4:3 ratio of the screen in those days.' Alongside typed text commands, *Domesday* used a tracker ball to push a pointer around the screen. Starting with a map of the whole country, the pointer could be moved to click on an area and progressively zoomed in, eventually getting to one of 23,000 'D-blocks', where a click would bring up local information.

Today such an approach has become unremarkably everyday, but it was startling novel in 1984. 'No one had had a microcomputer zooming around maps and zooming in. How do you do that? How do you indicate which way you're going? What's the grammar for moving in? For knowing where you are?' asks Peter Armstrong. 'That all had to be invented as we went along.' Another novelty was the 'surrogate walks' on

The National Disc, a series of photographic journeys around different locations such as a farm, a council flat and the Welsh market town of Brecon. To a viewer 30 years later, the similarities with mapping applications or Google *Street View*, not launched until 2007, are striking. Alongside the fancy graphical interfaces, *Domesday* also had a typed keyword search facility. However, in another innovation, *The National Disc* had a virtual reality gallery to wander through and access content by clicking the pictures on the walls.

A time capsule of 1980s Britain

Where King William had used scribes to record the wealth of his realm, the BBC followed with 15,500 schools and community groups, each assigned one or more D-blocks to cover. Schools were a vitally important part of the project. Not only were they spread across the country, but thanks to the government's efforts to fund school computers, they were already huge users of the BBC Micro. 'For schools it was a really good project,' recalls Peter Armstrong. 'They often said, well, we know our local area around our school better, and we've discovered things we never knew were there.' With BBC-issued guidelines, schools and groups compiled information, recording what was in their local communities and what it was like living in them. There were surveys of how much television people watched, what they ate, memoirs of daily life and much more besides. Finally, the floppy discs of data and three slides of the local area were posted off to the BBC to be checked and added to the project. 'That was the main work,' remarks Armstrong, 'it was a team of 25–30 people over two years and it was an absolutely huge amount of work.'

Because of the way it was created, *Domesday's Community Disc* often had the flavour of a school project, albeit on an enormous scale. Told largely from the point of view of children writing about their lives, *Domesday* often showed the 1980s through naive yet revealing minor details. The bitter 1984–85 miners' strike, for example, is recalled as a time of family arguments about money by the child of a mine worker. In 'Life in Brixton' a child on an inner-city estate, site of riots in 1981 and 1985, complained that because of the robbers and kidnappers in their block of meant they could not go out to play alone. Meanwhile in Ludlow, a class of nine-year-olds hoped that computers would not take over the world in the future, and that there would be jobs when they finished school.

Through countless little observations like these, *Domesday* hinted at the hopes and fears of 1980s Britain, be they socio-economic decline, technological change or even the Cold War. The entry on the Greenham Common cruise-missile base features peace protesters joking about the double meaning of *Domesday*. Other entries say much without saying anything. 'We found that some bits of Britain are not on the map because they're security sites of various kinds, so that was intriguing to find out,' reveals Peter Armstrong. In other cases current affairs influenced the coverage; the entry on Stretford in Greater Manchester is blank but for a note that the teachers were on a work to rule. 'There were some glaring gaps: most of London for a start,' recalls Andy Finney. 'The ILEA (Inner London Education Authority) was probably the only major local authority that used Sinclair Spectrums and it wasn't possible to do the data collection on a Sinclair Spectrum. It wasn't anything we had against Sinclair but just that the machine couldn't do it.'

Domesday succeeded abundantly in creating a time capsule of 1980s Britain, just as its creators hoped. 'It was partly historical, to create a portrait of Britain in the Eighties and lay it down like wine, and think it would get more and more interesting as time went on,' explains Peter Armstrong. Browsing through the *Community Disc* a quarter of a century later, it is impossible not to be struck by the changes in the country since the project. Shipyards, steelworks, mines, factories; *Domesday* recorded the twilight years of Britain's heavy industrial past, scenes soon consigned to history, in part by the changes to the economy that information technology helped to bring about. In contrast to despondent articles by unemployed people and photos of derelict factories, *Domesday* also recorded the green shoots of economic growth: surveys of how many children in school have a computer, descriptions of the new electronic devices in local businesses and ever-present redevelopment schemes.

Although the historical and educational aspects were obviously important, looking at the publicity around the system at the time, it is clear that the BBC had hopes for *Domesday* as an information resource for the present too. Project publicity outlined how it could be useful for local government, businesses, estate agents, journalists and travel agents. *The National Disc* in particular contained a mass of statistical data on everything from drinking habits to household appliances, which was presented as potentially useful in market research or local government. A wealth of multimedia data created by a million people, the equivalent of 300 paper volumes, and accessed through innovative data analysis and navigation tools, *Domesday* was astounding in its scope and potential utility. Yet there was one fatal flaw: the cost. 'We'd been told by Philips that the cost of the video disc player would be a few hundred pounds,' explains Andy Finney. As a piece of computer hardware, the system would also benefit from the government's 50 per cent discount on computer hardware. 'We felt we were realistic in thinking of these things in terms of thousands,' adds Finney.

Just as the project was on the final lap, Philips dropped a bombshell. 'The last three months, that was when we heard the terrible news... "terribly sorry but the promised price can't be met,"' sighs Peter Armstrong. 'And we'd completely relied on that for the whole business model; the projections for the number who would take it and everything.' Rather than a few hundred pounds, the total cost of a *Domesday* system, including the computer, came out at about £5,000, as much as a small car. The situation was made worse by a change in government support to offer schools 50 per cent off software rather than hardware. 'We thought it would be a third of the cost it turned out to be, and that it would have been in all the schools, it would have been in libraries and in all kinds of places, and a few individuals would buy it as an add-on to their BBC Micro,' explains Armstrong.

To those who saw *Domesday* at the time, it was extraordinary. 'They all absolutely loved it. Everyone had the same reaction,' explains Armstrong. 'They'd look up where they were born, a natural reaction in a way, but it seemed absolutely universal.' Ultimately about 1,000 *Domesday* systems were sold, meaning most of those who contributed were sadly unable to see the final result. Although a handful of other BBC LV-ROMs was released, including *Volcanoes*, and a nature reserve simulator called *The Eco Disc*, LV-ROM was soon overtaken by the cheaper CD-ROM technology.* *Domesday* stands as another example of what could be achieved with comparatively simple microcomputers and foreshadowed many future technologies, such as multimedia CD-ROM encyclopedias, map software and virtual reality walk-throughs. 'Many people who later claim to have invented things like online encyclopedias and tried to patent them found they couldn't because the BBC had what's called a prior art. They'd done it first,' explains Peter Armstrong.

Domesday could not simply be copied from its analogue LV-ROMs onto digital CD-ROMs without a great deal of expense and effort. Trapped on its obsolete disc format and with no resources to update it for new technology, *Domesday* achieved another innovation by becoming one of the earliest examples of digital obsolescence. By the early years of the twenty-first century, *Domesday* was only accessible on a dwindling number of original systems, and even the robust BBC Masters was not going to last forever. *Domesday* was regularly cited as a warning of what could happen to all

---

*CD-ROM was considered early in the *Domesday* project, but it was at an early stage of development, and in the absence of compressed image formats at the time, LV-ROM offered far more potential for storing and displaying photographs. Also considered was the experimental Picture Prestel, which was never rolled out to the general public.

electronic data in the future when technology moved on. It was not a problem that could easily have been foreseen in the environment in which it was created. 'Within the broadcast industry in the 1980s, we were used to working with technology that stayed around for decades,' remarks Andy Finney. 'The idea that this technology would disappear within a couple of years didn't even enter our heads.' For a time, it seemed possible that 1986's *Domesday Book* would be inaccessible in decades, while the 1086 original was still readable, albeit only to scholars of Latin, nearly a millennium after it was created.

Lost electronic worlds

Failures can tell us much about the history of technology. In a technical sense Prestel and *Domesday* both worked, and *Domesday*'s historical value will only increase with time. There was nothing wrong with the concepts behind them. Viewed in hindsight, both can be seen as visions of the future; ideas that would become common later, but realised within the technological constraints of the day, and unfortunately at prices that kept them out of the hands of many people. For several years *Domesday* was held up as an example of digital obsolescence. However, in the early twenty-first century a series of efforts was made to rescue the data and make it accessible on modern personal computers, albeit hindered by copyright issues and the idiosyncrasies of the original technology.

Significantly, in 2003 the original *Domesday* masters were backed up on a new, and hopefully more durable, format by the BBC and Public Record Office. In 2011, the BBC celebrated *Domesday*'s twenty-fifth anniversary by launching *Domesday Reloaded*, allowing people to access the *Community Disc* through the Internet.[6] While the *National Disc* and the pioneering environment *Domesday* used to access the data are generally only available on original systems,* much of

---

*An exception to this is the Domesday Touch Table installed at the National Museum of Computing at Bletchley Park in 2011.

Domesday is finally available to the people who contributed to it. In sad contrast, Prestel is a far better example of digital obsolescence. This online world, once inhabited by tens of thousands of people, has completely vanished, save for the memories of those who roamed it and screen shots of Prestel pages. Prestel and *Domesday* show the outer technical limits of comparatively simple microcomputers. There was nothing technical stopping 1980s home micros from becoming information terminals or communication systems, but economics and user preferences dictated otherwise until the 1990s. In the meantime, the major use of home computers would turn out to be games.

CHAPTER SEVEN

The Maturing of the Computer Game

Look through the pages of most national newspapers on 29 March 1983 and somewhere you will find a picture of a smiling, bespectacled teenager sitting next to a computer. His name was Eugene Evans and he was aged 16, from Liverpool and was apparently making a fortune from writing computer games. To the amazement of journalists, Evans seemed well on his way to becoming a millionaire, earning seven times more than his father, and casually discussing taking early retirement; all despite being too young to buy a house, drive a car or have a credit card. From *The Times*' 'Teenager with a Midas Touch' to the *Daily Mail*'s '£35,000 Whiz-kid!' it was no accident that the stories beneath the headlines were all very alike. It was less breaking news than inspired publicity campaign, orchestrated by Evans's employer, a software company named Imagine. 'Because he was so young and in such glamorous and exciting times, we made him one of the centrepieces for our PR campaign,' recalls Bruce Everiss, Imagine's head of marketing. The promotion of the teenage programmer was a shrewd move for the publicity-conscious Imagine, but by the time Eugene Evans was making headlines the home computer games industry was already a few years old.

There was little in the way of a video games industry in Britain when computing first spread to mass audiences. What microcomputer games there were tended to be simple, home-brewed efforts. Within a short few years, a whole new industry emerged and computer games took exciting and sophisticated new forms. As we shall see in this chapter, both the industry and the games it created were marked by the influence of contemporary British society and culture. Home computers opened up games creation to anybody with a computer and a grasp of programming, and there were no barriers to entry to the games market at first. Creating and selling games was relatively simple. 'It wasn't work. If we went to the pub and didn't come out with a game by closing time we'd have failed. Think it up, sketch it up, do the marketing, go down to the office and program it. It didn't take long,' recalls Mel Croucher, who launched one of the very earliest games companies, Automata Software, as an extension of his travel guide publishing business. 'Getting a game out there was simply a matter of getting a game out there. There was no approval process.' Games companies began in all sorts of low-key ways and brought in all sorts of people. Bedroom programmers turned kitchen-table entrepreneurs, creative teenagers launched family businesses with their parents, enterprising friends partnered up to make and sell games, and small businessmen began touting for trade as software publishers. 'I sent off my game to, I think, three different publishers, and got an answer back the next day saying, yes, we want to buy it!' remembers Jon Ritman of his start in the software industry. 'Offered me a ludicrously low amount of money, which I accepted because I had no idea… £150. God knows how much money they made out of it.'

There was a homespun quality to many of the outputs of these early companies; cassettes duplicated using domestic tape recorders at home, tapes shipped in cassette boxes with typed inlays, or in Ziplock plastic bags with photocopied instructions. The steady demand for type-in programs to fill the pages of programming books and magazines offered another way of getting software published, albeit as a paper listing rather than a cassette. For users, typing in a listing was cheap and educational, whereas cassettes were costly but convenient. For programmers the relative benefits of sending a program to a magazine or a software house were rather different. Not least finding a reliable way to get rewarded for the effort, when there were many less than entirely honest operations, as Simon Goodwin found out when he had a program accepted by a software publisher. 'After a while I received no royalties, so I went down and I was told, "Oh, no, nobody's really interested." And I discovered that actually the thing was on sale in the Ziplock bag hanging up in the shop.' Goodwin demanded and got his royalties, but realised that magazine listings offered a less risky income stream. 'I could get £30 a page for writing computer games, and it was possible to write a three-page game – if you had a bit of practice – in a day. And we're talking a student day, so you don't get up terribly early and you're finished by half five to catch the post.'

One of the downsides to a market with no barriers to entry was the lack of quality control. When anybody could write and sell a game, anybody did. Quality varied enormously and there was little guidance available as to what was worth buying before the magazines began reviewing software. The industry relied on mail-order sales at first, and there were few details in the small magazine adverts beyond vague descriptions along the lines of 'exciting space arcade game'. 'You wouldn't have a clue what you were buying by mail order,' recalls Simon Goodwin. 'There wasn't any way of explaining what it was. You'd get a name, a price and a platform. And after that you'd take a punt.' And were the games any good? 'They usually weren't. Occasionally they were. You'd go back to publishers you'd bought a good one from before.'

Manic Merseyside minors
There was a certain crudity to many early games – simple graphics, basic gameplay, badly laid out controls and the occasional game-crashing killer bug. Home computers were a new creative and technical medium. It took time for programmers to discover how to get the best from their hardware and to start experimenting with new game ideas. One of the earliest to get the killer combination of creative and technical brilliance just right *Manic Miner*, developed in 1983 by a Merseyside teenager named Matthew Smith. From the shrill rendition of *Blue Danube* on the title screen, through colourful screens of killer toilets and mutant telephones, to a Pythonesque game-over sequence featuring a

giant boot, *Manic Miner* was an acid trip of an action game. Like so many games of the time, it trod a fine line between fun and frustratingly difficult. Guiding miner Willy through the mine required almost pixel-perfect precision to avoid death from all manner of surreal hazards. Just how many people completed *Manic Miner* without resorting to cheating is highly debatable, but POKE-ing around inside a game to give an advantage was an accepted part of gaming. At a time when flickering graphics and awkward gameplay were not uncommon, it was notably smooth to play. That Smith managed to fit 20 unique screens of action into the Spectrum's 48k memory was thought quite an achievement. It also had the novelty of in-game music. The repetitive *In the Hall of the Mountain King* soundtrack beeping out through the Spectrum's tiny speaker was one of the first game tunes to imprint itself on the memories of a generation.

Manic Miner exemplifies two features common to 1980s video games. Firstly, it was a platform game, a two-dimensional, sideways-on world, where players could move left and right, and up and down between platforms, as they collected things and dealt with enemies. Platform games were relatively simple to program, and were one of the most common types of game of the day. Among the more prominent examples, both from 1983, were *Chuckie Egg*, a game of running up and down ladders collecting eggs and jumping over chickens; and the fast-paced *Jetpac*, a game of guiding a jet pack-equipped spaceman to assemble the parts of his rocket ship while zapping aliens. The same basic formulas of moving, jumping, platforms, enemies and collecting would feature in dozens of other variations over the 1980s. Secondly, *Manic Miner* exhibited the surreal streak that was a feature of many early British video games, an anarchic, weird and sometimes childish humour. As well as *Manic Miner*, the trend was pronounced in the creations of teenage programmer Jeff Minter, such as *Attack of the Mutant Camels*, a 1983 side-scrolling shoot-em-up that pitted the player's spaceship against giant camels; and in the wacky creations of Mel Croucher at Automata, of which more will be said later.

While it may have become archetypal, at the time *Manic Miner* stood out as a hit in a way few other titles had before. 'Instant winner', was the verdict of *Sinclair User*, which praised the sound and graphics, and the 'depth of concept'.[1] *Manic Miner*'s success created two of home computer gaming's earliest icons. The first was Willy the miner, who went on to star in the sequel, *Jet Set Willy*, the following year. Another surreal adventure, in which Willy had to tidy the mansion bought with his new-found mining wealth, *Jet Set Willy* was another hit despite originally containing a crippling bug that made it almost impossible to complete. The second icon was its creator, Matthew Smith. The zany, long-haired teenager became the archetypal star programmer who had made it big from writing games, with the rock-star lifestyle to match – or as he put it in an interview to *Sinclair User* 'partying, getting drunk and falling over a lot'.[2] Smith gained further fame by mysteriously dropping out of the industry and disappearing from public view, living for a time on a Dutch commune. He become a cult figure during his absence, even inspiring a website in the 1990s, devoted to pondering his whereabouts.

Inspired by an earlier game named *Miner 2049'er*, Matthew Smith originally cooked up *Manic Miner* working at home on his TRS-80. As he later told reporters, the computer had a habit of crashing whenever the kettle was switched on, leading him to generally work at night. However much it represented a new high in what bedroom programming could accomplish, at least part of *Manic Miner*'s success was down to its publication by Bug-Byte. Established in Liverpool in 1980 by Oxford graduates Tony Baden and Tony Milner, Bug-Byte was one of the earliest games companies to take on a more professional air. 'They actually had offices; it wasn't being operated from somebody's kitchen,' explains Bruce Everiss, who enhanced the fledgling company's marketing approach. Everiss replaced crude photocopied packaging and small ads with colour inlay cards and bold full-page colour adverts in magazines: 'We did proper advertising, using an advertising agency that would do properly designed adverts and proper campaigns, and we did lots of things in a professional manner that hadn't been done in a professional manner at all in the computer games industry before.'

Bug-Byte was the first of a cluster of games companies to emerge around Liverpool in the early 1980s, as the area turned into one of the centres of the nascent games industry. Like most high-tech clusters it was a rather incestuous milieu, built on personal connections that sucked in a variety of characters in informal ways. Teenagers hanging around the Tandy shop playing with computers, businessmen sensing new opportunities, and Saturday boys and salesmen from Microdigital. 'A lot of our staff and a lot of our customers still are in the industry in one way or another,' reflects Bruce Everiss. 'I think it's the thing that led, really, to so many computer games companies setting up in Liverpool, because there was the expertise, the enthusiasm and the knowledge.' In Bug-Byte's wake followed Software Projects, Psygnosis, Denton Designs, Imagine and others. The computer press of the time records a lively scene of people falling out with each other over creative differences or money, and joining competitors or taking their ideas to start new firms. Tales abounded of secret game projects, executives finding their telephones bugged, and programmers insulting rivals, when they were not driving around in their expensive sports cars. It was a brash and profitable new industry finding its feet, and at the centre of most of the hype was the enfant terrible of 1980s games companies, Imagine Software.

Programmers in Porsches

Founded in 1982 by former Bug-Byters David Lawson and Mark Butler, Imagine became one of the biggest gaming brands of the day. With a few exceptions, such as the bug-ridden but rather innovative war game *Stonkers*, much of their output was of middling quality. Typical of this were the distinctly average arcade games *Arcadia* and *Ah Diddums*, in which the player had to help a badly animated teddy bear escape its toy box. Both games were plagued by flickering graphics, irritating sound and poor playability, yet this did little to limit their commercial fortunes. Imagine prospered during 1982 and 1983, its titles regularly placed in the top-ten selling games charts. The (not very secret) secret to its success was a marketing effort that went beyond anything seen previously, even in Bug-Byte. 'Although the product was of an adequate and merchantable quality, I don't think that we ever produced anything that was massively groundbreaking,' reflects Bruce Everiss, who left Bug-Byte to join Imagine as operations director, with responsibility for sales and marketing. 'I think a lot of it was the impetus from the brand, the general image of Imagine, that people went and bought their games.'

Marketing was central to Imagine's success. Indeed, it was among the very first British games companies to fully exploit the idea that games were part of the entertainment industry, and not just about computers. 'We were not slow to make parallels with the 1960s pop movement that had been in Liverpool and included the Beatles. So I think it's no accident that the company was called Imagine Software,' recalls Everiss. 'We really did want people to know that there was a new, creative wave going through Liverpool.' Imagine's games were lavishly advertised in magazines with full-page colour adverts. The company made every effort to get its face in the news, sponsored a motorbike racing team and, for a time, discussed moving into the revolving restaurant that towers over Liverpool. 'What we were doing was very, very, very newsworthy, so we got a professional PR company, we issued press releases, then the world's press came to our door,' explains Bruce Everiss. 'That PR is what gave us our business. We got millions of pounds worth of marketing coverage, and it only cost us pennies.' The national media coverage that greeted millionaire-in-the-making Eugene Evans, in reality paid far from as lavishly as reported, was another example of Imagine's genius for publicity. Adding further gloss to this picture of success, Imagine rented its programmers' sports cars; that many were too young to drive them just added to the image.

The Beatles aside, there was another aspect to the Liverpool connection that deserves attention. The elevation of a video games-writing whizz-kid to celebrity status also tapped into something bigger. Eugene Evans's youthful success validated all the promises of children finding brighter futures through learning about computers. Yet perhaps the biggest surprise was not that Evans was 16, but that he was in Liverpool. The city was hard hit by the decline of industry and dockworking, with some of the highest unemployment in the country. Riots flared in the inner city, militant left-wingers gained control of the council and Yosser Hughes, the desperately jobless Liverpudlian from the hard-hitting television drama *Boys from the Blackstuff,* became a national icon of life on the dole. Liverpool was almost a tabloid byword for Britain's industrial and social decline. It was a proud city going through a bad patch. It was not just Evans's youth that caught journalists' attention, but that he was from a council estate in Liverpool. The *Daily Mail* even noted that while finding a job was the biggest problem for most Liverpool teenagers, Evans was unique in having problems deciding what to spend all his money on. Gaming magazine *Big-K* described the growth of the Merseyside games industry as electronic tendrils clutching bundles of money growing out of Liverpool's 'smouldering ash heaps'.[3] The apparent success of Evans and Imagine was virtually a local case study in the sort of prosperity and economic revival that information technology was predicted to bring. It was just a shame that it would be so fleeting in this case.

Imagine's eventual, spectacular demise makes it too easy to dismiss the firm as nothing more than marketing, but in several respects the company was an innovator. It made one of the early efforts to expand out of mail order and get its programs widely available in shops, as Bruce Everiss recalls: 'We had every *Yellow Pages* in the country… we rang every shop that we thought we could convert over to the dark side of selling computer games.' Indeed, the company started selling its programs overseas too, one of the earliest British games companies to go international. Rather than have programmers working at normal home computers, it invested in expensive SAGE IV development systems to speed up the process. At a time when games were often written by individuals, Imagine employed a team of specialists to support the programmers, such as graphic designers to storyboard its ideas and work up animations. However, the large staff, the specialist equipment, the offices and everything else were lavishly expensive. 'We had profligate overheads,' remembers Everiss. 'Every time we grew to a certain size we'd move to another building but not get rid of the old one.'

By 1984 the company was in trouble. 'Sales hit a brick wall because of piracy. Basically people went from buying games to copying them off their mates. And sales just collapsed,' recalls Bruce Everiss. 'Over one Christmas it flipped into being loss-making and sales going downhill. And it just happened like that.' Worse still, Imagine's cunning plan to corner the Christmas market by buying up tape-duplicating capacity so rivals could not use it had left it sitting on a warehouse of unwanted stock. To make matters even worse, a lucrative contract to supply *Input* magazine with software listings, reputedly worth as much as £11 million, fell through as resources were sucked into Imagine's grand plans for making 'Megagames'.

The Megagames – *Psyclapse* and *Bandersnatch* – were a suitably big idea, titles so advanced that they needed the extra power of a specially developed hardware upgrade, with the handy side effect of making piracy more difficult. With firm details shrouded in secrecy, their development was expensive and seriously delayed. In the absence of progress a series of teaser adverts continued to build the hype, with photos of Imagine's star programmers engrossed in their development equipment, and breakdowns of how many coffees and sandwiches they had consumed to date. To be priced around £40 when the typical game was typically between £5–£15, the Megagames were a commercially dubious proposition. Their delays and development costs were perhaps the final straw.

The cumulative effect caught up with Imagine in 1984, when the firm's unravelling was accidentally captured for posterity by a BBC documentary crew filming an episode of

Commercial Breaks. Rather than the success story they expected to collect, the cameras recorded a death spiral of development problems, a factional split among company directors, financial rescue attempts, unpaid suppliers and a growing sense of resignation. It culminated in Imagine's programmers being barred from the office by bailiffs. Broadcast for the nation to see, the last days in the bunker of the collapsing Imagine empire were as well publicised as everything else it had done. Imagine's collapse was dissected at length in the press in unflattering terms. It became something of a cautionary tale for the whole games industry, a warning about what happened when a company believed its own marketing hype rather than concentrating on the quality of its products. As stories emerged of unpaid advertising bills, poor financial controls and problems managing creative talent, it became clear that the company had fallen short of its glossy professional image.

Imagine may have failed, but other companies would emerge out of its ashes as staff moved on. Among them were independent developer Denton Designs, which found success with the surreal adventure *Frankie Goes to Hollywood*, based on the popular new-wave band; and Psygnosis, whose first release, the science-fiction action-adventure *Brataccas* was rumoured to be cobbled together from what had been done towards *Bandersnatch*, but reinvented for the more powerful computers of the later 1980s.* It says much about the power of Imagine's marketing effort that even at the end its brand was worth something too. The Imagine name lived on, sold on to Ocean Software, the other games company featured in *Commercial Breaks*.

Despite sharing screen time with the disgraced Imagine, Ocean would become a major success, one of the most

---

*Much later, Psygnosis scored a success far beyond anything achieved by Imagine by publishing the addictive puzzle game *Lemmings* (1991) and its sequels, on behalf of DMA Design. A few years later still, DMA Design would top the success of *Lemmings* with *Grand Theft Auto* (1997), the first of a long-running and hugely profitable series of crime-based adventure games.

significant games publishers of the 1980s and '90s. Based in Manchester, the company was started by businessmen Jon Woods and David Ward in 1983, building on their earlier Spectrum Games company. Ocean was initially a publisher that marketed the works of bedroom programmers, but it soon recruited an in-house development staff to produce its own software too. Gary Bracey's start as Ocean's head of development began as informally as most involvements with the games industry, with a conversation with Jon Woods. 'He told me "we understand business. What we need, while we're growing a bit, is for someone to manage the development side of video games,"' recalls Bracey, who ran a computer game shop in Liverpool at the time. 'I said, "Well, I play them a lot and I sell them so I know what people like." And so I went on board. In those days there was no discipline. We were inventing the business as we went along.'

Ocean's software came from a variety of sources. Some titles were sourced from smaller developers and bedroom programmers. Others, many based on conversions from arcade machine games or high-profile film licences, were developed by Ocean's in-house development staff. With an average age of just 19, they were a productive but lively group. 'It was completely undisciplined... you'd try to plan it out so people would work together, and quite often the older, more experienced ones would lend a hand, but they'd end up four weeks from completion and realise they had a fair bit of the game to go,' chuckles Bracey. 'Then having to work 24 hours a day for the next week in order to deliver, and that wasn't untypical.'

Based for much of the 1980s in the unlikely setting of a Quaker meeting house, Ocean's office arrangements reflected the two worlds that games companies increasingly needed to operate in. On the surface were spacious corporate offices for managing the business, marketing and sales. Underneath, in the coffee and cigarette fumes of the basement, were the dungeons of development staff at their computers. Much of the success of Ocean, and a big difference from Imagine, lay in successfully combining the worlds of marketing and development. 'The two often conflicted, because the developers wanted the best possible product, and marketing is only concerned with having a product to sell, on time. And that was a conflict,' remarks Bracey. But it was a conflict that Ocean managed successfully, on the whole, to keep a reliable flow of titles.

Ocean not only excelled at marketing, with big adverts, good press and retailer relations, and titles based on high-profile films, but it managed the creativity of developers to keep the games coming out. The style and quality varied enormously: platform games arcade conversions, adventure games, car games, sports games and more. A few titles, such as *Knight Rider*, were panned by reviewers, and others were of middling standard, but much of the output was solid and well received. Several games, such as *Frankie Goes to Hollywood* (published on behalf of Denton Designs), *Matchday*, *Daley Thompson's Decathlon*, and *Batman*, were critically acclaimed classics. Good or bad, individual titles faded in the context of how prolific the company was; it had released dozens of mostly successful games a year for different computers by the mid-1980s. 'We had a good sales force, a good marketing force, an excellent art component,' concludes Bracey. 'And a very, very prolific, creative and technically competent development team.' Success in the games developer world would increasingly rely on similar combinations of creative and business expertise.

Of moles and miners and missiles

The media interest in teenage tycoon programmers was just one aspect of a more complex relationship between games and 1980s society. Just as art, film, music and other media reflect the wider society they were created in, computer games took on – sometimes unlikely – themes from contemporary Britain. 'If you can't put your social and moral mores into your own work, what can you do?' argues Mel Croucher of Automata software. Based in a former wool shop in Portsmouth, Automata was the antithesis of Imagine, less a corporation and more a cooperative creative collective, where everyone earned the same £25-a-week wage. The company's early releases, many for the 1k ZX81, such as the 1982 eight-game collection *Can of Worms*, were simple but surreal, and often included songs and comedy sketches recorded on the B-side of the cassette.

Political themes came easily to Automata's games. Among these were the political management game *Dole*, and *Reagan*, in which the player had to dye the hair of the ageing US president to stop him starting a nuclear war. 'Absolutely political,' reminisces Croucher. 'I was trying to subvert the children of the country. Reagan was a warmongering tosser. There were three and a half million people on the dole at the time… there was a class war going on and I knew which side I was on.' Later Croucher recalls finding himself defending the political messages of his games in a radio interview: 'We went live on air and he asked, "Is this game not a front for CND?" I said, "No, it's not, it's overtly anti-nuclear."'

On the other side of the divide were games that turned the Cold War hot, notably Atari's iconic 1980 arcade game *Missile Command*, in which players had to intercept incoming missiles to protect their cities from nuclear destruction. Several commentators of the time described the premise as tasteless, but there was no shortage of versions for home computers. To the mainstream press of the time, gore and violence-filled 'video nasties' for the newly popular home video players were a far more important target of outrage than crudely animated video game violence. Although there were few moral panics on the scale of those that would greet violent games like *Doom* and *Grand Theft Auto* in the 1990s,[*] there were still reservations about the effects of video games. In 1981, Labour, MP George Foulkes became concerned by stories about children resorting to theft and vice to fuel their arcade machine addictions, and attempted to place greater controls over them. Foulkes's

---

[*]At least in Britain. The US had already witnessed its first moral panic over violent video games with the controversy over the 1976 arcade-machine game *Death Race*, in which the player had to run over stick figures. These were claimed by the game's developers to be gremlins, but looked rather more convincingly like pedestrians.

'Control of *Space Invaders* and Other Electronic Games' bill was defeated, after Conservative opponents objected to it as a 'socialist' restriction on free enterprise and people's personal freedoms to have fun. More generally, from browsing through computer magazines it is clear that some in the microcomputing world, both ordinary users and programmers, were concerned over video game violence, and worried that barbarous games would create a world of philistines.

'I just assumed that games were meant to be funny,' recalls Mel Croucher, one of the developers concerned by violent video games. 'The idea of killing stuff, simulated death on black and white screens, that was just so alien to me.' Croucher unexpectedly found himself facing criticism of a different sort from the tabloid *Sunday People* over Automata's allegedly 'sexy' games. 'They said I was trying to corrupt the morals of our country's youth,' recalled Croucher, after Automata provoca-tively advertised its games collection tapes as 'Adult' or 'Censored'. The potential of silly, simple ZX81 games with slightly rude titles, like *Vasectomy* and *Smut*, to corrupt the young was, to say the least, rather overblown, but Croucher's defence rested also on Automata's anti-violence stance: 'Would you rather teach your kids to kiss or to kill?'

While they rarely made much difference to the gameplay, contemporary themes featured in the offerings of many companies of the time. A good example was *Dennis Through the Drinking Glass*, a 1983 text adventure game starring Dennis Thatcher on a quest to find a gin and tonic in 10 Downing Street while avoiding Margaret. Social climbing from the dole to the heights of yuppie London society was the theme of 1984 text adventure *Hampstead*. The Falklands War inspired such titles as *Falklands '82*, *Bomb Buenos Aires*, and *Harrier Attack*. Yet perhaps the best example of how Thatcher's Britain flavoured the software of the day was the 1984 platform game *Wanted Monty Mole*.

Written by Peter Harrap, the son of a mine worker, the game was set against the background of the 1984–85 miners' strike. Players controlled monocled mole Monty on his adventure through a South Yorkshire pit, contending with picketing miners as he searched for coal to keep his family warm. The game won much free publicity for its chief villain, Arthur Scargill, general secretary of the National Union of Miners. To win, Monty had to infiltrate Scargill's castle and collect enough secret ballot papers to remove him from office, an unlikely democratic way to complete an action game. The game's publishers, Gremlin Graphics, even thought it best to make a donation to the Miners Welfare Fund to demonstrate their political neutrality in this highly emotive dispute. Of course, not all games so overtly reflected the society they were created in as *Monty Mole*, but there was undoubtedly an undercurrent of popular culture and current affairs in many titles of the time.

Tie-in games themed on various films and television programmes began to appear in numbers, often featuring ear-wrenching attempts at the original theme music played through the computer speaker. *Blockbusters, Spitting Image, Postman Pat, Minder, Bullseye, The Krypton Factor*, the games industry's attempts to recreate 1980s British TV in game form knew few boundaries, even if it sometimes resulted in unlikely scenarios for play. *Auf Wiedersehen Pet*, based on the hit TV comedy about builders who had left recession-hit Britain to work in prosperous West Germany, included the chance to play a Geordie bricklayer building a wall in Düsseldorf.* At their worst, tie-ins were mediocre attempts to cash in on an existing

---

*This is not to say that seemingly mundane activities could not be the basis of surprisingly enjoyable games, indeed there was something of a trend in turning innocuous daily activities into computerised entertainment. Jeff Minter's *Hover Bover*, for example, was based around mowing the lawn, carefully avoiding the risks of the mower overheating or neighbours trying to reclaim their borrowed lawnmower. Malcolm Evan's *Trashman* pitted players against speeding traffic in a quest to collect bins around the streets of Bath. Both were fun, with a streak of humour and good gameplay, and were well received by reviewers, proving that the game itself was generally more important than its theme.

franchise with a tenuously linked game. One of the worst was *Eastenders*, taking inspiration from the long-running soap opera. For £9.95 players got a collection of mini-games about pulling pints at the Queen Vic, washing clothes at Dot Cotton's laundrette and other tedious tasks described by *Sinclair User*'s reviewer as 'almost too awful for words'.

At their best, tie-ins allowed the industry to harness a good game to a recognisable brand, bringing the powerful combination of critical and commercial success. Programmer Jon Ritman already had a three-dimensional game in mind when he and artist Bernie Drummond started kicking around ideas for a theme. 'We need to find some sort of hero that people recognise,' thought Ritman. 'I was thinking of things like the gods, Thor, anything that people might recognise and I threw out Batman.' With the garish 1960s TV series enjoying a revival at the time, they showed a demo to Ocean Software, who sorted the licensing rights with DC Comics, with a few provisos. 'I'd given him some power-ups that I called Bat Pills. They were just like miniature Batmen, and DC Comics came back with Batman doesn't take drugs. So we just called them Bat Powers instead,' chuckles Ritman. Released in 1986, *Batman* earned a series of 90 per cent plus magazine reviews praising its graphics, inventive puzzles, the game's size and its little flourishes. 'You fit in what you can. *Batman* stopped development when I found out I had 12 bytes left in the entire machine,' recalls Ritman, who used the tiny space to make Batman tap his foot when the player left the machine idle. 'That was a well-spent 12 bytes. Nearly every single review carried that story, because it gave him character.'

As *Batman* shows, well-considered licences based on film and television could contribute to notably good games, and while they could impose a few creative limitations, they undoubtedly made good business sense too. 'The film titles were so successful because you were buying a brand; you were buying instant recognition,' explains Ocean Software's Gary Bracey. 'If we got it right, which we did fairly occasionally, and did a top game with a top title, then it went through the roof.'

Ocean became well known for games based on blockbuster Hollywood films and other big franchises. 'It guaranteed what we call the "Granny purchase",' explains Bracey. 'Granny goes into a computer shop wanting to buy little Johnny a game, and she doesn't know what Sensible Software's *Matchday* or *Whizkid* are, but she knows what *Top Gun* and *Robocop* and *Rambo* are.' The growth of big-name licences based on Hollywood films was another sign of the growing acceptance of computer games as part of the mainstream entertainment industry, not just as a diverting offshoot of hobbyist programming.

At first microcomputing had been exciting in ways that were perhaps more worthy, instructive and intellectual than they were straight-up entertaining. Games changed that, breeding a new computing culture that was more about consuming ready-to-run entertainment products than it was about creating or learning. As teenage boys retreated to their bedrooms to spend hours waggling joysticks with the curtains drawn, parents began to suspect that the allegedly educational computers they had bought as Christmas presents were perhaps unhealthily addictive and rather expensive toys. As with many other aspects of microcomputing, there was a gender aspect. Most of the games players were male, as were most of the games programmers and journalists. Researching the culture of microcomputing at the time, the academic Leslie Haddon noted that computer gaming, particularly around the school yard, was surrounded by a competitive, bantering and generally masculine context.[4] While girls played games too, from an early stage the wider culture of gaming was prominently male.

The transformation of the computer into a plaything went beyond just the act of actually playing games; rather it took on the characteristics of previous childhood entertainments. Older generations of schoolboys had competed to get the best collections of marbles, bragged about seeing the latest films, argued over which football team was best and gone round to each other's houses to play with train sets. 1980s schoolboys competed to get the biggest game collections and be the first to play the new releases, had passionate debates over whether the Spectrum or the Commodore 64 was best, and played video games at each other's houses. Computer games slotted into the childhood experience like so many other toys before them, and the industry grew on the demand this culture generated.

Much of it was encouraged by a new breed of magazines dedicated to video games, titles like *ZZap64*, *Crash* and *Computer & Video Games* (*CV&G*). They lacked much of the old dedication to explaining how things worked, the type-in programs and discussions of socio-economic effects. In their place were colourful screenshots, interviews with teenage programming stars, adverts, game maps, top ten charts, cheat codes and a fun informality that appealed to their young readership. There was always a creative tension in the work of gaming magazines. They made much of their money from advertising games, yet at the same time were tasked with writing impartial reviews on those same games. 'If you gave someone a bad review,' explains *CV&G* journalist Robert Schifreen, 'the first thing they'd do is ring up the publisher and say I'm going to take my advertising out. And any publisher worth his salt would say, "fine," and then they'd not bother doing it because they knew the magazine was worth advertising in.' From the games publisher's point of view it was not a matter of bias but of business. 'We may spend £5,000 advertising this particular game in a magazine… On the following page they give a crap review of 10 per cent, so it doesn't make sense for us to advertise that game, because the review is going to carry more weight,' explains Ocean's Gary Bracey, 'but we needed to advertise.' It was a delicate relationship, but it demonstrates just how much the games and magazine industries grew with each other. 'It was a symbiotic relationship. They needed us, and we needed them,' concludes Bracey. The success of this symbiosis was clear in the soaring sales of gaming magazines and of games themselves.

Pirates

A less welcome part of gaming culture, at least for the software publishers, was piracy. With new computer games typically costing around £5–£15 in the early 1980s, and cassette tapes very easy to duplicate, there was a clear incentive for all sorts of people to copy games. With intellectual property rights something few people were accustomed to, and copying and swapping an established part of early microcomputing culture, there was little taboo against it. 'It seemed to be completely moral,' notes Simon Goodwin. 'I've never held that it was, but we were accustomed to taping music off the radio.' School yards and many computer clubs were rife with informal software piracy. 'If you went along to a computer club,' recalls Goodwin, 'somebody would turn up with a suitcase and they would have hundreds of games and they would swap and collect them.'

Copies of copies made with twin cassette recorders became less reliable with each new generation of duplicate, so could only spread so far. More concerning for the industry were the professional copies that appeared on market stalls across the country, or were even slipped into official supply chains after being churned out by organised pirates with access to proper duplicating machines. Organised piracy too could be a surprisingly open activity at first, as Malcolm Evans found out when a prolific pirate of *Trashman*, New Generation's popular action game of rubbish collection, introduced himself to the company's staff at a computer fair. 'He had done very well out of our *Trashman* and he had given up piracy now and could he have a copy of *Travels with Trashman*?' remembers Evans. 'He had sold about 50 per cent of what we had sold of *Trashman*… my brother physically kicked him off the stand. It really was blatant.'

The industry fought back with a variety of methods, the start of a battle of wits between developers and pirates that continues to this day. Requiring people to enter codes printed on instruction sheets was common, but easily thwarted by photocopiers. A few games were shipped with a plastic prism device named Lenslok. This was supposed to unscramble an on-screen validation code when you put it up to the screen, but was fiddly to use and would not work at all if the game was shipped with the wrong prism. The lengths games developers went to thwart pirates is well illustrated by a story told by Simon Goodwin about his 1983 ZX Spectrum game *Gold Mine*. Yet another game with a mining theme, *Gold Mine was* actually about mining. Players dug underground looking for gold, avoiding flooding and other hazards, and trying to be strategic with their tunnel routes. 'I always liked the kind of game where the early decisions that you make influence the constraints later on,' explains Goodwin. 'An exploring game where you create a maze yourself was something I wanted to make.' The game sold well and got into the charts, partly, Goodwin suggests, because misguided parents got it mixed up with *Manic Miner*, but also because he had devised a copy-protection method to thwart bulk copying methods. 'I spent as long on writing that technique as I did on writing the game,' he recalls.

Stored after the program on the *Gold Mine*'s cassette was a short tone, which the game checked for when it loaded up. Neither a one nor a zero, the tone was undetectable by copying software and missed out on bulk pirated copies, which then would not work. 'It wouldn't say, "you are a pirate go away", but would do what every Spectrum owner dreaded most, and expected: it would say "R tape loading error",' explains Goodwin of the psychology behind the protection. 'That was going to cause them endless frustration and grief and maybe it was better to move and copy something else, and I think that was crucial to the game staying in the charts.' *Gold Mine* disappeared from the charts after the anti-piracy protection, complicated to implement by the legitimate duplicator, was discontinued by the publisher. 'It could be that the product life was short anyway, but I think that that could well have been a contributory factor,' sighs Goodwin. The impact of piracy was hard to measure. It undoubtedly happened on a large scale, and several bankrupt software companies blamed illegal copying for their collapse. By 1984, estimates of lost revenue from copying ranged as high as a barely creditable £100 million a year, but its impact was unquantifiable, a great unknown that bedevils games, and most of the other creative industries, to this day.

Quite apart from piracy, controversies over sexy games and violence, the rise of this new industry was not uncontested. Within the personal computing world, games were a challenge to the high aims of computer literacy. In the very first episode of *The Computer Programme*, computer expert Ian McNaught-Davis bemoaned people using computers just for playing 'silly' games as 'degrading' given everything else computers could do. Games did not depend on people developing a detailed understanding of the machine, just on being able to grasp a few simple controls and consume software. Letters to magazines complained about the misuse of microcomputers for playing games as a waste of potential, given how precious a resource computer runtime had been in the past. Yet the charge that games were a misuse of technology does not stand up when we consider the technical achievement of crafting software in the tightly confined computers of the day.

That so many good games would emerge in the constraints of these essentially simple platforms was a testament to the developing skills of games creators. While millions of ordinary people were learning BASIC, most games programmers moved on to learn the black arts of machine code and assembler. Instructing the machine in its own language saved memory and meant programs ran faster as BASIC commands did not need to be translated into the ones and zeros the computer could understand. Forsaking ease of use allowed programmers to create smaller, faster and more efficient programs, and for a time 'machine code game' was advertising jargon for 'it runs fast'. As they explored the computer and learned from what others had done, programmers found ways of doing things that the machines' designers had never expected. During 1983 and 1984 this maturing technical expertise would lead to some

masterpieces of the programmer's craft that reveal the great
leaps made in games development in a very short time.

An incredible use of technology?

It would need an entire book to adequately cover all the
innovation and creativity of early 1980s games developers. The
gaming scene was vast, with thousands of games of diverse
genres, produced by hundreds of companies, on dozens of
different platforms. However, an examination of just some of
the most inventive titles and techniques of the early 1980s
illustrates the great technical and creative achievements of
games developers. Many of the most innovative games of the
early 1980s originated on the ZX Spectrum, albeit they were
quickly ported to other platforms too. The machine was among
the most popular, meaning there were not only many people
programming for it, but a large market to supply. By 1984, over
3,500 games had been released for the machine in some form
or another.[5] The quality and sophistication varied enormously,
but it included a large number of critically acclaimed and
innovative titles. Curiously, the Spectrum itself was not as
optimised for games as some of its more expensive rivals. It
needed an adaptor to plug a joystick to it, the sound capability
was simply a beeper, and the way the machine produced a
colour display could create some odd-looking effects on
screen. Other machines had more sophisticated sound and
graphics, and provided built-in features to make writing games
easier. A good example is the Commodore 64, which not only
had an advanced sound chip, but the ability to use 'sprites',
graphical objects that made animations easier to create. 'The
trouble was, that guided everyone into making games that all
looked incredibly similar,' recalls Spectrum games programmer
Jon Ritman. The Spectrum had no such hardware support, yet
its simplicity and origins as a machine to be explored made it
a flexible medium to create games that did not have to obey
the rules. 'The Spectrum was just "here's a bit of screen". It's
laid out in a funny way, which is a bit of a pain,' explains
Ritman. 'But you just draw things. And you could do whatever

you want. It might not be as fast, but you can do whatever you want, and I think that as a result you got more interesting ideas on it.'

Many of the titles mentioned so far in this story have been action games of various types, but it would be entirely misleading to suggest that this was all that was on offer. Text adventure games were a hugely popular genre at the time. In 1983, nearly 130 were released on the ZX Spectrum alone, the same year that saw the launch of a dedicated computer adventure game magazine: *The Micro Adventurer*. At their best they were immersive works of interactive fiction, notably those actually based on books, such as *The Hobbit* and *The Hitchiker's Guide to the Galaxy*, which was co-created by its original author Douglas Adams. Very quickly they evolved beyond simple text games, as programmers started illustrating them and adding other dimensions to the gameplay. The most impressive example was probably *Lords of Midnight*, written by a former teacher from Liverpool, Mike Singleton, in 1984.

Drawing heavily on *The Lord of the Rings*, *Lords of Midnight* was a quest to defeat the Witchking Doomdark, but offered far more than 'YOU ARE IN A ROOM'-style descriptions and typed 'GO NORTH' commands. Rather, it was a mix of strategy war game and fantasy adventure, based around the remarkable 'landscaping' graphical technique developed by Singleton. The first-person perspective this provided created an impression of travelling through a vast fantasy land of citadels, villages, mountains and plains. It was a whole world for the player to explore, populated with enemies and potential allies, and like any good fantasy tale, the game even came with a map. *Lords of Midnight* was far more open-ended than typical adventures: there were multiple characters to control, and it could be played as an adventure to destroy Doomdark's ice crown, or as a war game by gathering forces to defeat Doomdark in battle. With 4,000 different locations and innovative gameplay, *Lords of Midnight* was one of the earliest games that could be considered an epic. The cast of characters, atmospheric surroundings, and enormous size and scope of gameplay made it a game that players could lose themselves in for many hours. Reviewers praised its well-realised world, landscapes and coherent storyline, attributes more often associated with books and films than mere games at the time.

Also visually impressive, but in a rather different way, was 1983's *Ant Attack*. Playing as either a boy or a girl character, a novelty in the male world of video gaming, the game's object was simple enough; players had to enter the lonely ruins of the city of Antescher, dodge the giant ants (or, more aggressively, blow them up with grenades) and rescue their significant other. What was striking was the world the action played out in. *Ant Attack* was one of the earliest home computer games with three-dimensional graphics, using a technique known as isometric 3D, where the objects in the game were drawn to look like they were solid rather than flat. The game's creator, Sandy White, was a trained sculptor. With little more than shaded blocks, White created a sprawling three-dimensional city for the player to explore. The isometric 3D technique was so novel that the game's publisher, Quicksilva, attempted to take out a patent on it, but it became a widely emulated technique on the Spectrum.

Isometric 3D was taken to another level the following year when Ultimate Play the Game released *Knight Lore*, an action-adventure quest of collecting the ingredients needed to stop Sabreman turning into a 'werewulf'. Ultimate, a trading name of Ashby Computers and Graphics, was rare among British games companies in already having experience of creating arcade machine games before the home computer boom. It became well respected for a series of superbly realised and highly successful computer games such as the platform game *JetPac* and action-adventure *Atic Atac*. The company cultivated an air of mystery; its lead developers, brothers Tim and Chris Stamper, rarely gave interviews, which paradoxically led to even greater press interest and a loyal fan base. Convinced that it had a winner, Ultimate delayed the release of *Knight Lore* for some months to avoid upsetting the market for its other

games. Whereas *Ant Attack* featured an expansive but essentially
static city where nothing moved save for the player and the
ants, *Knight Lore* used isometric 3D to create a miniature
interactive world. Essentially a three-dimensional platform
game, *Knight Lore* was a maze of claustrophobic dungeons that
exploited the extra dimension to good effect, with objects that
could be moved around, puzzles that needed to be solved in
three axes and hazards hiding behind things. The graphics were
also precisely detailed; the animated paroxysms of Sabreman as
he turned into a werewulf were a joy to behold. It was an
approach widely considered revolutionary; *Crash*'s reviewer
declared that it 'resembles nothing I've played before'. Other
programmers were impressed too. 'You could have heard our
jaws hit the floor basically,' recalls Jon Ritman of first seeing
the game. 'I looked at it and thought that's what I've always
wanted to do, as I saw it; to make a Disney cartoon that you
could play.'

After *Knight Lore*, isometric 3D became a staple of Spectrum
gaming. Indeed, so many games used the format that some
magazine reviewers seem to have got rather bored with it after
a while, but it was the basis for a number of inventive and
polished games. Three-dimensional games were generally more
technically demanding than two-dimensional ones, and few
players appreciated all that was required to make isometric 3D
work on a simple machine like the Spectrum. 'It required a
number of things,' recalls Jon Ritman, who employed the
technique to good effect in 1986's *Batman*. The smooth three-
dimensional animation as objects moved across the screen
relied on emptying a space in the graphic, then drawing into
the gap that was created. 'You work out the area of the screen
that's changed because something's moved,' explains Ritman.
'You work out the order of the room from the back of the
room to front, then you draw all the things that come in that
area that you need to update, in order, all the way to the front.'
To avoid the Spectrum's problem with colour clash, the action
in most isometric games was drawn in monochrome, albeit
with different colours used for different rooms and to display

information around the gameplay area. 'And then there was the physics, being able to move things around,' continues Ritman. It seems such a simple thing today, but having items moving around in a virtual world, not just scenes being drawn, but objects that the player could interact with, was curiously novel for the time.

A good game was not just about the graphics technique employed, but also about using it to make a fun experience that was large enough to entertain players for a good few hours. *Batman*, for example, had 150 rooms to explore of puzzles, enemies and items, requiring another set of techniques to fit the game into the confines of the Spectrum's memory. 'It required some intense storage, so the maps and things were incredibly condensed,' recalls Ritman. The following year Ritman and artist Bernie Drummond surpassed even this, with *Head Over Heels*, another detailed, and rather surreal, isometric game. *Head Over Heels* also offered some impressive gameplay innovations: enemies that homed in on the player's character as they moved, fiendish combinations of conveyor belts and enemies, and strange Prince Charles–Dalek hybrid creatures controlled by buttons within the game environment itself. Most notably, *Head Over Heels* had two characters with different abilities to control, the dog-like Head and Heels, who could be combined into a single symbiotic organism, allowing a number of different ways to play. When new, *Manic Miner* had been complimented for squeezing 20 two-dimensional screens of action into the 48k ZX Spectrum. A few years later *Head Over Heels* managed 300 three-dimensional rooms in the same computer; a striking demonstration of maturing programming techniques. Isometric games such as these were probably the most impressive displays of how far games programmers could push the simple capabilities of the Spectrum, creating what were essentially miniature interactive universes.

Playing God with the machine

One of the most ambitious conceptual developments on the Spectrum, though sadly a commercial failure, was Automata's

Deus Ex Machina. Based on Shakespeare's seven ages of man, the game followed a 'defect' in a dystopian future world from the 'DNA welder' through the stages of its life to eventual old age and death. The idea was a sophisticated one, but the realisation was extraordinary and almost impossible to describe. *Deus Ex Machina* was less to be played than to be experienced, a multimedia concept album of mini games, graphics, philosophy, music and poetic narration. 'I wanted to make a movie. A full-length movie, with a synchronised soundtrack, that you could be in. That's all I wanted to do. In 48k. Not very ambitious,' explains Automata's Mel Croucher with more than a hint of understatement.

A full-length movie with soundtrack was far beyond what should have been possible with a ZX Spectrum, but Automata was thinking outside the box in more ways than just the game's concept. 'We overcame how to get the sound. We overcame how to get an hour's worth of gameplay. We overcame how to get more memory into the computer than it actually had,' explains Croucher. *Deus Ex Machina* was split into two sections on different sides of the game's cassette tape, to be loaded up halfway through the experience.* The mini games themselves were a simple but surreal mix, involving such things as keeping DNA strands spinning or destroying the clots in a geriatric's blood-stream, but they were really secondary to the overall experience. Automata had a history of mixing media in its releases, often including music or sketches on the B side of the game's cassette. *Deus Ex Machina* took this mixing of media a step further and put a soundtrack on audio cassette to be listened to in time with the game.

For probably the first time ever, it would be a game with a celebrity cast providing the voices. 'I was just trying to get everyone I could get to. I was trying to get the most ludicrous people,' recalled Croucher, who tried to recruit monocled television astronomer Patrick Moore as the voice of a sperm in

---

*Splitting games into multiple episodes, each loaded separately, would become a more common practice later in the 1980s.

one of the mini games: 'Patrick Moore asked his mum's permission and she told him not to do it.' Despite this minor setback, the final cast was impressive, including former Doctor Who Jon Pertwee, peace campaigning historian E. P. Thompson, rock-and-roll star Ian Dury, and comedian Frankie Howerd playing the voice of the 'Defect Police'. 'They didn't have a clue what was going on, not a clue. It was just another radio jingle,' reminisces Croucher of the celebrities. The challenges of *Deus Ex* were overcome to the thoughtful lyrics of an ever-changing musical soundtrack; Jon Pertwee reading Shakespearean verse, Frankie Howerd's threatening remarks, and philosophical musing on video game violence, obeying orders and the nature of life. In spite of the sometimes serious tone, there was a streak of surreal humour to keep it fun, notably a mini-game about guiding a sperm to fertilise an egg, set to Ian Dury singing about being the fertiliser. 'Ian Dury, the whole sperm thing, I think it's hilarious,' chuckles Croucher. 'Getting people to fertilise an egg, come on! And enjoying it and bobbing around while they're doing it!'

The game ended with the poignant and inevitable death of the Defect, questioning the machine that created them. For Croucher, one of the satisfactions was the deep effect it had on many players: 'They put headphones on. They turned the lights off. They played it and they wept. They laughed. And at the end they wept.' Reviewers were puzzled over whether it was a game or a work of art, but they were united in praise and amazement. *Crash*'s reviewer went so far as to call it a 'milestone in computer history'. It was a startlingly creative experiment that blurred the boundaries of art and game to create something different and new. Unfortunately, Automata had difficulties getting the game into shops, and many people played it on pirate copies. After spending on celebrities, and reasoning that as *Deus Ex Machina* included a movie, a poster, an album and a game, *Automata* set the price at £15, making it an attractive target for piracy, but not in its entirety. 'Most people who had it, only had the game. Not the poster, or the soundtrack or the philosophy behind it. It was rubbish, this crude thing on the screen. What are you supposed to do with it?' sighs Croucher, who quit the games industry not long after *Deus Ex Machina*'s release and commercial failure. Other games may have stretched the Spectrum to produce more exciting gameplay or better graphics, but none was quite so impressively different as *Deus Ex Machina*.

Load new commander?

Not all of the gaming innovation was on the Spectrum. Indeed, the rather worthy BBC Micro was scene to a particularly noteworthy piece of conceptional and technical boundary breaking, courtesy of David Braben and Ian Bell's seminal 1984 space-trading game *Elite*. Players began the game on board a space station, with 100 credits, a minimally armed Cobra Mk III spacecraft, and a combat rating of 'harmless'. What happened next was largely up to the player. *Elite* was set in an open-ended universe of over 2,000 unique worlds, and offered countless opportunities for combat and trading, with no set path to follow; players' destinies were in their own hands.

As if that was not enough already, *Elite* offered a truly three-dimensional gameplay experience that went beyond any achieved on a home computer before. Isometric games, like *Knight Lore*, allowed movement in three dimensions, but their worlds were small and consisted of two-dimensional drawings of solid objects only viewable from fixed perspectives. *Elite*'s spaceships floated in a three-dimensional universe, free to move in any direction they chose, and when they did they seemed to change shape accordingly. Looking out from the cockpit of their Cobra, players could see the line-drawn space ships constantly shifting in perspective and size as their positions changed. The constant underlying number crunching that made it all happen was a serious test of the computer's hardware, and the cockpit display mixed the BBC Micro's display modes in a way its designers had never expected, but the effect was magical.

'Even before I had a computer I was mesmerised by the idea of making 3D graphics,' recalls David Braben. He did just that after his parents bought him an Acorn Atom, devising his own line-drawing techniques after finding the built-in methods too slow for smoothly flowing action. 'I spent ages pouring over these few lines of assembler,' recalls Braben. 'That was quite appealing. It's sort of like weeding.' At Cambridge, Braben teamed up with another student named Ian Bell, who had already published a number of BBC Micro games. At first, the idea was a three-dimensional space dogfighting game, graphically impressive but nothing conceptually ground-breaking, but as they talked the concept changed into something rather different. As Braben remembers it, the big ideas followed as a series of logical steps based on questioning the assumptions that many action games relied on. 'Why three lives?' asks Braben. 'Why not just make that one life three times as good? It was that sort of logic. What is the score a measure of? Is it my rank? Is it prestige? Is it money? And as soon as you ask the 'is it money?' question it's very hard to row back from that because you think, "oh, I could spend it on something for my spaceship".'

Money suggested new aspects to the game, such as bounty hunting, shopping for ship upgrades and trading goods between between planets. Several commentators have suggested a political symbolism in *Elite*. An independent trader in a universe devoid of society, setting out to make money and spend it on fancy ship upgrades, had a certain resonance with 1980s Britain, but it was more about game mechanics. 'We weren't intending to make a game that was overtly Thatcherite,' explains Braben. 'Elements of it came very much more from the game scene than, "I'd like to spend the score."' As well as money the other score was your combat rating, ultimately rising to the dizzying heights of 'elite' after 6,400 kills. Considering the frustrations of other games led to refinements such as enemies that were not impossibly tough and who might unpredictably run away. 'We were not competing with the player,' explains Braben 'We were entertaining the player and making it just hard enough to be rewarding.'

Squeezing all these ideas into the Model B BBC Micro was a challenge, particularly as much of the 32k of memory was taken up by systems software and unavailable to programmers. 'We had to fit the entire game into 22k,' explains Braben. 'I remember agonising that we were going to need at least 20 worlds for it to be interesting. How much memory can we afford? Almost none.' The solution was not to individually craft and store each planet, but to generate them all from a few lines of clever code as they were needed. 'That was a real nirvana moment,' recalls Braben. 'I suddenly thought that we don't have to have twenty, we have a hundred, we can have a thousand.' Even the unique short descriptions of each world that noted its statistics and notable features, such as fame for 'evil brandy' or 'ancient sitcoms', were computer generated from lists of words. 'We had a lot of fun with that,' chuckles Braben, although they did have to swap an entire galaxy when they discovered that their algorithms had spawned a planet named 'Arse'.

Gaming historians point to earlier games as precursors to *Elite*, but the world was not so interlinked in 1984, and Braben and Bell were largely unaware of them. *Elite* shared elements with earlier games, but nothing had really combined all these ideas together in such an elegant and imaginative way. What all of it added up to was widely recognised as something conceptually new: a blend of three-dimensional action arcade, stock-market trading and role-playing game, set in a free and essentially limitless universe. Depending on the choices you made, you could be an honest trader, asteroid miner, bounty hunter or anything else that you imagined. 'We started to realise that there are professions here, and you can play the game in so many different ways,' remarks Braben. 'The beauty from a writer's point of view is that it's the very same bit of code.' There was a moral element too. Get caught in space piracy or trading in contraband, and you would be branded a criminal and pursued by GalCop. Just like in real life, how you played the game in the *Elite* universe had consequences.

Compared to the confined worlds of most other games, *Elite* was vast and offered incredible freedom. The concept was too novel for the first publisher Braben and Bell approached to get its head around. 'Thorn EMI said it's a wonderful tech demo but we want three lives, we want a score,' recalls Braben. They found a readier reception at Acornsoft, the software publishing offshoot of Acorn. 'They knew how hard the problems were and they were really impressed. They said, "How did you do the 3D so fast?" The fact we'd got colour at high resolution on their computer, they said, "How have you done that?"' The innovative way the machine was used surprised even the designers of the BBC Micro. 'Some people found trade-offs we hadn't imagined,' recalls its co-designer Steve Furber. 'So David Braben's *Elite* program changed the display mode partway down the display in a manner that was sort of clearly impossible.'

Journalists reviewing the game were almost unanimously impressed. 'Undoubtedly a masterpiece of programming', was *Beebug*'s view on the BBC Micro version. 'One of the most imaginative games ever to be designed to run on a home computer', was *Crash* magazine's verdict on the Spectrum version, one of the many platforms the game was exported to. Yet not all the reactions to *Elite* were so positive. As the media historian Alison Gazzard points out, a sizeable number of people struggled with the advanced gameplay, the investment of time required and the brutal finality of losing the one life the game offered.[6] As anyone who repeatedly crashed into the space station while lining up with the tiny letterbox of its docking bay could attest to, controlling the ship in three dimensions could be tricky. That some people seem to have found trouble adjusting to it speaks volumes for what a different experience it was compared to the simpler games that predominated at the time.

In many ways *Elite* also marked the wider watershed moment the games industry was going through in the mid-1980s. It started off with a programmer seeing what their computer could do, but somewhere along the way *Elite* bridged the gap between hobbyist programming and professional development. Far from being finished in time to catch the post, *Elite* took about 18 months to bring to fruition after Acornsoft signed the game. Acornsoft's marketing was lavish, with the novelties of television adverts and a launch party at Thorpe Park theme park. The game shipped with Lenslok anti-piracy protection and even a novella setting the back story, by fantasy writer Robert Holdstock. It was very far from the small adverts and photocopied instructions that the games industry had started from.

From the bedroom to the boardroom

In a few short years computer games evolved from blocky graphics and elementary gameplay to offer far more sophisticated and varied entertainment experiences. Even the best games of 1981 looked almost prehistoric compared to those of 1984. It was not just a matter of improved computer technology, but of maturing developers and of creative freedom. The widespread uptake of home computers, combined with the games market's lack of barriers to entry, had democratised the development of computer games and allowed countless opportunities for creative interpretation. For a few years anybody with a computer and a grasp of programming could be a developer, but it was a situation that could not last.

Just as computer games had evolved, so too had the industry that made them. 'There was an immense change in the way games were developed and an immense change in the way they were distributed and sold,' remarks Bruce Everiss, who worked at several other software houses after Imagine. 'The only thing that remained constant during the time was that they were on cassettes. Everything else changed.' The shift to selling most games through shops rather than mail order brought in distribution companies and major retailers as market gatekeepers. This not only made it harder for new entrants, but added more middlemen to take their cut too. 'We were getting 80 to 90 per cent of the cost of the games when we were producing them ourselves,' recalls Malcolm Evans. 'At the end we were lucky to get to keep 20 per cent. We were selling many more so our income was about the same, but only if the game was successful. If not...'

By the mid-1980s, the games market's low barriers to entry had slowly risen up against new entrants, and it was harder for smaller companies to compete. Placing a small ad in a magazine and awaiting the mail-order cheques was no longer going to cut it. It was becoming more difficult for smaller companies to compete too. 'Our first advert had cost us £50,' recalls Malcolm Evans. 'When we pulled out of the games market, a full-page colour advert in just one magazine would cost £1,000, and distributors were only interested in your advertising budget.' The bigger firms could spend more on advertising, and their established positions naturally drew more press attention. 'If it was from a big company you'd want to review it, because if it's good you want to tell people, and if it's bad you want to tell people as well,' remarks *CV&G* journalist Robert Schifreen. 'If it's from a relatively small company, if it's good you tell people. If it's bad, there's no point.'

The market shake-up happened just as quickly as everything else in this new industry. In 1984 there were about 530 software companies and magazines producing ZX Spectrum games. By 1985, there were around 330. The same year, industry trade journal *Microscope* reported that a third of the market was held by just three companies, and that only five of the top 50 selling games came from small firms.[7] In any creative industry there will always be space for nimble newcomers with innovative products and, of course, new games developers emerged. However, the most successful new companies, such as Codemasters and Rare,* were often founded by people who already had some experience of the industry. The mainstream future of the games industry, at least until the disruptions of mobile gaming and the Internet, belonged substantially to the established players and to the big companies. Firms like Ocean

---

*Rare was founded in 1985 by Tim and Chris Stamper, formerly of Ultimate Play the Game. Codemasters, producer of the hit *Dizzy* series of adventure games, was founded in 1986 by brothers David and Richard Darling, both of whom had previously written games for budget publisher Mastertronic, and their father Jim.

successfully managed the messy creative processes to deliver a steady flow of titles, and had the contacts and the marketing nous to get them sold. By the early 1990s, the company was one of the world's biggest and most successful developers. 'When I started at Ocean, there were probably a dozen people in-house, a dozen developers,' recalls Ocean's Gary Bracey. 'By the time I left there were in the region of 120.' The extra people reflected a change in how games were developed. The hit-or-miss efforts of bedroom programmers were quickly overtaken by organised team efforts. A division of creative labour became common, between programmers, graphics artists and musicians, organised to keep the development pipeline flowing with the new titles the market needed. Not to mention people dealing with sales, marketing, licensing rights and all the other things required as gaming grew to become a mainstream part of the entertainment industry. 'It was rock and roll in those days, the Eighties and early Nineties,' reflects Bracey. 'Because it was creative we were innovating; we were inventing the industry as well as the games.'

The invention of this industry was one of longest lasting legacies of the computer boom, an illustrative fulfilment of the 1970s prophecies that microcomputers would create new high-tech industries. In 1986, retail sales for games were estimated at £120 million a year in Britain, a fraction of their value today, but a huge amount for something that was but a glint in a bedroom programmer's eye at the start of the decade.[8] By the mid-1980s, gaming was a well-established industry. It would have to reinvent itself constantly over the following years for new technology and changing market conditions, but it was here to stay. The rise of this industry, and of the gaming culture that went with it, profoundly changed home computing, undermining the ideas of computer literacy and overshadowing the creative enthusiasts. Games eventually became the dominant use of cheap home computers, the machines that the British microcomputer industry had grown up on, but this changing emphasis would have a profound influence on the fortunes of the home computer industry.

CHAPTER EIGHT

The Unmaking of the Micro

In December 1984 an unlikely scuffle broke out in the Baron of Beef, a Cambridge pub favoured by the city's high-tech scene, between rival computer company bosses Sir Clive Sinclair and Chris Curry. The reason for the fracas was a newspaper advert criticising the reliability of Sinclair's computers, and implying that an Acorn made a better Christmas present because buyers would not have to take it back in the New Year when it broke down. Witnesses reported that slapping and jostling ensued, before the two continued their disagreement at a nearby wine bar. The incident was overblown by a tabloid press delighted by the idea of brawling computing tycoons, but it was a hint that all was not well in the home computer industry by the end of 1984.

It would be a nice literary flourish to suggest that the glory days of the home computer ended then and there, but really there was no single dramatic moment when the home micro turned from wonder technology of the future into technological cul-de-sac. Nevertheless, 1984 was the beginning of the end for the home computer, as it was originally understood, and for many of the companies that made them. After being caught short by insatiable demand at Christmas 1983, manufacturers stocked up in anticipation of a repeat seasonal sales bonanza, which never came. Christmas 1984 was a disaster. Hundreds of thousands of computers went unsold, leaving the industry facing the dawn of 1985 with a multimillion-pound hangover.[*] Among the worst hit was Acorn, which had stocked up on Electrons after technical troubles had restricted its Christmas sales the year before. 'We couldn't make them fast enough in '83,'

---

[*]David Thomas in *The Amstrad Story* estimates that of the 1.7 million machines that were built in 1984, just 1.35 million were sold.

recalls Steve Furber. 'By '84 we'd cracked it but... unbeknown to us, the market had moved on, so there were a quarter of a million Electrons in a warehouse that we couldn't sell in the Christmas of '84.'

1985 brought a series of headlines about financial troubles in the home computing industry. Acorn shares plunged to a record low of 23 pence in late January, from a 1984 peak of 193 pence. Trading in Acorn shares was soon suspended and Sinclair cancelled plans for a stock-market floatation. On 1 February, Oric proudly launched a new computer, the Stratos. The next day, Oric went into receivership. It was bought by the French firm SPID a few months later, surviving as a largely French business for another couple of years. Computer prices tumbled during 1985 as computer manufacturers dumped stocks to raise funds and retailers slashed prices. In late 1984 an Acorn Electron cost £199, Sinclair's recently released QL was £399.99 and the new Commodore 16 was £139.99. A year later all three machines were half price, despite being bundled with generous packs of software and other goodies. The vicious circle of dumping and price cutting cost the companies producing the machines heavily. In June, the The Times reported that Acorn had made a £20 million pre-tax loss in the first half of 1985 alone.

Some sort of market shake-out had long been suggested in the press, but the victims were expected to be the smaller companies. Jupiter Cantab and Grundy had already disappeared before 1983 was out. Dragon Data called in the receivers in June 1984, but was pulled back from the brink thanks to a buyout from the Spanish Eurohard SA. A similar process was playing out in the US, albeit among larger companies for whom home computers were not the core business. Both Mattel and Texas Instruments dropped out of the market after losing the price war to Commodore. Atari persisted, despite being badly hit by a collapse in the video game console market, but was reckoned to have lost $500 million during 1983/84. Commodore remained a force to be reckoned with, but after the shock ousting of founder Jack Tramiel in 1984, the company

would lose much of its direction. Smaller companies and new
entrants to the market were always going to be at a disadvantage
in a market that favoured established firms. Yet as the likes of
Acorn and Sinclair began getting into noticeable financial
difficulties in 1985, it was clear that there was a much bigger
problem looming over the whole industry. Pundits began
comparing the cheap computer with the short-lived 1970s craze
for hula hoops. Why did people no longer want home computers?
Had a whole industry been built on a passing fad?

Maturing markets

We still have computers in our homes. However, they are of a
very different type to those of the early 1980s, separated by far
more than just technological development, but by profound
changes in how we expect to use them. What happened around
1984 was the unmaking of a particular type of home computer
and of the mode of home computing that went with it, and its
replacement by rather different types of computer and different
notions of what they were for. In part the home computer's
success was its own undoing. Growing computer familiarity,
the original raison d'être of the microcomputer boom,
undermined the need for introductory machines and the sense
that computers were there to be explored. A little of the
mystique and the urgent need for computer literacy faded as
computers become more commonplace. Programming became
less important with so much off-the-shelf software available.
For all but the most curious or dedicated, the computer
became more of a software player than an intricate puzzle to
be mastered. In magazines, type-in programs began a slow
decline in the face of ever more reviews for ready-made
software, and cover-mounted cassette tapes packed with
programs. The computer bought by parents to help the
children's education, but mostly used for games, became a
familiar story, written about in disparaging terms in computer
magazines as people were implored to exploit their micros'
capabilities to the full by trying something serious. In 1984,
market researcher Gowling reported the results of a survey

into computer attitudes among parents and children, recording growing doubts about the educational merits of computers bought for children.[1] Parents had started with ideas that computers would be good for skills development and technical familiarity, but found educational software simplistic, and worried that computers were just expensive games machines, the thing most home computers *were* being used for.

There is a close correlation between this sense of disillusionment with home computers and the rise of computer games. Use plays an important part in defining what a technology is. The torrent of games from the industry overshadowed the potential of home computers as useful household tools or worthy educational aids. The best example is the ZX Spectrum, originally designed with games more in mind than its predecessors, but still intended as an exploratory and general-purpose computer too. By 1984 about 400 educational titles, 400 computing tools and 900 assorted applications had been released on the Spectrum; clearly, at least some people found the Spectrum useful for accounts, word processing and other applications. However, in the same time frame, around 3,500 games were released for the machine. Any general-purpose aspirations of the Spectrum were overwhelmed by the gaming culture that had developed around the machine.

Cheap home computers became widely perceived as toys, not helped by the fact that many of them *were* toy-like in appearance and increasingly sold in toy shops, where they had to compete with other toys. 'All the computer companies were going bust in '84, and you know why?' asks Oric's Paul Johnson. 'The BMX bike. Home computers were toys, which were bought for children… It was a toss-up between a computer and a BMX bike.' After finding a Far Eastern supplier of cheap bikes, Oric came up with an inventive plan to save the company. 'If you bought an Oric you got a free BMX bike, but we couldn't get the letter of credit together because things were getting so rocky,' recalls Johnson.

Others had used home computers as far more than toys, in spite of the drawbacks of the machines on offer. Many people had tried to use basic home computers as useful tools, often going to some lengths to upgrade them to make them better suited as word processors, calculators and accountancy systems, hinting at a latent desire for more general-purpose utility. As users began to outgrow introductory computers, there was a growing sense that the future was not so much in simple introductory or games computers, but serious machines with the power for more sophisticated applications. In the world of professional computing, IBM's launch of the PC in 1981 had a profound impact. PCs were far too expensive for the home computer market at first, but the status of IBM helped to legitimise the idea of personal computers as useful tools for office-type applications in professional environments; why could the same not be true of computers in the home?

As early as 1983, industry pundit Martin Banks was musing in *Personal Computer World* that programs that offered tangible benefits to users were vital to the long-term survival of the home computer industry.[2] As 1984 drew to a close, the *Guardian*'s computer correspondent wondered if the 'Indian summer' of cheap computers was coming to an end, and predicted a final rush of first-time buyers before people moved upmarket to buy 'real' computers.[3] The low-cost, simple home computer was reaching a watershed moment. Its appeal among consumers, at least those not interested in games, was waning. For manufacturers the introductory computer market was beginning to turn into a race for the bottom, as prices were cut and stocks of discontinued machines were dumped. Yet at the same time there seemed to be a demand for more powerful and more useful machines, and even before the crash of 1984, several manufacturers were trying to move upmarket, towards more professional-styled 'real' computers. Not all of them would make it.

A quantum leap

After the overwhelming success of the ZX81 and ZX Spectrum, just what Sinclair might do next was a keen topic of speculation in the computer press. Journalists alleged that the ZX83 would be a professional computer rather than home micro, a portable business machine with built-in Microdrives for storage, and Sinclair's flat-screen television as a display. Considering that the first successful portable computer, the Osborne 1, had been a briefcase-size 'luggable' weighing 23 pounds and costing $1,795, the prospect of Sinclair cutting down the size and price of portable computing was an exciting one. There was also talk of a direct successor to the Spectrum, not to mention plans for the Low Cost Colour Computer, or LC3, later compared by Sir Clive Sinclair to a Nintendo console. 'The place was an ideas factory,' remarks ZX83 designer David Karlin. 'You wouldn't believe the number of ideas and conversations and different people's opinions about what things should be and what things might be.' Whatever the ZX83 turned out to be, there was an expectation that Sinclair would come up with something extraordinary, but then it did advertise for the best computer designer in the world to do it. 'I only discovered later that the job had been advertised as Sinclair wanted the best computer designer in the world, which I got mercilessly ribbed about by people for years afterwards,' chuckles David Karlin. Headhunted to develop the ZX83, Karlin had previously worked for Fairchild Semiconductor in California. While there he had been much impressed by the high-performance Xerox Alto and Xerox Star workstations developed by the nearby Xerox Palo Alto Research Center (PARC). The Xerox workstations introduced many innovations, notably a high- resolution screen with graphical user interface, soon to be adopted by Apple. They were top-of-the-line systems for demanding tasks, such as artificial intelligence work and office automation. 'I thought these were fantastic,' remarks Karlin. 'What you would be able to do with that kind of high-quality screen on a really good machine was just staggeringly obvious.'

Karlin's scheme for the ZX83 was suitably ambitious. 'What I wanted to build was essentially a sub £1,000 Xerox Star. It was going to have a big enough screen to be usable for real business work. The Xerox Star was ten grand... what we needed to do was build something that did what that did for a grand.' It was the sort of radical cost reduction that Sinclair had done so well at in the past, but there were other issues at hand too. The company had already been in talks with mainframe computer manufacturer ICL, the established British equivalent of IBM, over a collaboration on a business microcomputer. Yet set against this move into the professional market was the need to build on the success of the ZX81 and Spectrum. 'For Clive Sinclair the starting point was, what would be a better Spectrum that might take us in that kind of direction?' suggests Karlin, considering the situation over 30 years later. 'I think it's fair to say that in everything that followed, those two viewpoints were never actually reconciled. However, a sort of uneasy marriage of the two resulted in the QL.' In many ways the QL, as the ZX83 became, or Quantum Leap to give it its full name, seems a compromise between developing a true business computer and making a more powerful machine for the upmarket home computer user. 'All of the ingredients of my £1,000 Xerox Star were going to be in there,' explains Karlin. 'And a colour display, which I wasn't that bothered about, but a Spectrum successor games machine had to have colour.'

On the innovative and professional front, the QL had an 85-column screen for effective word processing, a 256 colour palette and fast, high-resolution, bit-mapped graphics far beyond those seen on most micros before. Rather than the unique user port of the Spectrum, the QL had serial ports to connect directly to standard peripherals. It also offered built-in local networking, available as an upgrade on the Spectrum, but once again the Xerox Star workstation was an inspiration too: 'There were all these workstations that were networked to each other and we looked at all these cool things we could do with them, and thought how fantastic it was. So that was totally obvious to me that it was something you should have,' recalls Karlin. There was innovation with the software too: built-in office applications developed by software house Psion; the new Super BASIC, offering the structured programming features that professional and education users favoured; and a sophisticated operating system named QDOS, developed by experienced software engineer Tony Tebby. QDOS offered an early windowed working environment and pre-emptive multitasking, the novel ability to have more than one program running at once, with the computer dividing processor time between the different tasks.

On the home and economy side, rather than use disc drives, the project had relied on a pair of built-in Microdrive high-speed tape recorders, slower than conventional floppy discs but readily available. At the heart of the machine was a new 32-bit processor, the first to appear in a home computer. The Motorola 68008 offered far more capability than the old Z80, but this too was a cost-driven compromise. The 68008 was the lower performance, budget version of the Motorola 68000. The 68008 was a 32-bit processor but with a narrower 8-bit data bus that took longer to transfer data to and from memory. To cater for games users there was a pair of joystick controller ports, and for the home user a television adaptor was added. 'I'd designed everything to have a dedicated display,' recalls Karlin. 'That got dropped and there was a reinstatement that it had be usable with a domestic telly as an option, and to be honest the QL's telly interface was bolted on at the end and wasn't very good.' Rather than go to the expense of a typewriter keyboard, the QL was instead fitted with a new evolution of the membrane, but with sculpted plastic keys offering a much-improved typing experience compared to the dead flesh buttons of the Spectrum. 'It had to have a proper keyboard,' recalls Karlin, 'but the keyboard had to be at a Spectrum-type cost.' The whole thing was wrapped up in an elegant case designed by Rick Dickinson.

Taken as an overall package, the QL was probably the most advanced home computer to date. Aside from the obvious economies, it really did offer a leap in capability over the Spectrum, Commodore 64 and even BBC Micro. Compared to existing professional machines, the QL was an advanced package of features at a surprisingly low cost. It was far slicker than the IBM PC, offering capabilities more like those found in Apple's revolutionary Macintosh, launched not long after it, but at a fraction of the price of either, just £399. Making the point abundantly clear, the QL's television advertising featured Sir Clive Sinclair taking a running jump over a row of more expensive competitors. Despite a few grumbles over the keyboard and the Microdrives, the general reaction after the QL launched in January 1984 was that it was an innovative, professional-looking machine which would probably shake up the market just as its predecessors had.Yet despite the advertising claiming that the machines would be shipped within 28 working days, there was one rather major problem: the QL was not actually finished. 'Six months later and six months better would have been a wonderful thing, I believe,' sighs David Karlin. 'Instead what we had were six months of pain.'

The technical details of what went wrong with the QL have been forensically examined elsewhere.[4] Suffice to say that what followed the launch was a difficult period when the development team did their best to get the troubled machine working and into production. 'When the machine came into manufacturing, all kinds of horrible stuff had to be done to make it just about work, and fairly heroic engineering efforts were made,' recalls David Karlin, 'but it really did only just work, and lots of them didn't quite work.'The biggest problem, according to Karlin, was in reliably transferring data between the Microdrives and the computer. However, there were also problems when software was late and buggy, and complications when a second processor replaced the planned purpose-designed ULA for controlling keyboard, sound and serial.

Overwhelmed by demand for its earlier products, the company was no stranger to criticism over delivery dates, but the QL took it to new levels. Sinclair took a beating in the press for the delays and for cashing mail-order customers' cheques when the machines were far from delivery. In April, QLs began to be shipped to customers, but with a curious addition sticking out of the back. 'We have a lump of firmware that is simply impossible to get onto the size chip that we can use on the board.What do we do?' recalls David Karlin. As an interim solution to get machines to customers while the designers completed a redesign, QLs were shipped with a kludge containing the missing firmware sticking out of one of the expansion ports, to much derision in the computer press.

The saga was damaging to the company's reputation and finances, and the QL delays became something of a cruel in-joke in the pages of magazines. One suggested that there was in fact just one QL doing the rounds, returned to Sinclair when it failed, then dispatched to a different customer to repeat the cycle. By July, kludge-less QLs were being shipped in volume to customers, but the machine's fortunes had been dealt a blow it would never recover from. 'I'm very sad at what might have been,' muses David Karlin. 'There was a slot in the computing world that was eventually claimed by Apple with the Mac. I think we had a really good shot at it, and we came two inches away from actually getting there... I think we did some fantastic work, but we clearly did a couple of things spectacularly wrong, and what's annoying is that the difficult stuff, the stuff that was really innovative and groundbreaking, we actually did really well in a way I don't think was bettered, not by Apple, not by anybody, for a good long time afterwards'.

Other companies slipped in their jump from home computer to business machine too. At about the same time as Sinclair was trying the QL, Commodore misjudged the market completely with a new, professional-styled computer, the Plus/4. While the QL had at least tried to advance technology, the Plus/4 was a backwards step, inferior in most respects to the older Commodore 64, yet more expensive and incompatible with the wealth of software that kept the C64 so popular. At the time Commodore was joining the race to the bottom in the home computer market with a new line of cheap, low-specification machines intended to undercut competitors: the lacklustre C16 and the rubber-keyed C116, intended as Commodore's answer to Sinclair. Commodore management then tried to turn them into business computers, by adding memory, built-in applications and a few other features to create the Plus/4. Derided in the press as the Minus/40, by 1985 £300 Plus/4s were being dumped at £49.95 at Dixons, only £10 more than the almost as unsuccessful C16.* The move from home micro to professional personal computer was not an easy one.† User expectations were higher, more capability was important and the abandonment of a trusted brand with a large software base was a difficult commercial decision.

There have been various explanations given for why the QL was launched prematurely: to fit into expensive, pre-booked advertising slots; to give Sinclair a financial boost before a planned stock-market floatation; or to beat the Apple Macintosh to market, which it did by 12 days. The Apple Mac was inspired by the same Xerox workstations that had influenced the QL, but with a $2,495 price tag and few of the same design economies, it was an unqualified success, a textbook exercise in style, marketing and innovation. The Mac's designers built the computer and floppy disc drive into the same simple, yet stylish box as the screen. With the disc slot positioned to give the compact computer a cheeky smile, they created a design classic. Underlying the style was a host of innovations: a powerful Motorola 68000 processor, the full version of the cut-down chip in the QL; a new 3½-inch floppy disc drive, far more compact than the older 5¾-inch discs; and most prominently a computer mouse driving a graphical user interface (GUI), the first on an affordable personal computer. So novel was a GUI to most people that reviewers had to explain the whole idea of what a computer desktop with its icons and windows was, and how you could click on things with a mouse pointer to make

*Yet again, while they may have been failures in Britain and the USA, Commodore's cheap machines would find some success in less-developed markets. The C16 was popular in Mexico and the Plus/4 in the Eastern Bloc.
†In 1985, Commodore launched the Commodore 128, a much-improved and largely compatible successor to the 64. Although the C128 faired better than the Plus/4, it was not the same success as the C64.

things happen, rather than having to type confusing commands. Not only was the GUI incredibly user-friendly, but it looked great too, just like everything else about the Mac.

It was a radically new concept for what a personal computer was, backed by a slick marketing campaign that cemented Apple's place as the computer company that did something different. Most famously, a 1984 Super Bowl advert, directed by Ridley Scott of *Blade Runner* fame, and costing around $500,000 to film, made headlines around the world. With the promise that Apple's 1984 wouldn't be like Orwell's *Nineteen Eighty-Four*, a colourfully dressed female athlete raced the thought police through a grey Orwellian world to smash Big Brother, a clear allusion to IBM, with a sledgehammer. Great successes have a way of overshadowing failures; Apple had tried to make a similar machine in 1983, the Lisa, which at a very expensive $9,995 had far less impact. However, with the Mac they scored a terrific success and created a revolutionary product that pointed to the way personal computers would develop in future.

In Britain, where the Mac was initially priced at around £1,975, it was simply too expensive to have quite the same impact as it did in the US, outside the circle of media and creative types who took to it with enthusiasm. There was a clear gap in the British market for something cheaper yet similarly innovative and professional, but with the failure of the QL it would be some time before it was filled. In the meantime, the 1984 break through computer in Britain would not be the Sinclair QL or the Apple Macintosh, but a machine from a new contender in the computer market, the Amstrad CPC464.

The Amstrad

The most remarkable thing about the CPC464 was not just that it offered a fresh concept, but that it was a success despite the odds stacked against any new contender in the computer market in 1984. Amstrad's founder was not one of the techie-turned-entrepreneur figures who had hitherto dominated British computing. Alan Sugar was a straight-talking salesman

from the East End of London, with a gruff persona and a
bottom line of giving customers what they wanted. Starting
out small, trading stereos from the back of a van, Sugar built up
Amstrad (a contraction of *Alan M Sugar Trad*ing) into a major
supplier of consumer electronics to the high-street chains.
Critics accused Amstrad's products of being cheap and cheerful,
but they were decent performers, and good value for money.
Car stereos, CB radios, hi-fi, video, televisions – Amstrad
successfully tried its hand wherever it might turn a profit, but
never at computers, at least until a Brentwood electronics
consultancy named Ambit received a visit from one of its
neighbours.

'Amstrad turned up in the autumn of '83, I suppose,' recalls
Ambit's Roland Perry, 'saying, "This is all very hush hush, but
we, Amstrad, want to enter the home computer market."'
Amstrad had something approaching a prototype to show, but
computer development had turned out to be a bit more
complicated than first envisaged. 'They said, "We've got this
couple of lads who said they're going to design the board for
inside it. They seem to be having a bit of trouble."' Amstrad's
computer was half finished. There was a case, but no working
computer to fill it with. 'The whole thing was finished down to
the hole you had to screw the top and bottom together,
everything. They said, "Can you just fit us a board in here?…
We need it in a couple of weeks, please."' An experienced
Cambridge-educated electronics engineer with a long
involvement with microelectronics, Perry explained that it took
around a year to develop such a machine from scratch. 'And
they said, 'Well, I'm sorry – you've only got three months.''

Perry began assembling a team to finish the machine. The
project was top secret at the time and the Amstrad logo had to
be taped over on the prototypes. Perry replaced it with the
code name 'Arnold', coincidentally an anagram of his own
name. The name also added to the subterfuge by hinting that
Ambit's mysterious client might be Arnold Weinstock, the
industrialist behind heavyweight electronics firm GEC. 'I
hawked this around my chums,' recalls Perry, 'and said we need

to fill this gap in here, and after a couple of weeks I put together a team of people who were foolish enough. They'd worked together on things before and some of them were hardware experts and some were software experts.' It was a hurried start to a time-pressured project, but Perry managed to recruit a set of small companies that could do it, notably MEJ Electronics and Locomotive Software. Typical of the pragmatism that sped the development, the original plan to use a 6502 processor was quickly dropped for a Z80, simply because Locomotive had recent experience creating a Z80 BASIC. A more technophilic company might have agonised over the choice, but Amstrad went with something that would work quickly.

Amstrad was a company driven more by the vision of a product than by introspective debate over its technical details. Perhaps unsurprisingly, one thing it did have ready was the case to put the computer in, which was central to the whole concept. Everyone else was selling a home computer that plugged into a television and a cassette recorder. Often, the bits did not work together at first, and at least some apparently faulty computers had nothing wrong with them apart from being incompatible with the television and cassette deck they were connected to. Amstrad's plan was to bundle the whole lot together: a keyboard computer with built-in cassette recorder, and monitor bundled in as well. 'We thought: it's big, and it's a bit ugly,' recalls Perry of first seeing the prototype. 'What we were really impressed about was that they'd got the injection moulding done. They'd got the keyboard done and everything was there. This was the whole thing. You didn't have to buy bits separately and plug it in.' It was another little step in user-friendliness, but had advantages all around. Building and selling a complete package avoided compatibility problems, meaning fewer faulty returns for retailers, and it had the unique selling point of not tying up the family television with a computer.

Amstrad had prior form at this sort of boxing up. In the 1970s it was common to build a home stereo from a separate radio tuner, tape deck, turntable, amplifier and speakers.

Amstrad pioneered the tower stereo, an all-in-one unit with everything built in, manufactured cheaply and sold at an attractive price. The CPC applied the same concept to the home computer. The old Commodore PET had done similar, but cheap micros had moved away from the all-in-one to cut costs. Amstrad had a genius in finding other ways to keep its costs down, not just by keeping the number of components down, but by sourcing parts and building products wherever they were cheapest, often in the Far East. Amstrad's complete computer was startlingly good value: £329 with a colour display, or £229 with a business-like green on black screen. There was much truth in Amstrad's advertising boasts of 'a complete workstation for the price of a home computer'. 'Workstation' just sounded so much more professional than microcomputer too.

The professional look was the other attraction of the all-in-one bundle. Dismissing Sinclair's machines as 'pregnant calculators', Sugar decided that his machine would be a home computer that looked like the sort of computer customers were used to seeing at an airport check-in desk. With its big case and screen, the CPC looked more like a 'real' computer than anything else in its price range. As the bottom dropped out of the cheap computer market, it was just the sort of package that would appeal to buyers looking for a more serious computer. However, Amstrad was careful to stress it could do games just as well. One advert, featuring a middle-aged man in a suit and baseball cap playing a racing game, reminded readers that the CPC could do business as well as '180 miles per hour'. The message was simple and effective – this was a genuinely general-purpose machine that was both fun *and* serious.

A new product in a mature market

The CPC was carefully designed to a price point. The colour monitor actually used a normal television tube, rather than the more expensive components of a higher definition professional monitor, but it still looked good. There were surprisingly few components laid out on the neat computer-designed motherboard, key to keeping the cost down. 'It became quite obvious to us that you needed to put as much of the electronics as possible inside one chip in a gate array,' recalls Perry. The trick, once again, was to use a ULA to do the job of dozens of other components. 'It was all terribly symbiotic; gate arrays are cheaper than lots of TTL, and you also can't copy them. We were very worried about people producing clones.' Not for the first time in the story of the British home computer, the curse of the Ferranti ULA struck. The design team visited Ferranti's factory in Manchester to check the first chips off the production line. 'We plugged it in to see if it worked, and it didn't! Damn damn damn!' recalls Perry. 'The main thing that was wrong with it was that the on-board crystal oscillator wouldn't oscillate.' Amstrad found a second supplier in Italy rather than waiting for the problems to be fixed. Time was money.

Established machines were supported by large back catalogues of software, against which new rivals struggled to compete. Instead of just hoping a CPC software scene would develop, Amstrad created one itself. About 50 prototype computers were hand assembled, with the logic that everything that the ULA was supposed to do was covered by built-in TTL chips in a Gate Array Simulator board. 'GAS boards. We had a sense of humour in those days,' laughs Perry. The GAS board machines were dispatched in great secrecy to software houses to build a stockpile of games and applications before the machine was even launched. When the CPC came out there were nearly 50 software titles available. To further support the machine, Amstrad was soon selling disc drives and printers, started a user club and published a magazine, *CPC464 User*. Alan Sugar's contacts with big-name retailers like Dixons, meant Amstrad could get the CPC straight onto the shelves across the country. The pieces were all in place to help the CPC become a major success.

There had been little precedent to guide the earlier computer companies. They were all pioneers in a new market where customer expectations had not yet formed. Amstrad was different. They learned from what went before and made a shrewd assessment of what customers wanted. On most home computers the cursor keys did not do anything until something was typed out on the screen to move the cursor around it. On Alan Sugar's computer they moved the cursor around the screen whether there was anything there or not, so a novice user playing with it in a shop wouldn't be disappointed by it not doing anything.* As the market-leading Commodore 64 offered 64k of memory, it was no coincidence that the CPC464 did too. Computer journalist Guy Kewney was even recruited to confidentially review the machine for Amstrad before it came out. 'Who do I make machines for?' muses Roland Perry, 'I used to make machines for magazine reviewers: it's not as strange as it sounds, because I made them for somebody who was reasonably skilled and adept at the machines... Something that passes that test will therefore almost automatically be good for your average family man who wants to buy a computer for the family.'

The CPC was a product well matched to a maturing home computer market, the right concept at the right time: a serious looking computer, good value with its bundled cassette recorder and monitor, and with plenty of software on offer. When it was released, on time, in June 1984, the CPC was a massive success. Journalists praised the machine as excellent value for money. Two hundred thousand CPC464s were sold that year,[5] many during the Christmas rush, at about the same time as a certain disagreement in a Cambridge pub, and as other manufacturers saw their sales crash. Always game for publicity, Amstrad promptly announced a new game, *This Business Is War*, featuring likenesses of Chris Curry and Sir Clive Sinclair throwing computers at each other, although it does not seem to have been released.

---

*Sugar's influence showed up in the manual too, which included a programming exercise on salaries, with such outputs as 'ASK FOR A PAY RISE' and 'ASK FOR A BIGGER CAR'.

1985 brought improved versions of the CPC with a built-in disc drive. In what was probably an economy measure, Amstrad adopted the otherwise obscure 3-inch disc drive. Little used by other companies, it became something of an Amstrad signature. More important was the release of another Alan Sugar concept, the PCW8256 word processor. For just £460,* the PCW was an all-in-one computer, 3-inch disc drive and green screen monitor, sold with a keyboard, printer and word-processing software. It was a neat and professional-looking product, an appliance for word processing, a machine explicitly sold as an application rather than as a computer. That it was also capable of running BASIC, games and other software were just bonuses to its primary purpose. However, with financial programs and other applications, the PCW eventually found some favour as a more general-purpose office machine too. Television adverts featuring a dumper truck of typewriters being unceremoniously tipped into a scrapyard made the primary point of the PCW abundantly clear. The PCW series were machines for people who wanted to type, not people who wanted to compute. Within eight months of launch Amstrad sold 350,000 of them.

For all their success as consumer products, as computers the CPC and PCW series were far from bleeding-edge technology. A *Personal Computer News* reviewer reckoned the CPC464 to be a very nice machine but 'rather old fashioned'. The Z80 CPU at the heart of Amstrad's machine had already been used in home computers going back to the old TRS-80 and NASCOM of 1977, but it did little to dampen appeal for the machines among those they were aimed at. Alan Sugar would later observe that his computers could be powered by a rubber band for all their buyers cared about the processor within them. The technology in itself was less important to

---

*Most sources list the price of the PCW as £399. However, while Amstrad's advertising of the PCW stressed the price prominently as £399, this was without Valued Added Tax (VAT) at 15 per cent, which was noted in rather smaller letters on adverts.

Amstrad's success than its clever application in well-priced and well-marketed consumer products.

Amstrad's rising fortunes stood in stark contrast to the struggles of other microcomputer makers at the time, perhaps most pertinently Sinclair, by now much concerned with non-computer projects. On a snowy day in January 1985, the long-awaited Sinclair C5 electric vehicle was revealed to a cynical press reaction. Just like the ZX80, the C5 was small and made of white plastic, but the minimalist personal vehicle shared none of the good fortune of the minimalist personal computer. A £399.99 battery-powered tricycle in a streamlined plastic shell, the C5 was capable of 18 miles per hour and could cover five miles on a penny's worth of electricity. Unfortunately, it looked terrifyingly vulnerable next to a heavy goods vehicle in traffic, and became an endless source of fun for newspaper cartoonists. It did not help the press reaction that it was manufactured by Hoover and was scurrilously rumoured to be powered by a washing machine motor. C5 production ended in August 1985, the affair having dented Sinclair's credibility and finances even more than the QL. It would be another 16 years before the success of the American Segway suggested that maybe there was something in the idea of an electric personal transporter after all.

Between overdraft and other debts, Sinclair owed a reported £25 million by mid-1985, a time when the press was filled with stories that newspaper baron Robert Maxwell was about to step in to save the company from financial disaster. Ultimately it came to nothing, and Sinclair bought time by offloading 160,000 pocket televisions and computers to Dixons for the bargain price of £10 million. Seeking to refresh the Spectrum, Sinclair had released the Spectrum+ in 1984, but the machine was a stopgap with few improvements beyond a QL-style keyboard, and met an underwhelmed reaction: 'no one in their right mind is going to buy the Spectrum+ if they already own a Spectrum', wrote Chris Bourne in *Sinclair User*'s review. The new machine also suffered from high failure rates, reputedly as high as 30 per cent, adding to Sinclair's financial problems. January 1986 brought the new Spectrum 128, a more comprehensive upgrade, with more memory, better sound and a host of other improvements. However, the big news came in April 1986 with the shock announcement that Clive Sinclair had sold his computer business for £5 million to Alan Sugar. That the deal was suggested to Sugar by Dixons said much about how the home computer business had changed to something far more retail influenced than driven by technology companies. For Alan Sugar it was a decisive way of expanding his 20 per cent stake in the home computer market into a decisive a 60 per cent majority.[6] Amstrad abandoned the QL,[*] not to mention a range of secret projects Sinclair had in the works, such as the Loki super-home computer and the Pandora portable, and went on to apply the Amstrad touch to the Spectrum. The Spectrum+2, sketched out by Amstrad before the buyout was complete, featured a built-in cassette player, joystick ports and typewriter-style keyboard, and finally optimised the machine into the games player that users had come to regarded it as. For Clive Sinclair, as he made clear in an interview with *Sinclair User*, it was a chance to escape a business that had become run of the mill, and go back to pioneering something new.[†] It was the end of an era. The Cambridge inventor had been replaced by the Brentwood businessman as the face of the British computer industry, and all had not been going well at Acorn either…

---

[*] The unfortunate QL would have a surprising legacy after one of the machines somehow got into the hands of a Finnish teenager named Linus Torvalds who learned to program with it, not least because there was so little software available. A few years later Torvalds, albeit working on a PC, developed the Linux kernel at the heart of Linux operating systems.

[†] Sir Clive Sinclair was back in 1987 with the Cambridge Computer Z88, an innovative portable computer. However, the market had moved on by this point, and while technically successful it was far from the commercial success of Sinclair's earlier machines.

The advantages of no people and no money

After the share price collapse, Acorn's finances were in a poor state by early 1985. The company escaped the receivers thanks to two multimillion-pound rescue packages negotiated with computer and office equipment giant Olivetti, which effectively turned Acorn into a subsidiary of the Italian firm. Olivetti bought rather more than it had bargained for when it saved Acorn. Aside from a few vague rumours in the press of an advanced new machine, and upgrades of the BBC Micro, Acorn had not released a new computer since the Electron in 1983. Behind the scenes the company had actually been rather busy working in secret on something called the Acorn RISC Machine – ARM, a completely new type of microprocessor. 'It was in the middle of the ARM development where Acorn's finances went through the floor, so that was fairly traumatic,' recalls Steve Furber. 'Olivetti had effectively committed to the rescue without really knowing about the ARM project at all. So we kind of treated it as sufficiently secret that we didn't even let people who were trying to invest money to rescue us know much about it.'

Around 1983, Acorn had been working on second processor expansions for the BBC Micro and considering what might succeed 8-bit processors in its next computers. Always technically focused, it was rather unimpressed by the performance of the new 16-bit processors available, particularly their slow interface with memory chips, and thoughts turned to why someone could not design a better processor. Or why could *they* not design a better processor themselves? 'We were toying with this idea,' recalls Steve Furber. 'The commercial microprocessors that we could buy… we don't like them, you know, so should we design our own?' Although Acorn had designed ULAs, microprocessor design was considered something of a black art requiring serious investment and resources. 'We started thinking that maybe we would have to design our own and this was clearly a ludicrous thing to think,' remembers Sophie Wilson. 'We went off to Israel to visit

National Semiconductor, and it was what you might expect, a big building full of engineers working away. And they weren't being that successful building the 32016.'* But they then took a trip to Arizona to visit microprocessor developers the Western Design Centre, which was working on a successor to the 6502 microprocessor. Instead of an expansive facility, they found themselves in a suburban bungalow staffed by a mix of engineers and students. 'They'd got some big machines, but basically it wasn't the shiny office block; it was quite a sort of cottage industry-type of design centre,' recalls Furber. 'We very definitely came away from that visit… with the idea that if they can design a microprocessor maybe we can.'

It was still an ambitious undertaking, but thanks to their university connections, a rather different type of processor came to mind than anything used in a home computer before. 'Andy Hopper dumped on my desk at work the first technical papers on RISC,' remembers Sophie Wilson. Over in the US IBM and postgraduate classes at Stanford and Berkeley universities had just published projects on designing RISC processors. 'That was interesting, because these were much simpler, even than the 6502… The Stanford team and the Berkeley team were small, so maybe we could do this.' The RISC philosophy was based on the observation that microprocessors with complex instruction sets, where a single instruction might execute a series of operations, were actually rather inefficient in practice. The key to a RISC processor was to use simpler instructions, Reduced Instruction Set Computing, and use the space saved on the chip to build in ways of executing them more efficiently, most importantly pipelining. Put simply, a processor typically works by fetching an instruction, decoding it into a form it can understand, then executing it. However, it only moves on to the next instruction when the first instruction is complete. Pipelining fed in new instructions continuously. As the first instruction is

*The 32016 was part of Motorola's new series of 32-bit microprocessors.

executed at the end of the cycle, a second was being decoded, at the same time as a third was being fetched. Pipelining was the difference between hand crafting and assembly line, a way of using the processor more efficiently, with consequent overall improvements in performance.

A RISC processor could be both simpler and more efficient than existing complex instruction set (CISC) designs, and the whole idea rather appealed to Furber, Wilson and, importantly, director Hermann Hauser. 'I did instruction design Tetris in my head for a long time and Hermann joined in the conversations,' recalls Wilson. 'This was one of the unique things about Acorn. The guy in charge was technically interested in everything and involved in everything.' As ARM was gestating, Acorn's fortunes declined alarmingly. Hauser's support for the new development was fortunate, and the research and development group escaped the redundancies hitting the rest of the company. 'Hermann had a lot of confidence in the group and its ability to generate ideas,' adds Steve Furber. 'We were in a quite well-protected environment.'

ARM1 took shape from 1983 to 1985, developed by a small team lead by Wilson working on the instruction set, and Furber on the architecture. It was a tall order for a small company, but they were a skilled team, and used to working closely together and clearly enthused by the task. 'Very exciting, designing our own processor having never tried it before,' remarks Furber. The inherent simplicity of the RISC concept was an undoubted strength too. 'Hermann's proud statement is that he gave us these two clear advantages: the first one was no money and the second one was no people,' chuckles Furber. 'The pressure to keep the ARM simple was very strong. If we'd allowed the complexity to grow at all then our chances of completion would have diminished very rapidly.' Wilson puts it even more bluntly: 'We had to design a simple, small processor because it was the only thing we were capable of designing.' To date RISC had largely been of pure academic interest and compromises had to be made to turn its academic concepts into a commercial product. As Wilson sums it up: 'Our slogan was simply MIPS for the masses. Millions of instructions per second for the mass audience. A processor that was cheap and high performance.'

On 26 April 1985, the first ARM chip prototype arrived at Acorn from chip fabricator VLSI Technology and was soon working. Later, Steve Furber rang a reporter to announce that they had developed their own new processor. 'This reporter simply refused to believe me,' laughs Furber. 'So it came as a bit of a surprise to everybody, not just us, when this processor worked.' Not only did it work, but it was fast and efficient. According to Furber, the ARM1 outperformed the contemporary Motorola 68020 despite being made of a tenth of the numbers of transistors.* ARM also had the seemingly supernatural ability to work without power. 'I set up the chip with an ammeter in the power-supply circuit, switched it on, started it running programs, looked at the ammeter and the ammeter was reading zero, which wasn't quite what I expected,' recalls Steve Furber. 'I discovered I hadn't actually connected the power to the chip, yet it was sitting there running programs.' It turned out that the chip was drawing power from the various components it was connected to. This low-energy consumption, far lower than they had expected, would prove to be enormously important in the future, but the original intent was simply to develop a processor for Acorn's new breed of computers.

After initially using ARM as another Tube second processor for the BBC Micro, Acorn released its new range of ARM-powered computers, the Acorn Archimedes, in 1987. At £799 for the basic model in the series, they were premium products but wowed reviewers with their spectacular graphics and high performance. A graphical user interface operating system, initially the rather basic Arthur, but soon replaced by the superior RISC OS, made the machines particularly user-friendly. Although the machine inspired much love among enthusiasts who recognised its powerful capabilities, its main use was in schools upgrading from BBC Micros. By the time the first Archimedes models

*25,000 transistors on ARM1, 250,000 on the Motorola 68020.

came on the scene in 1987, there were already several powerful rivals entrenched in the home and business markets.

The new order

The main rivals to the Archimedes in the home computer market, the Atari ST and Commodore Amiga, inspired as much fondness and rivalry as earlier micros had, but overall they had more similarities than differences. They both offered a powerful 16-bit 68000 processor, a real keyboard, floppy discs, breath-taking graphics and sound, extensive expansion and a mouse driven GUI. In short they offered Mac-like features, but with glorious high-resolution colour graphics, while the Mac was only monochrome, and at a fraction of the price. The ST was even nicknamed the 'Jackintosh' after Atari's new head, Jack Tramiel, ousted from Commodore but once again fulfilling his maxim of making 'computers for the masses not the classes' by taking on the Mac.[*] Commodore was so proud of the Amiga's graphics that at its gala launch it got pop artist Andy Warhol to show off its artistic potential by making colourful screenprint-style pictures of Blondie singer Debbie Harry. The racy machines set the pulse racing of many a computer journalist. Guy Kewney wrote in his review of the machine for *PCW* that the £1,500 Amiga was the computer he had wanted the industry to produce for the last two years, and reckoned it far faster than a Mac at less than half the price. *PCW*'s reviewer of the ST declared that it was the first machine to excite him since the QL dashed his hopes.

---

[*]The history of the Atari ST and Commodore Amiga is confusingly entwined. After being forced out of Commodore in 1984, Jack Tramiel responded in typically bellicose style by buying the struggling Atari in 1985 and using it to declare war on his old company. Unbeknownst at the time, Atari had been funding a small start-up called Amiga Corporation to develop an advanced computer chipset. Not favouring its chances under the new regime at Atari, Amiga Corporation quietly arranged to be bought up by Commodore, leaving Jack Tramiel to order Atari to develop a new machine to take on the one it had just lost.

Like the Archimedes, the Amiga and the ST were a generation ahead of the old 8-bit machines, but their higher prices and powerful capabilities created confusion as to whether they were home computers at all. Originally an Amiga cost around £1,500 and an Atari ST £750, putting them into the professional computer price bracket. *The Advanced Home Computer Course* thought that the Amiga suffered from an identity crisis as to whether it wanted to be a serious home computer, cheap business machine, or expensive and impressively powerful games machine. 'I'm still not sure whether to classify it as a home or business machine,' was *PCW* reviewer Peter Bright's verdict on the ST. The lowering of prices by about 1987, £399 for an ST, and the release of cheaper models, notably the £499 Amiga 500, nudged the machines more into the powerful home computer category, but the confusion remained and the reasons for it are understandable enough. The 16- and 32-bit machines were so unlike the 8-bit machines that they went far beyond the original conception of what a home computer was. In capability, design, use and marketing they became something rather different.

In its classic early 1980s guise, the home computer had been a comparatively simple technology that was there to be explored and programmed to do things. There was little between a user and the raw logic of the underlying machine, and by poking around with programming users could build up a feel for what was going on inside the box. The more sophisticated technology underlying the new generation of machines was far more complex, but it did not need to be understood in the same sort of way. Thanks to slick graphical user interfaces, GEM on the Atari, RISC OS on the Archimedes and Workbench on the Amiga, the new generation was far more user-friendly. However, they cast a veil over what was actually going on, computers were now to be used rather than understood. Learning to program these machines was far less prominently stressed. No longer were users confronted by the BASIC prompt inviting them to try their hand at a bit of code as soon as they switched on the computer.

The first thing seen when an Amiga was turned on was a hand holding a floppy disc, symbolic of the change in computer use. The built-in floppy disc drives on each machine made it far quicker and more convenient to load software than it ever was on an 8-bit with a tape recorder. People *could* program any of the new machines, but the expectation was that typical users would just use them as software players.

The marketing that advertised the machines had changed too. Gone were the explicit promises that the computer was a passport to the future, the excitement of a revolution in the making and the lure of learning to program. In their place was an increasing focus on power and capability as manufacturers sought to differentiate their products from the older home micros: 'New Amiga 500. Now other home computers are just toys', proclaimed one Amiga advert. The versatility of the machines remained an important part of the pitch, but the vague advertising patter that the machines could do anything, up to and including running a power station, was superseded by specific claims about software. Buy an Archimedes for 'power to handle word processing, spreadsheets and project planning more quickly', explained one Acorn advert. Gradually, adverts and reviews started differentiating between the different breeds of microcomputer. The new machines were *personal computers*, the old ones merely *home computers.*

By about 1986, home computing in its original form had been overshadowed by something new. The next generation of home computers were not simple devices to be explored, understood and programmed for fun and entrainment, but powerful general-purpose personal computers for running software. Of course, there were still enthusiasts out there programming for themselves, but much of the excitement and the imagination had gone out of microcomputing. The computer had become an everyday tool, just something to be used. What happened to the new generation of so-called home computers that succeeded the 8-bit micros is a story for a different book, but not one with a happy ending. The new order, while reasonably successful for a time, would never have such a clear run of the market as the older machines had. The Archimedes did well in schools, and the Amiga and ST became very popular for gaming. However, in the home and in professional environments, there were powerful rivals facing the home computer of the later 1980s, most notably the IBM standard PC and a new range of Nintendo and Sega games consoles.

The tap-dancing elephant in the room

The earlier Pong machines and Atari consoles had not made much impact in Britain as it went through the growing pains of computer literacy. After the computer literacy agenda faded, leaving video gaming well established in British homes, the path to market was open for a new generation of consoles in the latter half of the 1980s. Neither the 6502-cored Nintendo Entertainment System (NES), nor the Z80-based Sega Master System offered particularly advanced technology, but they were convenient appliances for gaming, the main thing home computers were being used for anyway. Why wait ten minutes for a tape to load on your micro when you could slot a cartridge into an NES and be playing a big-brand game like *Super Mario Bros* a minute later? The Japanese home computer invasion had never really arrived, but where MSX had failed, Nintendo and Sega succeeded.

The Archimedes never grew a substantial games base, but the Amiga and Atari ST were the platforms for a golden age of innovative gaming during the later 1980s and '90s. Titles such as *Cannon Fodder, Lemmings, Carrier Command, The Pawn,* and *The Secret of Monkey Island*, exploited the new hardware in fun and impressive ways that 8-bit programmers could only dream of.* However, the European release of the Sega Mega Drive and Super NES in the early 1990s offered 16-bit consoles

---

*Although it is a testament to the skills of 8-bit programmers that they were able to make respectable, if not quite as slick, conversions of 16-bit titles for veteran machines like the ZX Spectrum and Commodore 64.

with the power to compete with 16-bit computers. In a fickle
market that thrived on novelty, the new consoles offered
something fresher and more fun than a machine with a
keyboard. The release of new hand-held consoles like the
Atari Lynx and Nintendo Game Boy added more rivals, and
all of the consoles were far cheaper than fully fledged personal
computers. By Christmas 1991, Dixons was selling Atari STs
for £299.99, but a Sega Mega Drive was only £129.99.

Things were changing in the serious sector of the personal
computer market too, largely due to the growing influence of
the IBM PC standard and the cold hand of conformity it
represented. Quite apart from the convenience offered by
standards and compatibility between different computers, the
IBM PC came to dominate the personal computer world for
two key reasons. Firstly, it was from IBM. Secondly, anybody
could make one. For decades, IBM had dominated the
mainframe computer business through firm management, a
well-respected brand and carefully planned technological
advances. Other than a brief experiment in making $10,000
portables in the early 1970s, IBM was slow to move into
personal computers. IBM was the computing establishment
and had little to gain from starting a revolution. Microcomputers
were mere toys in comparison to its data-processing machinery,
and the sober-suited IBM man was part of a different world
from that of the hippies, enthusiasts, inventors and entrepreneurs
who had spawned the microcomputer. Apocryphally, one
analyst likened IBM developing a personal computer to an
elephant learning tap dancing. Despite this, it was a matter of
faith among other industry pundits that at some point IBM
would enter the personal computer market, and that when it
did, its impact would be significant.

The IBM PC was announced in August 1981 to much
excitement from journalists and computing professionals.
IBM's advertising campaign showed the PC helping silent
movie star Charlie Chaplin advance to modern times, yet it
could have been a metaphor for how the PC pulled IBM into
the microcomputer era; Apple even published a sarcastic advert

welcoming IBM to the personal computer market. However, there was little especially modern about IBM's $1,565 PC. It was largely a solid application of existing technologies rather than anything particularly innovative. Faced with a 12-month deadline, the PC-development team broke from the normal IBM way of doing things. Rather than rely on in-house IBM technology and expertise, they subcontracted development work and bought off-the-shelf technologies from outside, such as the Intel 8088 processor. The DOS operating system was licensed from Microsoft in a deal that would make its founder Bill Gates, a billionaire. Hoping to spur the development of software and hardware peripherals, IBM gave the PC an open architecture, meaning that others could easily produce things to run on it.

With this background, IBM did not own the PC. With enough lawyers, engineers, a few licence payments and a bit of reverse engineering, companies could start manufacturing legitimate 'IBM PC compatibles' or 'clones'. Already the Apple II, ZX Spectrum, Tandy TRS80 and other machines had been copied around the world, legally or otherwise. With the PC, IBM gave the world an open computer architecture to adopt, backed by its prestige. In the mainframe computer days it was said that no one got fired for buying IBM. Compared with the risks of devising a new design of computer and worrying about getting people to write software for it, a PC clone would be guaranteed support and a market. All over the world companies began producing PC compatibles – Eagle, Compaq, Columbia, Hyperion and many others besides. People could even build one themselves at home if they bought all the parts.

IBM's entry into the market is often explained as the moment when the personal computer became respectable, as the established giant of corporate computing gave its stamp of approval to this upstart new technology. Yet the launch of the IBM PC made barely a ripple in the British home computer market. When it was launched in Britain in 1982, there was a certain excitement among journalists and industry pundits, but there was far wider interest in the new ZX Spectrum and

BBC Micro. The PC was explicitly a business machine, lacked the excitement of games or the worthiness of education, and was far too expensive. Yet as the dozens of idiosyncratic machines battled it out for a share of the cheap home computer market over the early 1980s, IBM's PC architecture gained ground in the professional computing sphere, and the appearance of cheaper IBM clones made the machines more affordable.

By the time the new generation of more expensive home computers tried to stake a claim as 'real' computers in the mid-1980s, the PC was well established in that position. The ease of use and technical superiority of the new machines mattered little in a market increasingly adopting the PC standard. 'Although the Archimedes was clearly vastly superior to a PC in every important performance aspect, it struggled in the market because the market had become very PC focused,' explains Steve Furber. 'A machine with the Archimedes' capabilities, so far ahead of the competition at the time, in a different environment, would have done a lot better.' Much the same could be said of the Amiga and the Atari ST, which were probably undermined by their gloriously rich games and user friendliness. As the *Guardian*'s computer correspondent Jack Schofield noted of the Amiga, for many people 'anything easy or attractive cannot be serious computing'.[7] By contrast, slow graphics and basic sound made the PC a disappointing entertainment platform. The text-based DOS operating system, used by most PC users until the widespread uptake of Windows 3.1 in the 1990s, was hopelessly old fashioned and complicated compared to a GUI. Yet in its boringness the PC was indisputably a serious computer. The growing prominence of the PC meant the very idea of a unique computer with its own idiosyncratic design, propriety operating system, individually crafted software and disregard for standards came under existential threat.

At the time rumours surfaced that familiar names of the British home computer industry were going to make PC clones, but few did. For some, financial troubles stymied plans to make clones. 'The galling thing was we'd already started the development of a PC clone, before Compaq,' recalls Oric's Paul Johnson. 'We'd designed a PC clone that we could build for £200.' With stereo sound and superior graphics to the IBM original, and a highly integrated chip set (now referred to as core logic) to save costs, it could have been a breakthrough product. Yet it was thwarted by Oric's financial difficulties and a lack of funding to bring it to fruition. 'This was so much cheaper than anything anybody else had come up with and we'd actually got a chip set for doing this,' sighs Johnson. 'Oric could have been something really, really big.'

For other firms the issue was perhaps more philosophical. What is a standard but a generally agreed way of doing things? This was not what the most important British computer companies had been about. Whether it was Acorn taking inspiration from cutting edge university research, or Sinclair with its inventive minimalism, they were innovative companies whose thinking was not conducive to simply following what others did. On the terms of many British computer designers, IBM had not done anything special. 'When I use a PC today I cannot understand why a machine with 1,000 times more processing power has a worse user response than the machine I was using in the late '80s at Acorn,' remarks Steve Furber. 'Well, I do know why it is, but it still seems the wrong answer.'

IBM turned making personal computers into a commodities business more than the innovation game it had been for many firms before. Perhaps unsurprisingly, the British computer company that took most enthusiastically to the PC clone was the businesslike Amstrad. IBM's original PC was an over-engineered Rolls-Royce of a computer. Amstrad took the lessons it had learned from making low-cost home computers and applied them to the PC. The basic model of Amstrad's 1986 PC clone, the PC1512, was just £460 (with VAT), putting the PC into the home computer price bracket for the first time. Price apart, it would take some years, the adoption of the more user-friendly Windows operating system and better entertainment provision to turn the boring PC into an appealing domestic appliance, but gradually the PC forced its way into the home. Squeezed between the PC and the new generation of games consoles, Amiga, Archimedes and ST production ended in the mid-1990s.* The advanced machines barely outlived the 8-bit home computers they were supposed to replace.

A failed technology?

The 8-bit home computers that survived the fallout of the mid-1980s crash were fated to enjoy a few more years of active semi-retirement. After equipping themselves with various models of BBC Micro and Master, along with software and educational resources around them, schools were in no hurry to replace the sturdy machines. The Beeb would remain a familiar sight in British schools into the late 1990s, if not beyond. Indeed, Acorn only stopped making Masters in about 1993. The ZX Spectrum+2 (as built by Amstrad), Commodore 64 and Amstrad CPC 464 all lasted in production as cheap games computers into the early 1990s, supported by a vast back catalogue of games and a continuing trickle of new titles. Surprisingly, it was thought worth revamping the old machines by creating new versions, such as the disc-drive equipped Spectrum+3, Commodore 64GS games console and improved Amstrad CPC464 Plus, albeit to limited commercial success. By the time official ZX Spectrum production ended in 1992, the basic design was a decade old. It says much about its versatility, the importance of its software base and its place in popular culture that the Speccy lasted so long; indeed, souped-up Spectrum descendants were still being made in Eastern Europe for some years after its official end of production.

---

*After the Archimedes, Acorn developed a further line of ARM-powered professional computers, the powerful RISC PC, which lasted in production, despite the relatively limited interest in the machine, until 2003.

The ultimate disappearance of the cheap home computer as a distinct type of computer makes it tempting to write off the whole idea as a failure. The model of computing the home micro originally espoused was overshadowed by the mid-1980s by general-purpose personal computing; most of the companies that made home computers pulled out of the market or went out of business; and the dominant IBM PC architecture owes little to the world of home computers. A more upbeat interpretation would be that the home computer was a remarkable success, when we view it as a stepping stone in computer technology, and on its original terms of reference as a passport to the future.

In 1980 the computer was a mysterious technology to most people, shrouded by misconceptions and widely misunderstood. The original idea of the home computer had been to change that, to make computing accessible to the general public, fuelled by an expectation that it was going to be important. No one really knew what was going to happen next. In retrospect, the whole computer boom could have been a giant experiment to see what happened when millions of people were handed a computer and told *how* to use it, but less *what* to use it for. The computers that started the boom were blank slates, massively flexible machines waiting for someone to find a use for them. Over the early 1980s the home computer introduced millions of people to the idea of what computing was, spawned countless new uses for the machines, and gave birth to a software industry so people did not have to program for themselves. That few wanted an introductory computer after a few years was not a mark of failure, but of success. The familiarity bred by the home computer paved the way for all the other information technologies that have transformed our lives over the subsequent years.

Today the computer, in whatever form, is a boringly everyday technology. We have grown used to machines that can conjure virtual universes on our desktops, send messages around the world in moments and put unquantifiable amounts of information at our fingertips. We take for granted incredible technologies that were almost beyond the imagination of science fiction a few decades ago. The greatest legacy of the 1980s home computer boom is a world where computers no longer fill people with awe or trepidation, but one where we just accept these machines and the incredible things they do as perfectly normal. We live in a world where people stopped worrying, learned to love computers, got bored with them, then moved on to exploit information technology throughout their lives without thinking about it as special or particularly intimidating. The greatest lasting legacy of the home computer boom is the digital world we live in now, but the aftershocks are still with us…

Epilogue: Back to the Future?

Last Christmas my parents bought me a computer. They have prior form at this sort of thing. Back in the 1980s they gave my eight-year-old self a Commodore 64 (mainly wasted on playing games), then spoiled me with an Acorn Archimedes in the '90s (it actually did help with the homework, but the games were better on friends' Amigas). For Christmas 2014, I unwrapped a Raspberry Pi, the £25 computer touted in the media as the heir to the BBC Micro, ZX Spectrum and other early 1980s micros. A simple little machine developed in Cambridge, just like its 8-bit predecessors, the Pi is a credit card-sized computer intended to make programming and learning about computers easy and fun. Much like the microcomputers of the 1980s, the Pi is a computer to be understood rather than merely used, yet it is not just the technology that invokes the 1980s but the hopes attached to it.

The Pi has been hailed by the media and politicians as a fix to the looming skills shortage in the British high-tech economy. It is the device that will empower a new generation to understand computers and learn to code. It is not just a product, but a movement. The Pi has inspired books, computer magazines, 'Raspberry Jams' where users get together with their Pis, after-school computer clubs, a cottage industry supplying gadgets to plug into it and a community of users learning from each other through online forums. The machine was so popular when it was launched in 2012 that the website crashed under the demand, a very modern revisiting of the lengthy delays for mail-order 1980s machines. In these and in so many other respects, the rise of Pi resembles the 1980s microcomputer boom in miniature, and this is not a coincidence. The Pi is a very conscious recreation of 1980s computing for the twenty-first century.

'It starts with: where the hell did all the students go? It starts with us waking up in 2005 struggling to find people to study computer science at the University of Cambridge,' explains Eben Upton who worked at the Computer Laboratory at Cambridge at the time, and is now the CEO of Raspberry Pi Trading Ltd. 'We'd coasted for a couple of decades on the back of the computer literacy initiative in the early 1980s and suddenly it evaporated.' In his spare time Upton started building simple computers at home, and in 2008, by then working at semiconductor giant Broadcom, he found his interest piqued by an email conversation circulating around the University Computer Laboratory. It had the title line 'Redo BBC Micro' and suggested that a modern-day BBC Micro could interest children in learning about computers, leading them to computer science at university and jobs in the high-tech economy. 'There was a missing piece. The recruitment woes were down to the lack of a bit of hardware,' explains Upton. 'And this idea from about 2008 that we could do something that was in this sort of area, and it kind of went from there.'

The original hope was to create a successor to the BBC Micro, but early discussions among the growing number of people backing the idea encountered an uncanny echo of a situation faced by the Computer Literacy Project's founders. 'Raspberry Pi has a really good brand now, but we didn't want a brand. We wanted to call it the BBC Micro,' explains Eben Upton. 'We discovered that the BBC can't do that anymore. You can't have a state industry like the BBC turn up and compete in the computer industry!' In other ways the Pi has been fortunate in aiming not to repeat the mistakes of the earlier British computer companies. 'It's a source of inspiration and cautionary tales,' remarks Upton. 'It showed that there was a market for a thing nobody really thought there was a market for... and that people like hacking on stuff.' Thanks to worldwide distribution through the Internet, the Pi benefits from the economies of scale of a large market unthinkable to earlier home computer companies. While a few imitators have appeared since its launch, the Pi has not yet had to fight dozens of close competitors; indeed, much of the British high-tech industry has united in praise of Pi. As of early 2015, five million Pis have been sold, far more than the Raspberry Pi Foundation's 'wildest dreams' of perhaps selling 100,000. 'It turned out, like in the 1980s, that there was a latent demand for this stuff,' notes Upton. Indeed, the need for some sort of educational computing device has been widely felt.

The lack of computer science graduates has also become a concern to the games industry. Once the bête noire of computer literacy, video games companies have become vocal lobbyists for computer education, alongside the growth of their economic and cultural clout. In late 2014, NESTA estimated that there were over 1,900 games companies in Britain, contributing about £1.7billion to the nation's gross domestic product.[1] A few of its products, notably the *Grand Theft Auto* series, have even reached the status of cultural exports. New platforms, distribution through online stores, crowd funding, mobile gaming and indie games companies have all contributed to an industry that is probably more diverse now than at any point since the boom years. Once again small programming projects and individual efforts, particularly mobile phone apps, have become viable. Few of the companies from the 1980s endured the evolution of the industry, but many of the people have, building careers on the start home computers gave them. 'A lot of people, me included, were put into a wonderful position when we were very technically literate at a very young age,' explains David Braben, now CEO of games developer Frontier Developments, after a 30-year career in the games industry started with *Elite*. 'I'm very lucky enough to have been there at the right time to take advantage of it.'

'The BBC Micro went into schools in very big numbers and that created a familiarity,' explains Braben. 'We had computer science A levels and O levels, and by the mid-'90s applications were at the highest level they've ever been.' In the early 2000s, computer studies in schools shifted to Information and Communications Technology, ICT, with more emphasis on using technology than on understanding how it works and programming. 'I had stand-up arguments with certain politicians about this. I thought it was unforgivable what they were doing,' recalls Braben, who became one of the co-founders of the Raspberry Pi Foundation in 2008: 'What I hope we've done is given to people who are motivated to play with technology today, the opportunity to do what we did.' Others intimately involved with developing British computers in the 1980s also seem to see the Pi as the heir to the sort of computing they helped to create. 'Raspberry Pi buzz is kind of the first time I felt an echo of the buzz that the BBC Micro generated in the early '80s,' remarks BBC Micro designer Steve Furber.

Powering the Pi is something more than a spiritual legacy of the home computer boom, an ARM microprocessor, descended from the chip dreamt up at Acorn in the mid-1980s. In 1990, Acorn set up Advanced RISC Machines (ARM) as a joint venture with semiconductor firm VLSI Technology and Apple. Rather than manufacturing chips, ARM built up partnerships with technology companies across the world, designed the technology, then licensed it out. By 1999, Acorn's stake in ARM was worth more than the rest of the company, and after a complex series of financial manoeuvres they went their separate ways.* Still headquartered in Cambridge, ARM Holdings, as the company is now known, went on to become the most significant British high-technology firm of recent years. Its relatively modest financial results (profits were a mere quarter billion pounds in 2014) completely understate its significance. 'ARM has been monstrously successful. I mean, it's the flagship of the UK's semiconductor industry today,' concludes Steve Furber, now a professor at the University of Manchester. 'It still doesn't make anything; it just does designs and licences them.' In a way, ARM is a very real manifestation of another dream of the 1980s computer boom; a company

---

*The remaining parts of the Acorn computer business became Element 14, and survives today in Cambridge as part of wireless and broadband communication giant Broadcom.

that makes its money from making knowledge rather than making physical things. As of 2015, some 50 billion ARM processors have been sold around the world by ARM's various partners. As well as the unseen ARM chips embedded into the systems around us, they turn up in many of the new high-tech devices of recent years. Android tablets, Apple iPhones and iPods, Amazon Kindle e-readers and smart televisions are just some of the places where this legacy of the 1980s home computer boom might be found quietly working away.

A revolution revisited

Behind 1980s computer literacy and the home computer boom was an idea of information technology as a transformational force. It was not just about education or computers, but about using information technology to rejuvenate the economy and society at large. Behind the Pi are similar hopes. 'We're getting another bite at the cherry. White Heat all over again,' suggests Eben Upton, invoking the 1960s 'White Hot Technological Revolution' and its vision of a new Britain forged through science and technology. 'Computing is the cheapest way to get you into engineering. What you're really teaching people is to think like an engineer,' argues Upton. 'This is an attempt to reboot that enthusiasm. What will we see out of it? We'll see one or two generations of start-ups… You'll see businesses will find it easier to recruit qualified, motivated young engineers.'

Computer literacy is back on the agenda. So too are the concerns that originally led to it. The declarations of a microprocessor revolution have long faded, but its underlying view of computers as a disruptive technology is as applicable today as ever. The news over recent years has been filled with stories of traditional businesses facing competition from information technology-driven rivals: London black cab drivers protesting against Uber, the smartphone application that allows anyone with a car to be a taxi business; high-street bookstores, music shops and electrical retailers being put out of business by Internet retailers, e-books and downloaded MP3 music files.

The list of such disruptions is long and varied, but the essential process at work would be familiar to 1970s information technology prophets like Christopher Evans. Indeed, in many ways we are still living in the same information technology revolution that was widely predicted in the 1970s. The electronic smart gadgets and disruptive technologies of the twenty-first century are but new implementations of older ideas.

Much as the home computer boom was fuelled by the recession of the 1970s and early '80s, since the economic downturn of 2008 there has been growing momentum behind a modern-day computer literacy. Once again, computer education is seen as a solution to a deficit in the understanding of information technology, and ultimately as a way of regenerating the economy. In 2011, the NESTA *Next Gen* report into the future of the games and visual effects industries highlighted how a skills shortage was disadvantaging Britain in the face of foreign competition. *Next Gen* placed much of the blame on deficiencies in computer education, and called for a renewed emphasis on computer science in schools rather than ICT. In 2012, a Royal Society report on computing in schools, chaired by Steve Furber, recommended a 'restart' of computing in schools, including an emphasis on engaging children with programming. At about the same time as the Royal Society report, Education Secretary Michael Gove declared an end to unimaginative ICT in schools, and its replacement by teaching that promotes a more fundamental understanding of how computers work. The hope, again echoing the 1980s, is 'skills which the jobs of the future and, for that matter, the jobs of the present, demand,'[2] as Gove put it in a speech to the BETT educational technology conference. The technology and the terminology have changed, and the current buzz phrase is 'digital literacy', but the promises and hopes attached to information technology remain the same.

Over the last few years the BBC has launched a renewed effort to get the nation, particularly children, interested in computers. 2015 is the year of the BBC's 'Make it Digital' scheme, a large-scale effort to inspire greater understanding of the opportunities of new-information technologies. A *Doctor Who* game to introduce programming concepts, and a drama on the creation of *Grand Theft Auto*, seem rather far from the worthiness of *The Computer Programme*, but there is a similar hope to interest, inspire and instruct. Having overcome the objections of commercial rivals, the Corporation plans to give away a million Microbit educational computers, similar in concept to the Raspberry Pi, from late 2015. Britain is rediscovering computer literacy, for much the same reasons as it grasped the original iteration so tightly. 'I want to have a functional industrial economy in 40 years' time when I come to draw my state pension,' concludes Eben Upton. 'I want to grow old in a First World country, and we're not going to have one if we don't fix this.'

1980s computer literacy advocates hoped that computing would bring about a new sort of high-technology Britain. Information technology and its understanding has become entwined with economic development. There were 6.8 million people employed in manufacturing in Britain in 1979. By 2010 there were just 2.5 million in the sector. The jobs that have replaced traditional manufacturing have been in services, software, the financial sector, creative industries and other areas dependent on information technology. This reorientation of the economy was widely predicted in the 1970s as a consequence of microprocessors. Political and economic factors, globalisation and the neglect of the British manufacturing industry from the 1980s have undoubtedly been major forces in this shift. However, computer literacy and the computer boom helped to pave the way for this very different sort of economy, by creating a workforce familiar with information technology.

For many people in Britain, 1980s home computing really was a passport to the future. 'In the area around Cambridge any number of people cite their experience of playing around with the BBC Micro, whether it was like me principally with software or whether it was soldering up little boards,' observes David Braben. 'They got such a technical familiarity they've now gone on to found big-tech companies.' The broader trend was confirmed in a 2012 report on the *Legacy of the BBC Micro*,[3] in which many respondents to a survey of former users commented on the importance of their earlier microcomputing experiences to their current jobs in the technology and creative sectors. Much the same can be said of the other machines of the 1980s, not least the ZX Spectrum, which far outsold the BBC Micro. 'I've spent some decades in the computer industry, recruited no end of software engineers and bumped into loads of people whose early experience of computing was with the ZX Spectrum,' recalls Richard Altwasser. 'I think there are a large number of people out there who can look back and say, "Why did I have a career in computing? Well, the ZX Spectrum was an important part in that."'

8-bit nostalgia

Legacies are normally bequeathed by the dead, but the machines of the home computer boom are still very much alive and enjoying an active retirement. One aspect of this is how popular culture has appropriated 1980s home computing and the feelings of nostalgia it evokes. Home computers appear on nightclub flyers for '80s nights', on retro T-shirts and as passing reference in jokes and news reporting.[*] In 2009, the BBC broadcast *Micromen*, a well-received drama based on the rivalry between Acorn and Sinclair in the 1980s. Filled with in-jokes and cameos, and portraying Clive Sinclair as far more of a mad genius than he ever was in real life, *Micromen* was something of a caricature, which made for greatly enjoyable television precisely because it appealed to something people were already

---

[*]Two favourite examples of recent months came from the run-up to the 2015 UK General Election, when Labour Party leader Ed Milliband declared his love for *Manic Miner* in a radio interview; and comedian and journalist Charlie Brooker sparked a Twitter debate over which home computer each political party leader had owned as a child.

familiar with. A fond retelling of history, *Micromen* was not entirely historically accurate, but nostalgia never is.

The machines themselves are also still going surprisingly strong. Retrocomputing, collecting or using old computers, has become a popular passtime enjoyed by many thousands of people. The hobby seems driven by a quirky mix of enduring design appeal, nostalgia, collecting and personal fondness for technologies that once played a part in the collectors' lives. Much of it has been enabled by the countless websites and Internet forums devoted to old computers. Online, individuals and communities have built up vast archives of games, magazines, adverts, interviews and all manner of home computer-related ephemera. Internet auctions have enabled a thriving trade in old computers, and machines that once would have changed hands for a few pounds in a 1990s car boot sale now fetch high prices on eBay. Not all the activity is virtual, but much of it is enabled by a large community of interest. In late 2013, Elite Systems, originally a 1980s developer of ZX Spectrum games, managed to crowdfund a replica ZX Spectrum keyboard to be connected to tablet computers. Each year brings fresh retrocomputing books, many self-published or crowdfunded by nostalgic fans: fondly produced histories of computers and companies, encyclopedias of classic games and memoirs from home computer pioneers. In an appropriate touch, there is even a magazine devoted to the subject, *Retro Gamer*, now running for over a decade. The home computer is a nominally obsolete technology enjoying an active second life.

The old games have survived just as well as the computers. Not only do people retrogame on original machines, but emulators for playing on modern computers and mobile phone recreations have made classic titles accessible without original hardware. More ambitious still has been the reimagination of classic games for new computing platforms, carefully treading the line between remaining faithful to the spirit of the original and exploiting new technology. A good example is *Elite: Dangerous*, a new version of a fondly remembered original, released in 2014. 'We've tried to get the feeling of enjoyment of the earlier *Elites* but put it in a proper modern context,' remarks David Braben. 'It's an astonishing change, but what it's enabled us to do is some very interesting things.' Alongside modern graphics and new paths to follow through an open-ended universe, *Elite: Dangerous* is impossibly larger than the original, with 400 billion star systems to explore in a galaxy accurately modelled on the Milky Way. That it was made possible thanks to £1.5 million crowdfunded from 25,000 people, presumably mainly fans of the original *Elites*, is another sign of enduring appeal.

To many of those involved in 1980s microcomputing, the ongoing interest has come as something of a surprise. 'I think if you'd asked me to predict that in 1982, I certainly wouldn't have done,' reflects Richard Altwasser on the continued appeal of the ZX Spectrum more than 30 years later. 'I don't get the retro thing,' remarks games programmer Jon Ritman. 'But it's very nice that I probably get one email every couple of weeks now from somebody... to tell me how much of their school life I ruined. And I always write back "another notch on my keyboard!"' Emulation and modern recreations have kept classic games alive on new platforms, but for many people only the original hardware will do.

Old microcomputers are highly collectable. Much like stamps or coins, computers are aesthetically interesting as individual items. You can 'collect the set' from specific manufacturers, or search for the rare and unusual. In 2014, an original Apple I, one of perhaps 50 still in existence, sold for $365,000 at auction. Few other machines command such exceptional prices, yet at any time there are hundreds of people bidding in online auctions for vintage computers, software and even peripherals. Yesterday's technology of the future has become today's collectable from the past. 'Collecting computers is no different from collecting anything else,' argues Jason Fitzpatrick. 'You start off buying the machines you once had in childhood, [then] you start thinking, "well, there's the machines I couldn't afford and now they're cheap I'm going to get those too…" Then the ones that weren't even released in this country, and then you start looking for the rarer and more exotic machines. That's what happened with me. It's a habit that kept on growing into a huge collection.' To judge from various vintage computer Internet discussion groups, most computer-collection machines end up hoarded away, displayed almost as art, or even actively played. Jason Fitzpatrick's collection had a rather different fate: 'I saw the light and decided that this is pointless. So I decided I either had to do something with this, or I stop doing it.'

Today Fiztpatrick is director of the Centre for Computer History, a museum in Cambridge with a rich collection of machines and archived computing paraphernalia. Key to the centre's appeal has been its attention to the social history of computing and the personal resonance between its collection and its visitors. 'We're always getting people talking about how nostalgic they are,' observes curator Jeremy Thackray. 'People get in touch with computers that they last used years ago and they suddenly find themselves typing things they'd completely forgotten.' To a certain generation, 1980s computers are not soulless artefacts, but bonds with past experiences. Embedded in their plastic and electronics are distant memories of *Granny's Garden* at school, saving pocket money to buy games, learning to program with parents and a million other lived experiences. 'You give them so much information – you put a lot of yourself into those machines I think. It sounds weird, but you do build a personal relationship with them,' argues Fitzpatrick.

The centre's collection has grown with donations from people in search of a good home for their once-treasured microcomputers. 'Quite often you get this little after-question, when they hand it over: "You will look after it, won't you?" It's like a pet they've taken to the vet,' muses Jason Fitzpatrick. 'And I think that's why the museum has been so successful, because we look at this from the personal point of view, not just the bits and bytes.' In common with the Pi and the wider rediscovery of computer literacy, there is an educational focus to the centre's work too. With modern computers built to be used rather than understood, the instructional value of the simpler 1980s machines is as relevant as ever. 'These machines are really useful for understanding what a computer is and how it functions, and that comes across particularity well when we have school groups in,' notes Jeremy Thackray. Another attraction of the centre's exhibits is the chance to play with them; indeed, it is an important part of the interpretation strategy. 'Number one on our list is to have them working,' explains Thackray. 'We don't want the object in question to be a lump of plastic that people stare at. We want them to actually use it.'

The technology may have dated, but the essential appeal of the home computer as a creative machine to do *something* with remains as viable as ever. People are still creating new things with old computers. A good example is the demoscene, a subculture of users that spread across Europe from the late 1980s and is still thriving today, driven by graphic artists, musicians and programmers, creating artistic demo programs. Somewhat akin to hobbyist computing, demos rely on an intimate understating of the hardware and its quirks to create audiovisual displays once thought impossible on such simple hardware. Lively mixes of high-resolution graphics, smooth and swift animations, and surprising visual effects set to music, demos are a modern-day incarnation of the technical and creative expression of early microcomputing.

Games programmers too are still creating new titles on machines long abandoned by commercial publishers. A steady trickle of new titles for old computers appears each year, particularly on the machines that were once most popular, like those of Commodore and Sinclair. 'The reason I do it is exactly because the machines are so very limited in their capabilities,' explains programmer Bob Smith, creator of over two-dozen new ZX81 and Spectrum games. 'Being a programmer foremost, it's a great challenge for me to try and make these machines do things that they weren't considered capable of back in the day.' Just as in the 1980s, people are exploring what microcomputers can do and pushing the technology to make them do more. In a twist on the updating of old classics like *Elite*, for new platforms, several of Smith's projects are interpretations of new games, such as *Quack*, a ZX81 version of the hit mobile phone game *Flappy Bird*. 'I like to try to pick games that would suit the retro machines,' adds Smith. 'Not only to ease the conversion to a playable game, but also to prove that some modern games are simply very good ideas, which could work on any machine.' Like many retrogamers, Smith uses editors and emulators on a modern PC, rather than original hardware, to create the titles. Modern development tools and not having to suffer the idiosyncratic keyboards of the original Sinclair machines speeds development, but the last stages have an appropriately authentic touch. 'The final games are tested on real machines,' explains Smith. 'Which is very important to me.' At the start of the 1980s the home computer was a technology for people to experiment with and discover what they could make it do. The same is still true three decades later.

Long after the crash of the computer market, the closing of production lines and a gradual slide into technical obsolescence, the home computer is still very much alive. In the twenty-first century people are still playing around with home computers, seeing what the technology does and using them to create. The legacies of the machines are all around us, embedded in popular culture and personal life stories, buried in the histories of the technologies we use today and in the companies that make them. Originally conceived as a way to make new-information technologies acceptable and accessible for everyone, the biggest legacy of home computers is a world where computer technology is commonplace. As times goes by the original machines will stop as their electronic components degrade and fail, but their legacy will remain, perhaps refreshed anew. As I was finishing this book, news broke of the launch of a new Sinclair computer. The Sinclair Spectrum Vega, a reincarnation of the Spectrum as an ARM-powered console with 1,000 built-in games, pre-sold its entire initial production run within 36 hours of being offered to the public. Through the Pi, the Vega, popular culture and the retrocomputing community, the 1980s home computer has proved to be a remarkable survivor. The signs are that it will remain so for quite some time to come.